The Passing of Postmodernism

THE SUNY SERIES IN
POSTMODERN CULTURE
Joseph Natoli, *Editor*

The Passing of Postmodernism

A Spectroanalysis of the Contemporary

JOSH TOTH

Published by State University of New York Press, Albany

© 2010 State University of New York

For information, contact State University of New York Press, Albany, NY
www.sunypress.edu

Production by Cathleen Collins
Marketing by Anne M. Valentine

Library of Congress Cataloging-in-Publication Data

Toth, Josh.
    The passing of postmodernism : a spectroanalysis of the contemporary / Josh Toth.
        p. cm. — (SUNY series in postmodern culture)
    Includes bibliographical references and index.
    ISBN 978-1-4384-3035-5 (hardcover : alk. paper)
    1. Postmodernism (Literature).   2. Semiotics and literature.   3. Criticism.
4. Poststructuralism.   5. Derrida, Jacques—Criticism and interpretation.
I. Title.

    PN98.P67T68 2010
    809'.9113—dc22

                                                                    2009021169

10 9 8 7 6 5 4 3 2 1

For those who haunt everything I do:

Dad, Mom, and (of course) Danica and Marlow

Thou art a scholar; speak to it, Horatio.

—Jacques Derrida, *Specters of Marx*

Contents

Acknowledgments

There are a number of people without whom this project, too, would be "still incomplete." At the top of the list are Thomas Carmichael, Tilottama Rajan, and my partner (in everything), Danica Rose. All three provided invaluable and tireless guidance, guidance that defined my thinking from start to end. Many thanks go, also, to Linda Hutcheon, Alison Lee, Martin Kreiswirth, and Daniel Vaillancourt (all of whom kindly identified errors and offered advice). Finally, I would like to thank both Neil Brooks and Clay Dion; their support and friendship helped me to endure any number of frustrations along the way.

Scattered portions of the following text have appeared in previous publications: "A *Différance* of Nothing: Sartre, Derrida and the Problem of Negative Theology" (published in the Berghahn journal *Sartre Studies International*) and "Introduction: A Wake and Renewed," which I co-authored with Neil Brooks as the Introduction to *The Mourning After: Attending the Wake of Postmodernism.* (*The Mourning After* was published as part of Rodopi's Postmodern Studies series, edited by Theo D'haen and Hans Bertens.)

Front cover illustration: Alex Golden. "Untitled" (Front View), 2006. From "Waving and Clapping" series. Oil and inkjet on canvas, 44 × 85 inches. Reproduced by kind permission of the artist.

Back cover illustration: Alex Golden. "Untitled" (Back View), 2006. From "Waving and Clapping" series. Oil and inkjet on canvas, 44 × 85 inches. Reproduced by kind permission of the artist.

CHAPTER ONE

The Phantom Project Returning

The Passing (On) of the
Still Incomplete Project of Modernity

There is no more hope for meaning. And without a doubt this is a good thing: meaning is mortal. But that on which it has imposed its ephemeral reign, what it hoped to liquidate in order to impose the reign of the Enlightenment, that is, appearances, they, are immortal, invulnerable to the nihilism of meaning or of non-meaning itself.

—Jean Baudrillard, *Simulacra and Simulation*

(*Marcellus*: "What, ha's this thing appear'd againe tonight?" Then: *Enter the Ghost, Exit the Ghost, Enter the Ghost, as before*). A question of repetition: a specter is always a *revenant*. One cannot control its comings and goings because it *begins by coming back*.

—Jacques Derrida, *Specters of Marx*

CONCIERGE: What is it? Will there be more?

RAY: Sir, what you had there is what we refer to as a focused, non-terminal repeating phantasm, or a Class-5 full-roaming vapor. Real nasty one too.

—Ivan Reitman, *Ghostbusters*

Introduction

"Let's just say it: it's over" (*Politics* 166). Postmodernism, that is. Or so Linda Hutcheon claims. For Hutcheon, "the postmodern moment has *passed*, even if its discursive strategies and its ideological critique

1

continue to live on—as do those of modernism—in our contemporary twenty-first century world" (*Politics* 181, my emphasis). Hutcheon's
announcement rings—and I imagine this is her intention—like a death
knell, the final word. Indeed, the entire epilogue to the second edition of *The Politics of Postmodernism* reads like an epistemological obituary.[1] Hutcheon employs phrasing that is usually reserved for funerals,
or extended periods of mourning: postmodernism has "passed." Of
course, Hutcheon *really* means "passed" in a temporal sense, that the
postmodern moment is now *in the past*. Yet it is difficult, if not impossible, to ignore the metaphysical connotations of "passing." So, let's
just say it: postmodernism is, according to critics like Hutcheon, dead.
It has *passed*. It has, in other words, *given up the ghost*. Such phrasing,
though, resounds with ambiguity, inviting a number of questions: What
ghost? Given? Passed on?—where?, to whom? When, or where, did this
passing/giving begin? Is this ghost that postmodernism has "given up,"
is this thing that has "passed on," that which Hutcheon claims continues to "live on?" Is it the same thing that lived on after modernism,
and therefore lived on (in) postmodernism? This seems to be, then,
a question of the paranormal, of possession. What is this thing that
lives on, moving from host to host? But I have already generated more
questions than I can, at this point, possibly answer. What is important
to note, for now, is that the death of postmodernism (like all deaths)
can also be viewed as a passing, a giving over of a certain inheritance,
that this death (like all deaths) is also a living on, a passing on.

Perhaps the fall of George W. Bush's cynical administration (with
its reliance on tenuous truth claims and its blind support of neoco-
lonial capitalism) and the massively popular rise of Barack Obama's
overtly "sincere" administration (with its renewed faith in global ethics
and transparent communication) finally signals the culmination of a
grand epochal transition, but one thing is clear: Hutcheon (in 2002) is
already quite late in arriving at the deathbed of postmodernism.[2] The
deathwatch began, one could argue, as early as the mid-1980s. In 1983,
the British Journal, *Granta*, published an issue entitled "Dirty Realism:
New Writing in America." Introduced by Bill Buford, this "new" realism
was presented as an initial step beyond the pretensions of postmodernism. This revival of some type of "realism" was further solidified by
the American writer Tom Wolfe in his 1989 "literary manifesto for a
new social novel." In fact, by 1989, the demise of postmodernism was,
for most, an inevitability. With the First Stuttgart Seminar in Cultural
Studies—"The End of Postmodernism: New Directions"—the fate of
postmodernism seemed sealed. By the mid-1990s, the phrase "after
(or beyond) postmodern" could be found on the cover of any number of critical works.[3] In other words, since the end of the 1980s an

increasing number of literary critics and theorists have announced, or simply assumed, the end of postmodernism. The race is on to define an emergent period that seems to have arrived *after* the end of history.

As I suggested above, the critics who participate in this theorization of the end typically highlight a recent shift in contemporary narrative that is marked by the growing dominance of a type of neo-(or, "dirty")-realism, and by an increased theoretical interest in the issues of community and ethical responsibility. Indeed, the recent shift in stylistic privilege—from ostentatious works of postmodern metafiction to more grounded, or "responsible," works of neo-realism—seems to echo the recent ethico-political "turn" in critical theory, a turn that is perhaps most obvious in Jacques Derrida's late work on Marxism, friendship, hospitality, and forgiveness. In line with this theoretical turn, and in the *wake of postmodernism*, a growing body of cultural and literary criticism has dedicated itself to the recovery of various "logocentric" assumptions. The recent collection of essays edited by Jennifer Geddes, *Evil after Postmodernism: History, Narratives, Ethics*, might stand for the moment as an example of this shift in critical concern.[4] In terms of narrative production, then (and as I demonstrate in chapter 3), the suggestion we get from those critics and writers who seem to have arrived *after postmodernism* is that the stylistic elements that have been typically read as emanations of (what most writers and critics now view) as a subversive and nihilistic epistemological trend have been undermined by a new discourse that is no longer overtly concerned with the impossibility of the subject and/or author and the need to avoid a grounded, or situated, commitment to the political. However, as Klaus Stierstorfer points out in his introduction to *Beyond Postmodernism: Reassessments in Literature, Theory, and Culture*, this return to seemingly prepostmodern ideologies has been somehow tempered by the lessons of postmodernism:

> Whether it is the more universal interest in the possible foundations of a general or literary ethics in a world of globalisation, or the more specific and local issues of identities, scholars and writers alike nevertheless continue to find themselves in the dilemma of facing the deconstructive gestures inherent in postmodernist thought while at the same time requiring some common ground on which ethical agreements can be based. Hence some form of referentiality, even some kind of essentialism is called for. (9–10)

In terms of the apparent shift to a type of neo-realism, we might say that some form of mimesis is called for—that is, some type of renewed faith in the possibility of what postmodernism narrative has repeatedly identified as impossible: meaning, truth, representational accuracy. But as Stierstorfer notes, this shift to some type of (what I call in later chapters) "renewalism" is not simply a backlash in response to post-modern narrative production; it is neither a reactionary return to the ethical imperatives of modernism nor a revival of the traditional forms of realism that proliferated in the nineteenth century. Postmodernism, to a certain degree, persists. Consequently, this seemingly progressive movement *out of* postmodernism is confronted at the outset by two pressing questions: has postmodernism, as Linda Hutcheon claims, finally "passed?"; and, if so, what is or can be *after* postmodernism? With these increasingly focal questions as a point of departure, I will consider the possibility that, while heralding the close of a moment in cultural and epistemological history, the current discussion ironically highlights the inevitable *persistence* of postmodernism. That said, I am not interested in arguing simply that what comes after postmodernism remains informed by postmodernism; this is, obviously, and as I demonstrate throughout, the case. I am interested in demonstrating that the current epistemological, or cultural, reconfiguration—a reconfiguration that maintains many postmodern "traits"—betrays the inevitable persistence of what Jacques Derrida might refer to as the "inheritance," or "specter," that animated postmodernism in the first place.

Functioning primarily as a cultural critique (or, rather, as a critique of contemporary cultural critique), the following chapters will thus approach the issue of postmodernism's passing in a manner that recalls Jacques Derrida's analysis of Marxism in *Specters of Marx*. In line with the theoretical mode Derrida assumes in order to locate in both Marxism and deconstruction a past revenant, or ghost, of "emancipatory and *messianic* affirmation, a certain experience of the promise" (*Specters* 89), my study of the death of postmodernism will function as a type of two-pronged "spectro-analysis," or "spectrology." What I would like to suggest is that postmodernism (as a privileged epistemological "configuration," or cultural dominant, encompassing both narrative and theoretical discourse) was *haunted* by a certain teleological aporia, a promise of the end represented by a type of humanism, a certain faith in historical progress, a sense of justice and/or meaning. The recent critical identification, or attempt to theorize, the end of postmodernism seems to speak to the fact that this aporia, or specter, necessarily continues to persist, even in the wake of the recent abandonment of postmodernism's formal characteristics. A certain necessarily persistent specter—what Fredric Jameson seems to identify as both the "return of the repressed" and the "utopian impulse" in *Postmodernism, Or, the Cultural Logic of Late Capitalism*, and which is ostensibly at work in all epistemological reconfigurations—compels movement, even if that movement is a narrative or theoretical attempt to exorcise what haunts and compels. Still, I do not intend to deny the reality of what we might tentatively refer to as a type of epistemic break with the postmodern; rather, I am interested in the way in which this current "break" recalls, or reenacts, the postmodern break with modernism—that is, the way in which any such break, or epistemic rupture, can be viewed ironically as both complete and partial.

To a certain extent, and in the same way that a work like Jameson's *Postmodernism* is interested in postmodernism as a unique stage in what is, ultimately, a much larger historical progression, the following discussion is interested in postmodernism and its apparent passing insofar as it is indicative of a certain spectrologically induced pattern of epochal "shifts," or "breaks." Postmodernism is viewed here as a unique epistemological configuration that is defined by the way in which it attempts to "deal with" a certain ineffaceable and transhistorical specter. Via a focus on the passing of postmodernism, then, I want to suggest that it is possible to understand cultural shifts in aesthetic and theoretical discourse/production as "epistemological reconfigurations." Rather than employing a rhetoric of complete epistemic ruptures—that is, a rhetoric of epochal breaks that, *à la* Foucault, conceives of seismic epistemological upheavals that leave no residual traces of a previous "archive of knowledge"—it is, I would argue, more useful to view each identifiable epochal, or epistemic, shift as *another* configuration, as another epistemological attempt to deal with a certain persistent and ineffaceable specter, a certain persistent and ineffaceable teleological aporia. From this perspective, an epoch remains understandably definable (or, perhaps, to a certain degree, synchronically exclusive) while also remaining quite understandably partial, an inevitable continuation of the past. Each epistemic break is always, or *only*, a reconfiguration because its formation is necessarily contingent upon the fact that something (a specter) always and necessarily passes on. Of course, before we can attempt to relocate this specter in the current, or emergent, period *after* postmodernism, it is necessary to first locate it within the postmodern itself. For this reason, each of the following chapters begins by first establishing the specter's (non)presence in canonical works of postmodern theory and narrative. Only by first observing the specter at work in postmodernism can we begin to map its trajectory across the "great epistemological divide" that defines this epoch that has arrived *after* postmodernism.

However, in order to establish the exact theoretical framework that will inform the subsequent discussion, it is necessary to inspect, or spectro-analyze, the original theorization of what we have come to accept as postmodern. In what ways was the theorization of the term "postmodern" influenced by the very specter I propose to locate and relocate? In what ways does the logic of the original postmodern debate inevitably realize, or announce, this specter? This chapter functions as a spectrological recuperation of that debate. By re-approaching a number of the significant "accounts" of postmodernism, my goal is to track the specter in question through as well as *in* a number of different perspectives, or theoretical positions. So, while it may at times look the part, what follows is not simply or only a review of what has come before concerning the problem of postmodernism and historical shifts. My purpose in the following sections is to provide, rather, a type of "spectral genealogy" of the various attempts to theorize postmodernism. By locating the ostensible specter of postmodernism within the various and seemingly conflicting theories articulated about and during the postmodern period, this genealogy should go a long way in terms of establishing the fact that a specific spectral impulse *effects* certain recurring discursive formulations in a given episteme. What follows is thus both a cursive survey of the postmodern debate (as it occurred within, and as an effect of, the postmodern episteme) as well as an articulation, and initial employment of, the spectrological framework that will inform the following chapters.

Before I begin, though, a final word on method. While I am interested in the discussion surrounding, and the reality of, a "postmodern break," this is not an attempt to finalize the debate concerning that break, or shift; I am not concerned here with definitive dates marking the beginning or the end of postmodernism. Obviously, dates will be important to any discussion of historical periodizations—and I will certainly make suggestions concerning the moments of reconfiguration here discussed—but this is an attempt to theorize the way in which the general concept of such ruptures is undermined by a specific spectral persistence. Ultimately, I am not interested in the exact moments of epistemological change. As I explain below, these epistemological configurations seem to recede gradually as new and emergent configurations become dominant. In other words, the spectral reconfigurations identified in the following pages are better understood via Raymond Williams' concept of residual, emergent, and dominant periods than they are via the Foucaultian sense of spatially conceived epistemes that exist entirely independent of one another.[5] The specter I propose to examine can be said to persist simultaneously in several distinct epistemological configurations (although, at any given time, a specific epistemic configuration might be in a position of "dominance"). This will make more sense as we move, finally, into a discussion of the postmodern debate as it occurred up to postmodernism's apparent *end*.

Ruptures and Specters

Employed loosely in Arnold Toynbee's multivolume *Study of History* (eight volumes of which were published between 1934 and 1954), the term "postmodern," written "post-Modern," was used to describe a late-nineteenth-century epochal shift: the end of a "modern" bourgeois ruling class and the growing dominance of an industrial working class. I do not wish to get lost in the early history of the term, but Toynbee's initial theorizing of *a* "post-Modern" period of Western civilization is a useful point of departure; it inaugurates a long tradition of viewing the postmodern as an ultimately unsuccessful break with the motivating assumptions of (a) modernity. According to Perry Anderson in *The Origins of Postmodernity* (perhaps the most recent and most comprehensive history of the term), Toynbee "was scathing of the hubristic illusions of the late imperial West" (6), which saw the culmination of the Victorian period as the end of history itself. For Toynbee, "the Modern Age of Western history had been wound up only to inaugurate a post-Modern Age pregnant with imminent experiences that were to be at least as tragic as any tragedies yet on record" (Vol. 9, 421). The Western world—which, for Toynbee, primarily included France, Britain, Germany, and America—had come to believe that "a sane, safe, satisfactory Modern life had miraculously come to stay as a timeless present. 'History is now at an end' was the inaudible slogan of the celebrations of Queen Victoria's Diamond Jubilee in A.D. 1887" (421). What is interesting about Toynbee's discussion of a post-Modern period is his willingness to chastise the assumptions of such a period. Toynbee ultimately demonstrates that the very conception of an "end of history" is ironically animated by a desire for an as yet unrealized end of history. The end of history is only possible, Toynbee seems to suggest (in a manner that will echo in the following discussion of Derridean spectrality), because it is never fully actualized in any real sense. As Toynbee points out, the desire for an end of history necessarily persisted even as the Western ruling class announced, or assumed, the arrival of a finally posthistoric epoch:

> German, British, and North American bourgeoisie were nursing national grievances and national aspirations which did not permit them to acquiesce in a comfortable belief that "History" was "at an end"; indeed they could not have continued, as they did continue, to keep alight the flickering flame of a forlorn hope if they had succumbed to a *Weltanschauung* which, for them, would have spelled, not security, but despair. (423)

A far cry from the current, now virtually institutionalized, parameters of the term, Toynbee's concept of a post-Modern introduces an issue that has never ceased to inform the modern/postmodern debate: the issue of historical breaks and the culmination of history itself. Toynbee seems to anticipate the recent claim that postmodernism has been as unsuccessful as modernism in terms of heralding, or representing, a final break with the past. Of course, Toynbee's modern/postmodern periodizations are essentially equivalent to what literary critics conventionally identify as Victorian/modern (or what, in economic terms, someone like Jameson, following Ernest Mandel, might associate with market/monopoly stages of capitalism). After all, Toynbee marks the postmodern epoch as beginning with the Franco-Prussian war. Nevertheless, his discussion of *a* post-Modern is of considerable interest. The attempt to theorize a postcontemporary moment that is, in some regard, an unsuccessful or incomplete break with the ideology of a past modernity or historical trajectory is a useful segue to a discussion of the specter that informed modernism long before it was inherited by postmodernism. In fact, Toynbee's discussion of a post-Modern period can be neatly tied to the current understanding of modernism. In a manner that recalls the typically accepted date for a postmodern break with modernism, Toynbee seems to mark the 1950s as the end of a distinctly post-Modern period. Not only does Toynbee seemingly view the "Modern and postmodern chapters of Western history" as now past, he suggests that, by "A.D. 1950, the expansion of the Western Society and the radiation of the Western culture had brought all other extant civilizations and all extant primitive societies within a world-encompassing Western Civilization's ambit" (413–14). Pointing to the reality of an apparently emergent multinational period of cultural and economic growth—that is, a period of unprecedented globalization—Toynbee argues that "perhaps for the first time in the history of the Human race, all Mankind's eggs are gathered into one precious yet precarious basket as a consequence of the Western Civilization's world-wide expansion" (415). Simply put, Toynbee's understanding of a post-Modern period can be usefully employed as way of understanding the modern episteme, in our contemporary sense of the period, and its subsequent "passing." Moreover, Toynbee's use of the terms Modern and post-Modern to describe the shift from a period still marked by its explicit faith in the assumptions of the Enlightenment to a period that defined itself as the end of progress itself, highlights the inherent connection between (what we consider today as) modernism and postmodernism, while also giving us an interesting framework within which to view the current epochal shift.

About the time Toynbee was working out his epochal parameters, the term "post-modern" was more favorably applied to contemporary aesthetic developments by the American poet Charles Olson. In a text that Anderson seems to view as a "lapidary manifesto" of the post-modern, Olson begins by stating that "My shift is that I take it the present is the prologue, not the past" (250). What is ultimately a brief biographical introduction, this apparent "manifesto" concludes with Olson identifying a small group of "modern" writers who he believes prefigured the arrival of a distinctly postmodern period of aesthetic production (within which he locates himself):

> I am an archeologist of morning. And the writing acts which I find bear on the present job are (I) from Homer back, not forward; and (II) from Melville on, particularly himself, Dostoevsky, Rimbaud, and Lawrence. These were the modern men who projected what we are and what we are in, who broke the spell. They put men forward into the post-modern, the post-humanist, the posthistoric, the going live present, the "Beautiful Thing." (207)[6]

As Anderson explains, Olson's becomes the first "affirmative conception of the postmodern" (Anderson 12).[7] Obviously distinct from Toynbee's earlier usage, Olson's "post-modern" nevertheless echoes Toynbee's in the sense that, as Hans Bertens somewhat begrudgingly notes (while discussing Michael Köhler's take on Toynbee and Olson), it "indicates a new episteme—to use Foucault's term—in the history of Western culture"[8] (Bertens 11), while also implicitly calling our attention to a certain modernist revenant, a persistent drive (what Anderson calls a *Stimmung*, or mood) whose presence, at least from a certain post-modern perspective, is indicative of a failure to be wholly and finally POSTmodern. These initial occurrences of the term—occurrences that hardly affected later theorizing of a postmodern period—suggest that, whatever the final definition of the postmodern became, it, like modernism before it, was unable to escape a certain aporia that seemingly animated previous epochs. I am referring here to the contradictory impulse toward, or aporia surrounding, the possibility of a type of "final answer." As I explain more fully below, this particular aporia that animates any given epoch is often, if not always, identified by, and seemingly confronted or resolved in, a succeeding epoch. This particular aporia is, we might posit tentatively at this point, what "passes on," what is "given up"—the one essential ghost of an epistemological period, or what I will call here the specter of postmodernism.[9]

While most agree, Anderson included, that Toynbee and Olson are the first Anglophone critics to employ the term "post-modern"—and that, after them, "The referent of the postmodern lapses" (Anderson 12) and does not resurface until the late-1950s—Bertens, in "The Postmodern *Weltanschauung* and its Relation to Modernism," discusses John Berryman's reemployment of Randall Jarrell's 1946 use of the term to describe the poetry of Robert Lowell. In an attempt to give Olson's various and often unclear uses of the term more contemporary relevance, Bertens quotes Jerome Mazzoro's *Postmodern American Poetry*, highlighting Mazzoro's argument that Olson's, like Jarrell's, understanding of the postmodern can be easily identified with the term's contemporary usage, even if such usage refers more typically to fiction than poetry.[10] According to Mazzoro, both Jarrell and Olson ultimately conceive of the postmodern as a radical break from, what we might call today, modernism's logocentric assumptions; while modernism attempts to bypass, or improve upon, language acts as the unstable mediator of reality, postmodernism refuses to differentiate between language and the reality it represents.[11] Whether or not this is an accurate definition of Olson's, or even Jarrell's, conception of the postmodern, Bertens is correct in one regard: Mazzaro's interpretation of Olson's definition(s) is remarkably similar to what will become the dominant understanding of postmodernism.[12] More importantly, Mazzoro's ability to read Olson in such a way suggests that Olson's struggle to employ the term is also a struggle with the very contradictions that will become the primary concern of the "postmodern debate." On the one hand, Olson's "postmodern" is unable to distance itself entirely from modernism and (I will propose tentatively here) the specter of an Enlightenment project that continued to haunt, and thus animate, the modern aesthetic sensibility. On the other, Olson's "post-modern" is a complete and utter break with the motivating assumptions of what many would define today as modernism. It is this apparent contradiction that I want to continue highlighting, as it is—or, at least, this is what I want to suggest—the key to understanding postmodernism's *passing*.

In the early 1960s, the postmodern became associated with a "fall" from modernism. Critics like Irving Howe and Harry Levin employed the term "post-modern" to describe what they saw as distinctly negative developments in contemporary literature. For this first "real" wave of postmodern critics, the postmodern is viewed as an aesthetic setback. Levin, for instance, describes the postmodern epoch as a distinctly reactionary and "anti-intellectual" trend, a lamentable return to ideologies that modernism had only recently demystified. Anticipating theorists like Habermas, Levin's postmodern is a neo-conservative interruption of a distinctly modern—or, rather, *radical*—period of cultural production: "This realignment corresponds with the usual transition from *enfant terrible*, who is naturally radical, to the elder statesman, who is normally conservative" (309). In a similar manner, Howe's postmodern is marked by the absence of strong belief systems, the loss of a moral center, or ground.[13] This loss of traditional authorities is, for Howe, symptomatic of a "mass society":

> By mass society we mean a relatively comfortable, half welfare and half garrison society in which population grows passive, indifferent and atomized; in which traditional loyalties, ties and associations become lax or dissolve entirely; in which coherent publics based on definitive interests and opinions gradually fall apart; and in which man becomes a consumer, himself mass-produced like the products, diversions and values he absorbs. (426)

As a result of this mass societal state, "vast numbers of people now float through life with a burden of freedom they can neither sustain nor legitimately abandon to social or religious groups" (427). While it is, perhaps, more closely related to phenomenological or existential theories of subjectivity and freedom,[14] Howe's understanding of mass society clearly anticipates the more recent discussions of late-capitalism and the death of the subject.

Levin, for his own part, makes similar observations about the postmodern state of economic and societal growth. In fact, Levin's postmodern epoch is initially associated with what we might understand today as a Baudrillardian sense of mass production, simulation, and hyperreality:

> this is reproduction, not production; we are mainly consumers rather than producers of art. We are readers of reprints and connoisseurs of High Fidelity, even as we are the gourmets by virtue of the expense account and the credit card. For our wide diffusion of culture is geared to the standardizations of our economy, and is peculiarly susceptible to inflationary trends. The independence of our practitioners, when they are not domesticated by institutions of learning, is compromised more insidiously by the circumstances that make art a business. (313)

Of course, Levin (and, I imagine, to a lesser degree, Howe) is seemingly still enamored by the illusion that modernism was an unprecedented period of artistic autonomy, a period in which the market failed to penetrate the elite arena of "high" cultural production. Still, both Levin and Howe seem to anticipate the ways in which the effects of rapid societal modernization would be read by future postmodern writers and theorists. And the fact that Howe explicitly identifies a certain "threat" to the subject is, particularly, worth noting. Howe's conception of a postmodern period, while associated with a canon of writers we would hardly recognize today *as postmodern*[15] is, as Bertens points out, "important in its early recognition of the role that epistemological and ontological doubt would play in postwar American literature" (14). More significantly, though, it is important (as is, to a lesser degree, Levin's understanding) in terms of its initial recognition and articulation of what later critics would come to identify clearly as a cultural and epistemological "break" or "rupture," a definitive shift from modernism to something explicitly *not* modernist—whether that "something" is an improvement or not.[16]

By the mid-1960s, and into the 1970s, critics like Leslie Fiedler, Susan Sontag, and Ihab Hassan were outwardly celebrating just such a "rupture," or epistemic upheaval (if we can return to the Foucaultian terminology discussed above). This turn to a distinctly positive view of postmodernism is perhaps best exemplified in Fiedler's virtually ecstatic pronouncement, in "Cross the Border—Close that Gap: Post-Modernism," of the *passing of* modernism:

> We are living, have been living for two decades—and have become acutely conscious of the fact since 1955—through the death throes of Modernism and the birth pangs of Post-Modernism. The kind of literature which arrogated to itself the name Modern (with the presumption that it represented the ultimate advance in sensibility and form, that beyond it newness was impossible), and whose moment of triumph lasted from a point just before the First World War until one just after the Second World War, is *dead*, i.e., belongs to history not actuality. (344)

Like Sontag—who, in *Against Interpretation*, celebrates the postmodern aversion, or outward resistance, to final meaning(s), authorial intention, and thus interpretation—Fiedler conceives of the postmodern as "apocalyptic, anti-rational, blatantly romantic and sentimental; an age dedicated to joyous misology and prophetic irresponsibility; one, at any rate, distrustful of self-protective irony and too great self-awareness" (Fiedler 345). If such apocalyptic pronouncements give us a somewhat uneasy sense of déjà vu, it's not surprising.[17] The claim, here, that modernism is *finally* dead (and not just dead, but—with empathic italics—*dead*) is remarkably similar to the postmodern death notices mentioned above. It is at this point—that is, the point at which the postmodern debate begins to include outward celebration—that I can begin to tie together the initial portion of this survey, while further articulating the spectrological argument proposed above.

That the death of modernism was read as the end of history[18] and the teleological assumptions of history, that its death marks the birth of a finally postmodern, posthistoric aesthetic sensibility devoid of positivist assumptions and humanist imperatives, has several crucial implications. These implications—implications that I have already touched on in the above discussion of Toynbee's "post-Modern" epoch[19]—are all the more germane to our discussion if we consider the fact that the theorizing of modernism's "passing" has been neatly echoed in the more recent pronouncements of another epochal death: the death of postmodernism. On the surface, there are two ways to look at this. From either perspective, though, the majority of postmodern analysis since the first considerations of Toynbee and Olson must be viewed as inherently flawed. *Either*, as critics like Gerald Graff[20] have suggested from the beginning, late modernism has been mis-recognized as POST-modern—that is, the *true end* of modernism; *or*, postmodernism *was indeed a break* with modernism, but it was ultimately unable to be what the majority of critics claimed it was: post-ideological.[21] But which is it? Or, is there another possibility?

Andreas Huyssen, to a certain degree, had much of this worked out back in the mid-1980s: "Either it is said that postmodernism is continuous with modernism, in which case the whole debate opposing the two is specious; or, it is claimed that there is a radical rupture, a break with modernism, which is then evaluated in either positive or negative terms" (Huyssen 182). Given the recent development of an epoch/episteme that has emerged *after* postmodernism, it would seem that the "rupture argument," as I suggested above, can only be maintained if the effect of the rupture is considered a failure, an unsuccessful and ultimately temporary postmodern—an *almost-*(truly)POSTmodern. But Huyssen seems to anticipate a way out of this dilemma. Viewing the either/or sensibility animating much of the postmodern debate as a failure to understand the most useful insights of Derridean deconstruction, Huyssen suggests that the postmodern—rather than being *either* continuous *or* wholly discontinuous with modernism—is *both* continuous *and* discontinuous. This is apparent, Huyssen points out, in the term itself; "postmodern" inscribes within itself the very term (i.e., "modern") that it defines itself against. Ultimately, though, Huyssen's argument and apparent answer to the dilemma with which we are now confronted reaffirms the very binary he wishes to avoid. Huyssen eventually goes on to describe a series of movements *out of* modernism, a series beginning in the 1960s with a type of "anti-modernism" and seemingly culminating in the 1970s and 1980s with an almost complete epochal transformation into what we might think of as postmodernism proper. Huyssen essentially categorizes the postmodernism of the 1960s as a rebellion against certain strains of high modernism: its institutionalization, via the New Critics, within academia and its consequent failure as a subversive and critical avant-garde. By the late-1970s and early 1980s, though, postmodernism ceases to be simply anti-modernist, abandoning the concept of the avant-garde altogether and splitting into two separate strains: one that manifests itself as an affirmative culture of eclecticism with little interest in critique or subversion and another that manages to resist and critique the status quo while abandoning avant-gardism and/or basic modernist assumptions. Huyssen is particularly interested in the latter form of postmodernism and the possibility of its eventual transformation into a cultural dominant. What is important about his argument is that he sees the postmodernism/anti-modernism of the 1960s as a type of postmodern "pre-history" (195), as if the postmodernism that begins to emerge in the 1980s is almost finally and truly POSTmodern. The sense we get is that, even by the mid-1980s, postmodernism has not yet finally emerged—that, while it *has been* both continuous and discontinuous with modernism, it will eventually be something wholly different, something truly POSTmodern: "what appears on one level as the latest fad, advertising pitch, and hollow spectacle is part of a slowly emerging cultural transformation in Western societies, a change in sensibility for which the term 'postmodernism' is actually, at least for now, wholly adequate" (Huyssen 181).

In a way, then, Huyssen can be read as the first critic to theorize a period *after* postmodernism. That the term "postmodern" is "wholly adequate" in terms of temporarily describing a final shift to something wholly other than modernism is tantamount to saying that true POSTmodernism will not actually be identified *as* "postmodern"—a term that, according to Huyssen, cannot help but intimate a latent connection to modernism. From this perspective, Huyssen does indeed theorize a (for lack of a better term) POSTmodern rupture; but the rupture he theorizes is delayed, or prepared for, by a period of anti-(or, post)MODERNISM. Huyssen's still forthcoming postmodern episteme is thus equivalent to what is currently described as the period *after* postmodernism. Hutcheon, in fact, does a similar thing. Hutcheon doesn't *really* announce *the death* of postmodernism; rather, she seems to suggest that what has been mistakenly thought of as postmodernism is dead and that POSTmodernism has finally become a reality—so much so that it requires "a new label of its own" (181), one (we might assume) that no longer implies a connection to the past.

Unfortunately, all this leads us back to the initial problem: either we "jumped the gun" when we first started identifying aesthetic production and social dynamics as postmodern, or the postmodern we correctly identified was unable to live up to our expectations. Both options, of course, ultimately become conflated; whether the past fifty or so years was just a continuation of modernism or an unsuccessful version of postmodernism, the fact remains that a truly POSTmodern epoch, with a name of its own, remains to be seen. And, besides, wouldn't an unsuccessful postmodernism, by definition, be a continuation of modernism anyway? As a possible way out of the problem, and as a way of salvaging the majority of postmodern criticism, I want to focus on Huyssen's suggestion that the postmodern is both continuous and discontinuous with modernism—but I would like to dismiss as somewhat facile the importance of the term itself; it seems to me that modernism is as continuous/discontinuous with the epochs that preceded it as is postmodernism, and the term "modernism" does not include references to the Enlightenment, romanticism or Victorianism. In this sense, I would like to employ a theory, or rhetoric, of ironic continuity/discontinuity as a means of understanding the death of postmodernism (as well as postmodernism itself). Nevertheless, the various versions of this particular position are not entirely in line with the direction I'd like to take such a theory. Some, like Huyssen, fail to sustain a wholly ironic viewpoint; others, like Hassan, employ a sense of continuous discontinuity in order to reaffirm a sense of historical trajectory, or progress. Still, Hassan's suggestion that a period, or epoch, is "both a diachronic and synchronic construct" (Hassan 88) is a useful one. But instead of viewing the seemingly discontinuous, or synchronic, as the effect of an almost arbitrary system of categorization that gives definition to an otherwise smooth historical trajectory (as Hassan seems, in the end, to be interested in doing), I want to suggest that it is as incorrect to say that "modernism and postmodernism are not separated by an Iron Curtain or Chinese Wall" (Hassan 88) as it is to say that postmodernism, like all periodizations, is simply an illusory construct that obscures the reality of what is actually a much larger and unified historical movement. I'm not willing—nor do I think it is useful—to wholly abandon the rhetoric of the rupture.

Importantly, this critical sense, or theorizing, of a rupture is itself an identifiable symptom of the postmodern. As Jameson notes, "The postmodern looks for breaks, for events rather than new worlds, for the tell-tale instant after which it's no longer the same; for the 'when-it-all-changed' . . . or, better still, for shifts and irrevocable changes in the representation of things and of the way they change" (*Postmodernism* ix). There is no better example of such thinking than that of Michel Foucault. The seismic upheavals identified in *The Order of Things* and *The Archeology of Knowledge* can be read, I would argue, as a poststructuralist counterpart to the postmodern, or markedly "Anglo-American," appeal to ruptures discussed above. Similarly, and while remaining wary of any simple conflation of poststructuralism and postmodernism,[22] we might usefully (if tentatively) approach the apocalyptic "ends" repeatedly articulated in the poststructuralist discourse of the 1960s and 1970s—including Barthes' death of the author and Derrida's "ends of man"—as distinctly postmodern realities, born of a certain epistemological configuration that aimed to severe all ties with history, to be (as Lyotard might have it) radically new. This is not to deny that certain shifts have occurred—or, even, that certain "ruptures" have occurred. On a certain level, Foucault's posthistoric conception of synchronically defined epistemes remains a useful one; his announcement in the concluding portions of *The Order of Things*, like Derrida's at the end of "Ends of Man,"[23] functions as an accurate foretelling of what the postmodern would become: the end of a distinctly modern mode of representation and the absence of a certain, relatively short-lived, concept of the individual as the subject and object of knowledge. What I want to suggest is that the postmodern debate—and, now, the discussion of postmodernism's death—can be read as symptomatic of some type of ineffaceable "inheritance" that carries across these seemingly self-contained, or exclusive, epistemes (or, better, epistemological configurations). Primarily, though, I want to avoid falling into the trap of simple historical analysis. In looking at the postmodern debate, or the phenomenon that is the subject of that debate, I'm not interested in demonstrating that the proclamation of an end of history (or the end of anything else—postmodernism included) was nothing more than a miscalculation, that, as Anderson attempts to demonstrate in the *Origins of Postmodernity*, the claims attributed to a postmodern way of thinking can be traced backward as progressive developments of temporally and geographically contingent modes of thought, developments that ultimately reaffirm the persistence of what we might think of as a type of Hegelian and/or Marxist historical advancement.

Yet, and at the same time, I'm interested in demonstrating that the various complete and utterly unbridgeable ruptures identified by "the postmodernists" share a *certain history*, a certain genealogy, that the postmodern theory of "ruptures" was indeed (at least on one level) effected by a certain shared experience, a certain experience of the past.[24] Let me put this differently. Certainly, it is entirely possible to identify certain breaks, or shifts—even if it is, perhaps, going too far to say, along with Foucault, that in terms of *other* epistemes, like modernism, "There is *nothing* now, either in our knowledge or in our reflection, that still recalls even the memory of that being" (*OT* 43, my emphasis). What I would like to suggest, instead, is that it is possible and *more useful* to conceive of such breaks as moments of epistemological *re*configuration. By conceiving of historical periodizations in such a way we can avoid the rather simplistic alternatives: either such periods are (1) artificially categorized moments in a much larger and inevitable historical trajectory, or (2) synchronic and utterly exclusive epistemes. Viewed as a series of nonprogressive *re*configurations—as *re*configurations of, as I explain more fully below, a certain essential spectral relationship—periodizations as such can be more easily understood as both continuous and discontinuous with their predecessors. At the same time, any given epistemic reconfiguration can be understood, in line with a more Jamesonian view, as a type of cultural dominant, even as other residual and emergent configurations continue to persist and influence each another—like wheels within wheels. The conception of epochal or epistemic shifts (i.e., reconfigurations) here proposed allows us to account for seemingly evident ruptures while simultaneously making room for a certain underlying spectral persistence, a certain *shared history*.

After all, if the horror films of the last century have taught us anything, it's that even after the break is complete, after the dead are finally separated from the living, something always manages to come across from *the other side*—or rather (and I'm not just speaking of essential horror plot devices) something *must* come across; it's absolutely essential. What I'm suggesting is that postmodernism—like all such "epistemes"—is, if we employ Derrida's phrasing, a "double and unique experience" (*Specters* 15). The experience of any given episteme is always, then, to a certain degree, an experience of déjà vu. It is this sense of déjà vu, I would like to suggest, that has animated the postmodern discussion, a discussion that has, and which continues to, struggle with postmodernism's relation and/or lack thereof to modernism, its seemingly contradictory impulses and its more recent passing. What we have—in modernism, in postmodernism, and now *after* postmodernism—is a series of repetitions, or returns. A persistent revenant. Yet each of these revenants—as that which comes back, a ghost—is always also original, unique. Here, then, we can begin to employ the metaphor of the specter: that which is and (yet) is not, that which returns *for the first time*, that which "*begins by coming back*" (*Specters* 11).[25]

It is with this ironic, or paradoxical, metaphor in mind that I want to continue my inspection of the postmodern debate. By viewing the postmodern as an episteme defined on both sides by certain discernable "ruptures," while understanding it as a periodization or epistemological reconfiguration animated by a certain persistent specter or inheritance (passed on to, and in turn, by, modernism), we can begin to see a way out of our current dilemma. Modernism and postmodernism and, now, this newly emergent epoch can indeed be viewed as singular events, or epistemes; they are also, though, epistemological *re*configurations, *re*configurations of an unavoidable relationship with a certain repeating—we might say passing, or "passed on"—aporia: a certain inheritance, a certain specter.

Exorcisms Without End

In *Specters of Marx*, Derrida argues that Marxism was haunted by various spirits. According to Derrida, one of these spirits cannot be ignored; it cannot be ignored because it compels movement—that is, critical, aesthetic and/or revolutionary movement. But a spirit, Derrida insists, arrives, or manifests, as a ghost, a specter. It is both seen and unseen, present and absent; or, if we employ Derrida's earlier terminology, the spirits of Marxism exist only as trace and differance. What is interesting about Derrida's "essential" specter—and the use of the possessive has double significance, for Derrida (like Marx before him) possesses, or is *possessed by*, the very specter he is discussing—is that it is associated with "emancipatory and *messianic* affirmation, a certain experience of the promise" (89). The specter of Marx—the one that Derrida is concerned with, the one that continues to haunt and thus compel deconstruction—is the one motivating spirit haunting all past idealism(s): faith in god, humanism, meaning, telos, truth, and so on.[26] Ironically, these "spectral effects," these *ideological tendencies*, are the very "opiates" of which Marx (at least according to Derrida) would like to rid the world. Yet the very specter, or teleological aporia, that compels the ideological tendencies to which Marx is opposed animates the discourse of Marxism, the discourse that is intent on exorcising all specters *once and for all*. Simply, if more crudely, the specter of a "true and final" state of communism haunts, and thus compels, the subversive implications of historical materialism; the very ideal of communism is, Derrida seems to suggest, wholly contrary to the anti-ideal-ist discourse that is ultimately animated by *the possibility of communism.* And it is, as I've already intimated, this specter of the messianic, of the promise "to come," that *effected* the very shape of postmodernism as a cultural dominant.

That being said, I'd like to move slowly at this point. To fully understand Derrida's argument—and, in turn, to make it fully appli-cable to a discussion of the passing of postmodernism as an episteme—we need to keep in mind that a specter is always a revenant (i.e., *of the past*) *and* a promise, or sign, of the future, a future to come. It returns from the past to herald the future. The ghost of Hamlet's father is, as Derrida's analysis of *Hamlet* demonstrates, a useful point of refer-ence. The dead King *returns*, but his return as a revenant speaks to the possibility of a future, a time when justice is fulfilled, time is back "in joint" and the revenant is allowed to rest, dissipate, dissolve *finally*—at which point *the future would be present*; the possibility of the future, of the promise, would cease to be a possibility (for the condition of a promise, of its possible fulfillment, as Derrida asserts on numerous occasions, is its impossibility). The specter of Marx can be understood, then, as the animating factor in all past ideological revenants that beckon toward the *horizon* of the future. The specter represents the promise of a future that is forever "to come," or what Derrida refers to as "a messianic without messianism" (*Specters* 59). Now, I have repeatedly associated the specter in question with a certain inherited aporia, namely, a certain teleological aporia.[27] This is because this aporia can be defined as a desire for, or latent belief in, finality, a faith that will never be *finally* "worked out" of our (epistemological) systems/configurations. This is because it animates those very systems. However, and here is where the issue of postmodernism begins to converge with Derrida's discussion of Marxism, these discursive systems (or, in the specific context of this paper, epistemic configurations)—at least since the beginning of what Foucault marks as the modern episteme—have been opposed to, if not entirely frightened by, ghosts. The irony, as Derrida argues, is that the "hostility toward ghosts, a terrified hostility that sometimes fends off terror with a burst of laughter, is perhaps what Marx will always have had in common with his adversaries" (*Specters* 47). According to Derrida, then, the specter that "is haunting Europe"[28] (i.e., commu-nism) is as troubling to Marx's opponents as the specter motivating our blind faith in bourgeois ideology, exchange value, and religion is to Marx(ism). So, Derrida asks: "But how to distinguish between the analysis that denounces magic and the counter-magic that it still risks being?" (*Specters* 47). The war against Marxism, just like the war

Marxism wages against the presumption that ideology, or the immaterial, is *real*—that it is the ultimate source of historical development—"is a war against a camp that is itself organized by the terror of the ghost, the one in front of it and the one it carries within itself" (*Specters* 105). What is always desired in these wars against ghosts is to "exorc-analyze the spectrality of the specter" (*Specters* 47)—that is, to conjure the specter, to make it *be* finally and thus to exorcise it finally. But, "to conjure" (as an act of calling into being or as an act of exorcising, for the one is ultimately the same as the other)[29] is an act compelled by the specter of an end[30]—or, put differently, a certain teleological impulse.

Let's put this as simply as possible: the primary injunction of the specter, its promise of emancipation, is to be rid of all specters. The promise promised is a world without ghosts, a world that is post-ideological: the future as present, the end of history. However, and this is Derrida's main (ethical) point: the promise of such a world *is a specter*. It is only possible because it is impossible. Yet, its possibility compels movement. Ideally, for Derrida, we need to respect the specters of emancipation, not as the promise of a definite telos (which promises the end of the specter, of the promise, of the future, etc.), but as a certain non-teleological eschatology, a repeating promise of the end represented by a type of radical democracy, a sense of justice and/or meaning, deconstruction completed finally and *at last.* But I am not, at this point, interested in our *ideal,* or ethical, relationship to the specter of the messianic; rather, I'm interested in looking at the way in which this specter, or teleological aporia (for, I would argue, this specter continues to compel teleologies rather than non-teleological eschatologies) is seemingly "conjured" by a given epoch. Moreover, I'd like to suggest the possibility that what we might identify as an epistemic rupture occurs at the point when it is impossible to avoid the fact that a given epistemological reconfiguration is animated by the very revenant that was apparently conjured/exorcised by that episteme in the first place. This will make more sense if we look at Derrida's discussion of Marxism *as* communism:

> There is nothing "revisionist" about interpreting the gen-
> esis of totalitarianisms as reciprocal reactions to the fear
> of the ghost that communism inspired beginning in the
> last century, to the terror that it inspired in its adversaries
> but that it turned inside out and felt sufficiently within
> itself to precipitate the monstrous realization, the magical
> effectuation, the animist incorporation of an emancipatory
> eschatology which ought to have respected the promise, the
> being-promise of a promise. (*Specters* 105)

Communism, Derrida suggests, should never have proclaimed itself as the promise finally realized; it shouldn't have attempted and/or claimed to conjure the specter once and for all, to make it real and thus exorcise it as a specter, as a promise. For the promise, as specter, ceases *to be effectual* if we believe that it has been actualized. The promise of emancipation (of meaning, of truth, etc.) no longer animates; it dominates as an apparent reality, an imperative.[31] At the point when ghost busting outdoes itself, when a given epistemic configuration—such as modernism or postmodernism—becomes institutionalized and thus an imperative (because it has forgotten about ghosts, for it believes it has finally conjured/exorcised all ghosts), the specter returns with new ferocity and a new reconfiguration is necessary to deal with it. In the case of Marxism, a discursive rupture[32] seems to have been "the effect of an *ontological* treatment of the spectrality of the ghost" (91). Something similar, it would seem, can be said for *all* cultural production affected by the modern episteme, of which Marxism is arguably only a discursive effect.

With its faith in genius, its heroic literature and architecture, high modernism sought "with prophetic elitism and authoritarianism" (Jameson, *Postmodernism* 2) to challenge and dismantle the false ideologies of the past—ideologies of representation, religion, reason, and so on—by producing cultural artifacts capable of emancipating the masses—or, at the very least, capable of pointing toward that emancipation. We might argue, while risking the accusation of oversimplification, that modernism's "ontological treatment of the spectrality of the ghost" is most obvious, in terms of aesthetic production, in its assumptions surrounding, and its privileging of, the autonomous subject, the man of genius, and the elite ability and/or appreciation for aesthetic innovation.[33] Postmodernism, on the other hand, as innumerable critics have pointed out, seems to dismantle or "deconstruct" these modernist assumptions. As even a quick glance at Hassan's now famous chart of modernist/postmodernist distinctions will reveal,[34] postmodernism exposed the elitism and exclusivity (or, what Derrida would call, the "onto-theology") that haunted the modernist project. For instance, where modernist architects like Le Corbusier and Frank Lloyd Wright built structures that stood as monuments of inspiration, stressing the difference between high and low culture, the postmodernists—in an attempt to renounce "the high-modernist claim to radical difference and innovation" (Jameson, *Postmodernism* 63)—built structures that (according to a someone like Jameson, at least) blended into, or "mirrored," the contexts in which they were erected.[35]

This distinction, of course, applies to literary production as well. While, for the most part, the work of modernists such as Eliot, Pound,

Hemingway, and Faulkner stands aloof from the otherwise indistinguishable masses of pulp, the work of the postmodernists—such as Vonnegut, Barth, Pynchon, Coover, and Acker—attempts to dismantle the distinction between pulp and literature, low and high culture.[36] The now canonical postmodernists tend to employ corrosive self-reflexivity in an attempt to forego any pretence to originality or genius. The typical postmodern subject, like Pynchon's Slothrop, disintegrates into a scattered collection of discursive fragments, nothing more than a type of Foucaultian "author-function."[37] Yet, and as I demonstrate in chapter 3, postmodernism's final days are marked by a heightened awareness that postmodernism failed to escape the binaries it sought to subvert, that the books and buildings of high postmodernism are just as "monumental," just as "elite," as the masterworks of high modernism. Put differently, postmodernism's passing is marked by the pronounced realization that the insistence on groundless self-reflexivity (in architecture, literature, or whatever) ironically became *another* ethical and "elitist" imperative, an imposing suggestion that "responsible" narratives *do not* allow a ground to persist. Given the above discussion, this realization could be said to signal the fact that modernism did indeed "give up the ghost." If modernism attempted to deal with its specters by "ontologizing" the spectrality of ghost (i.e., by determining *as false*, or illusory, all things immaterial), then we might say, if somewhat hastily, that postmodernism "conjured" its spectral inheritance by rejecting all things material or real, by determining *as false* all seemingly stable distinctions.[38] In both cases, though, the animating motivation—that which "passes on"—was the specter, or the promise, of a certain telos, the end of the aporia of spectrality. In modernism, the spectrality of the ghost was challenged by the promise of absolute materiality (as we see in a work like Joyce's *Portrait of the Artist*, which insists upon the absolute autonomy of the author/subject); in postmodernism, the exorcism was animated by an absolute denial of the possible materiality of the ghost (as we see in, say, Tom Robbins' *Even Cowgirls Get the Blues*, which refuses to privilege the author as anything more than another fictional construct). Either way, the ghost's ironic spectrality—its presence *and* its absence, its possibility *and* its impossibility—was challenged and eventually denied altogether.[39] And, as I have suggested numerous times already, this specter continues—as it is what "passes on"—after postmodernism. In fact, it is possible to refer to this epistemological reconfiguration after postmodernism—just as it is possible to refer to the episteme *after modernism*, as a period of mourning, a period in which we struggle to get over (i.e., conjure/exorcise) that which has *passed*, or that which *is past*. Still, before moving on to a discussion of

the ways in which the specter of postmodernism returns *after* postmodernism—that is, before considering the fact that the passing of postmodernism refers both to its death *and* its inevitable persistence—it is
necessary to return to and thus conclude the above "spectroanalysis"
of the postmodern debate. By way of a return, though, I'd like to look
at the concept of the specter from another perspective.

Kenneth Burke argues that all dominant discourses—what he calls
"terministic screens"[40]—should be understood as "mystifications." While,
according to Burke (and, here, we must return again to the issue of
Marxism), historical materialism is a demystification of Hegelianism, it
is also a type of remystification. Any given discursive "answer" to another
discourse is always a (de/re)mystification.[41] This "mystifying" process
seems to persist *ad absurdum*, apparently without beginning or end. Yet,
Burke seems more than willing to accept the apparent necessity of this
inescapable process of mystification, referring to it, at times, as a type of
"spiritualized" (*Rhetoric* 114) rhetorical compulsion. With this in mind,
Burke's conception of discursive dynamics can be understood as pre-
(or, proto)spectrological. As such, it gives us another perspective from
which to approach the issue of postmodernism's "passing." Employed
on a larger scale—that is, in terms of epistemes—Burke's argument
highlights the way in which one epistemological configuration seems to
"answer" the problems of another while simultaneously persisting in the
same problematic act: mystification, or spiritualization. Each episteme is
compelled by the promise of an end (telos) to the spiral of mystification—"spiral" in the sense that each mystification is both a return and
a unique event—that animates the spiral in the first place. We could
probably trace this spiral back before Plato—and Derrida, or Burke,
might have such a history in mind—but, for my purposes, I want to
focus on the fact that what we see spectrally persisting or "living on"
in modernism and postmodernism, and now *after*, is most easily recognized as a revenant of an Enlightenment project. Put differently, I'd
like to locate the origin (albeit, a contingent origin, an origin unique
to the context of this particular book) of postmodernism's essential
specter—or, rather, its spirit of an emancipatory teleology—in the basic
assumptions of the Enlightenment.

The (Phantom) Project Still Incomplete

With the theory of the specter and of mystification in mind, I would
like to return now to the above "survey" of the postmodern debate via a
discussion of one of postmodernism's staunchest, and most influential,

critics: Jürgen Habermas. For Habermas, postmodernism is a type of interruption, an interruption of what he refers to as the still incomplete project of modernism. Since the late 1960s, Habermas argues, the *"spirit* of aesthetic modernity has ... begun to age" ("Incomplete" 4, my emphasis).[42] For Habermas, the project of modernity—as distinct from a modern period or epoch—is marked by a connection to the past, a desire for the new and a certain "longing for an undefiled, an immaculate and stable present" ("Incomplete" 3). On the one hand, "Modernity revolts against the normalizing functions of tradition" while, on the other, "The modern avante garde spirit ... opposes at the same time a neutralized history, which is locked up in the museum of historicism" (4). This subversion of history, a subversion that is ironically animated by a sense of a dynamic history moving toward "an as yet unoccupied future" (3), is at the heart of what Habermas sees as the project of modernity: "The project aims at a differentiated relinking of modern culture with an everyday praxis that still depends on vital heritages, but would be impoverished through mere traditionalism" (13). Ultimately, Habermas' project of modernity embraces the aims of the Enlightenment, aims Habermas sees as the responsibility of modernity to realize. In the article I've been citing, "Modernity—An Incomplete Project" (also known as the "Frankfurt Address"), Habermas associates this project, specifically, with a desire to recover a certain unity of the disciplines, disciplines separated into three distinct and specialized spheres: science, morality, and art—or, "cognitive instrumental, moral practical, and ... aesthetic expressive rationality" (8): "The project of modernity formulated in the 18th century by the philosophers of the Enlightenment consisted in their efforts to develop objective science, universal morality and law, and autonomous art, according to their inner logic. At the same time, this project intended to release the cognitive potentials of each of these domains to set them free from their esoteric forms" (8). The separation of these fields, and the subsequent specialization of knowledge—that is, the separation of forms of knowledge from the average citizen—leads to the increased threat that (what Habermas refers to as) the "life world," "whose traditional substance has already been devaluated, will become more and more impoverished" (8). The sense we get is that the project of modernity aims to seal the rift between these specialized forms of knowledge and the "life world" that they are ultimately meant to serve.

What is important to note, though, and what I want to stress here, is that, according to Habermas, this project repeatedly *and perhaps necessarily* encounters various obstacles. For the most part, these obstacles come in two distinct varieties. Either the project stumbles upon the belief that "the aesthetic and the social world" are absolutely irreconcilable—at which point the "utopia of reconciliation" fails to be an animating goal—or, in reaction to such absolutism, the project attempts to actualize itself by dissolving all distinctions. Habermas views the surrealist movement as an example of the latter.

After describing the surrealist movement as an attempt "to level art and life, fiction and praxis, appearance and reality to one plane" (10), Habermas points out that "A rationalized everyday life . . . could hardly be saved from cultural impoverishment through breaking open a single cultural sphere—art—and so providing access to just one of the specialized knowledge complexes" (10–11). It is useless, if not dangerous, to insist that *everything* is art. Put differently—and in such a way as to begin drawing some connections between the project of modernity and the concepts of the specter and mystification discussed above—Habermas, like Burke (and, to a certain degree, Derrida), sees the attempts to actualize a project of Enlightenment, a project aimed at an "utopia of reconciliation," as necessarily resulting in various incomplete solutions. These "incomplete solutions" could be called, if we were to use Burke's words, " 'high abstractions' [that, necessarily] omit important ingredients of motivation" (114). Habermas puts it this way:

> Reification cannot be overcome by forcing just one of these highly stylized cultural spheres to open up and become more accessible. Instead, we see under certain circumstances a relationship emerge between terrorist activities and the over extension of any one of these spheres into other domains: examples would be tendencies to aestheticize politics, or to replace politics by moral rigorism or to submit it to the dogmatism of a doctrine. (11)

This claim is, as we have already seen, echoed in Derrida's discussion of the Marxist failure to respect the spectrality of the specter. The suggestion that a certain dogmatism results from the very attempt to manifest the "project" (or, if I can begin to reemploy the terminology delineated above, "the specter") of emancipation recalls—or, rather, anticipates—Derrida's suggestion that such a project is only useful if its actualization remains deferred. The fact that Habermas understands just this point is all the more apparent when he seemingly turns on his own advocacy of the Enlightenment project: "artistic production would dry up, if it were not carried out in the form of a specialized treatment of autonomous problems, and if it were to cease to be the concern of experts who do not pay so much attention to exoteric questions" (12). At this point, it would appear that Habermas is employing paradoxical, if not spectrological, logic. This aspect of Habermas' thinking cannot be overstressed.

Consider Anderson's account of Habermas' understanding of modernity: "the 'project' of modernity as [Habermas] sketched it is a contradictory amalgam of two opposite principles: specialization and popularization" (39). Anderson, of course, reads this contradiction as a type of failure: "How was a synthesis of the two at any stage to be realized? So defined, could the project ever be completed?" (39). Certainly, Habermas' argument has its problems; but those problems are, I would argue, a result of his claims that the major "poststructuralists" (from Bataille[43] to Derrida) are young conservatives and that postmodernism is a neoconservative trend complicit with societal modernization. What Anderson seems to forget is that Habermas' definition of modernity refers less to an epoch than it does to a certain spirit of emancipation "passed on" since the Enlightenment. Its very impossibility or contradictory nature—its spectrality, if you will—is an essential characteristic, a characteristic that, I'm suggesting, Habermas is intent on demonstrating. When Anderson refers to "the *pathos* of Habermas's later theory, which simultaneously reaffirms the ideals of the Enlightenment and denies them any chance of realization" (44, my emphasis), he has, to a certain extent, missed the point. If Habermas voices any pathos, it is in his claim that postmodernism—as well as the anti-modernism of the poststructuralists—has given up on the possibility of the project, the specter, the promise. Arguably, for Habermas, postmodernism, anti-modernism, and premodernism (Habermas locates three separate strains opposed to the project of modernity) have ignored the specter, denied the specter, or looked to the wrong specter respectively. Such a claim is, of course, pure conjecture, but that's beside the point. What Habermas identifies as the still incomplete project of modernity can be identified as a certain specter of the Enlightenment, the manifestation of a spirit of emancipation (as I defined it above). While, in "Modernity—An Incomplete Project," he focuses on the impulse toward unification, the project of modernity can be understood more broadly, as later work by Habermas intimates,[44] as the spirit of utopianism/emancipation. What Habermas fails to see is that what he calls "postmodernism" and "anti-modernism" are symptoms of an emergent epoch, or epistemological reconfiguration, that continue to be animated by the specter of a still (and, perhaps, *always*) "incomplete project of modernity." This argument can be further clarified if we look at the way in which Habermas' argument ultimately and *spectro-*

logically conflates with that of Jean-François Lyotard, the advocate of postmodernism *par excellence.*

Jameson argues that Lyotard's first major work on postmodernism, *The Postmodern Condition*, is "a thinly yeiled [sic] polemic against Jürgen Habermas's concept of a 'legitimation crisis' and vision of a 'noisefree,' transparent, fully communicational society" ("Foreword" vii).[45] This "crisis" can be aligned with what Habermas describes later in the Frankfurt Address as the interruption, or abandonment, of a still incomplete project of modernity. From this perspective, Lyotard's "report" can be read as advocating the very crisis that Habermas laments, a crisis that has been fostered in the field of science (science being Lyotard's primary concern in *The Postmodern Condition*) by theorists like Thomas Kuhn and Paul Feyerabend. That is, as Jameson suggests, Lyotard's "post" is roughly analogous to Habermas' "crisis"; what Habermas views as a legitimation crisis Lyotard celebrates as a radical break from the imperative of legitimation.[46]

Lyotard associates this collapse of legitimation with a corresponding collapse of "metanarratives," the grand narratives that previously functioned as the grounds upon which knowledge was legitimated in the first place. Lyotard identifies these metanarratives, or narratives of legitimation, as those assumptions that, up to the postmodern period, or moment of "crisis," have tended to validate the claims of dominant groups. These grand narratives offer totalizing, or teleological, conceptions of social dynamics. They are, in short, both idealist and ontological narratives of emancipation.[47] The crisis that Habermas speaks of is, then, associated with the "de-legitimation" of these "unifying" grand narratives. Lyotard puts it this way: "We no longer have recourse to the grand narratives—we can resort neither to the dialectic of spirit nor even to the emancipation of humanity as a validation for postmodern scientific discourse" (60). For Lyotard (and, we might say, for Habermas too), the term "postmodern" is thus defined "as incredulity toward metanarratives" (*Postmodern* xxiv). In place of these grand narratives, Lyotard identifies an infinitesimal number of "little narratives." The rules of any "little narrative"—what Lyotard also describes as the rules of a language game that is in constant "play" with an unlimited number of other language games—are, and *must be*, susceptible to change and cancellation. Because consensus is always interrupted, or made impossible, by the continuously shifting or "temporary" contracts of any given interpretative community, legitimation no longer has any claim to permanence; it is spatially and temporally specific.

Through his discussion of little narratives Lyotard works to demonstrate that any latent desire for stable consensus—or, in other words, any desire for a still viable and unifying metanarrative—is fundamentally at odds with the current liberating acceptance of, what he terms, the "paralogical" nature of radically heterogeneous language games:

> as I have shown in the analysis of the pragmatics of science, consensus is only a particular state of discussion, not its end. Its end, on the contrary, is paralogy. This double observation (the heterogeneity of the rules and the search for dissent) destroys a belief that still underlies Habermas's research, namely, that humanity as a collective (universal) subject seeks its common emancipation through the regularization of the "moves" permitted in all language games and that the legitimacy of any statement resides in its contributing to that emancipation. (66)

Legitimation for Lyotard is no longer rooted in any stable consensus, or unifying goal (i.e., telos); rather, language games are now "legitimated," as Jameson puts it, by "a search, not for consensus, but very precisely for 'instabilities,' as a practice of *paralogism*, in which the point is not to reach agreement but to undermine from within the very framework in which the previous 'normal science' had been conducted" ("Foreword" xix). In this way, Lyotard's postmodern is ultimately aligned with the radically new, or wholly heterogeneous. This is particularly clear in Lyotard's later essay (published three years after *The Postmodern Condition*): "Answering the Question: What Is Postmodernism?" Here Lyotard almost entirely blurs the distinction between postmodernism and the high-modernist imperative of experimentation. Postmodernism is now the ultimate form of avant-garde cultural production: "A work can become modern only if it is first postmodern. Postmodernism thus understood is not modernism at its end but in the nascent state and this state is constant" (79). Modernism is, in this sense, postmodernism *after* its radical heterogeneity, or "newness," has been (at least partially) absorbed, or assimilated—that is, *after* it becomes "understood" and, for that very reason, ceases to be wholly other/new.

Almost immediately, then, Lyotard's conception of the postmodern—which is seemingly inseparable from his critique of the apparent utopianism of Habermas—seems to turn on itself, becoming the very thing to which Lyotard would like the postmodern to be wholly antithetical.[48] Lyotard's vision of postmodernism becomes, itself, a metanarrative.[49] Consider, for example, Lyotard's claim, cited above, that the *end* of "the pragmatics of science" is not "consensus" but "paralogy."

Lyotard can certainly claim that the postmodern *realization,* or *accurate representation,* of the un-totalizable heterogeneity, and instability, of language games "destroys" the possibility of Habermas' implicit belief in a legitimating, or unifying, narrative of collective emancipation. However, the very fact that Habermas' "move," or participation in a certain language game, is denied, or de-legitimated, as implicitly determined by false rules (if only because *all* rules are false, or illusory) allows us to locate in Lyotard the very impulse toward consensus he ostensibly rejects. Lyotard's paralogy becomes a type of ironic revival of the belief that humanity—which is now viewed as a heterogonous mass of discursively determined nodals[50]—"seeks its common emancipation through the regularization of the 'moves' permitted in all language games and that the legitimacy of any statement resides in its contributing to that emancipation" (*Postmodern* 66). The only difference between Lyotard's version of Habermas' latent faith and Lyotard's own revival of that faith is the fact that now, in paralogy, legitimacy is determined by a statement's implicit *or* explicit denial of the possibility of legitimation. As Habermas fails to make (at least, obviously) such a statement, his "move" in the language games of postmodernism is necessarily illegitimate. This apparent conflation of Lyotard and Habermas' superficially opposed positions is, perhaps, most obvious if we consider the way in which both theorists ultimately desire a return to the imperatives of high modernism, the avant-garde, the possibility of critical change, and a more enlightened understanding of reality.

This brings me to the crux of my argument. Lyotard's discussion of the postmodern ultimately highlights the way in which Habermas' "project" remains an animating feature within the postmodern *even though* an absolute denial of that project is the defining characteristic of the postmodern. The project—or, we might say at this point, the specter—returns through, or because of, its denial. Both Habermas and Lyotard fail to see this; it is, in fact, this joint failure that ultimately effects, at least in my reading, an ironic theoretical convergence. Habermas (the modernist) is too focused on the possible materialization of the specter, while Lyotard (the postmodernist) is deceived by its apparent lack of materiality. The most obvious counter to this claim is, of course, the fact that Lyotard hardly seems, at least in "What Is Postmodernism?," to be talking about what we have come to consider postmodernism. It seems quite likely that Lyotard is simply mistaking postmodernism for some strain of late, or *latent,* modernism. If this is the case, then it's not surprising that Lyotard's argument ultimately converges with Habermas': they are both opposed to that which is considered to be *truly* postmodern. Still, I'd like to suggest that Lyotard's return to a type of high-modernist imperative is simply an ostentatious effect of the postmodern specter I've been attempting to locate. As I have stressed throughout this survey of the postmodern debate, postmodern theorists have repeatedly noted—or, at the very least, demonstrated in the very logic of their arguments—that the postmodern is, in some way, both continuous *and* wholly discontinuous with modernism. Moreover, Lyotard's understanding of disparate and eternally shifting language games, or "little narratives," can be aligned with the most canonical representations of a postmodern epistemological "shift:" Foucault's discursive networks, Barthes' "texts," Kristeva's intertextuality, Derrida's linguistic bricolage, and so on.[51] All of which, I will add, if only tentatively at this point, are animated by this specter I have been discussing, the specter that is (albeit, in a more obvious fashion) lurking about in Lyotard's pages.

We can now turn to the work of Jameson directly. From a certain perspective, I would argue, Jameson's take on the postmodern is in fundamental agreement with the spectrological argument I have been sketching throughout this chapter. While I do not wholly agree with Jameson's claim that "Lyotard is in reality quite unwilling to posit a postmodernist stage radically different from the period of high modernism" (xvi)—for this argument cannot account for Lyotard's discussion of language games in *The Postmodern Condition*—Jameson's identification, within Lyotard's work, of "the persistence of buried master-narratives" (xxii) suggests an implicit awareness of a certain specter necessarily at work in postmodernism. In an attempt to reconcile Lyotard's claim that all master narratives are illusory with his paradoxical "faith" in the emancipatory nature of "small narrative units at work everywhere *locally* in the present social system" (xi), Jameson suggests the possibility that "This seeming contradiction can be resolved . . . by taking a further step that Lyotard seems unwilling to do . . . , namely to posit, not the disappearance of the great master-narratives, but their passage underground as it were, their continuing but now unconscious effectivity as a way of 'thinking about' and acting in our present situation" (xii). As Jameson himself points out, the persistence of these seemingly effaced legitimating narratives—narratives that motivate all forms of action, or deliberation—can be connected to what Jameson calls, elsewhere, "the political unconscious." Moreover, this conception of a "persistent" yet repressed political unconscious can be read as an early description of what Jameson will later come to refer to as the utopianism of the postmodern, or the "return of the repressed."

It is important to note that a certain shift in "tone" can be identified in Jameson's later work on the postmodern. Take, for example, the development of his most well-known essay: "Postmodernism: Or, the Cultural Logic of Late Capitalism." In its first published manifestation, "Postmodernism and Consumer Society," the cultural production of late capitalism is described in a distinctly pejorative manner, a manner (no doubt) that allowed someone like Hutcheon to denounce Jameson's position as blind to the critical nature of postmodernism. According to Hutcheon, Jameson fails to distinguish between the socioeconomic period of late-capitalism and the cultural production that occurs within that period. Jameson does not, according to Hutcheon, distinguish between postmodernity and postmodernism. As a mode of cultural production, postmodernism, in Jameson's work, is wholly complicit with the inherent assumptions of late-capitalism, or what David Harvey identifies as a period of flexible accumulation. If we look exclusively at "Postmodernism and Consumer Society," Hutcheon's position is certainly feasible. However, if we move into an analysis of the final manifestation of Jameson's paper (never mind his foreword to Lyotard's *Postmodern Condition*, which actually predates Hutcheon's *Politics*)—that is, if we look at the introductory chapter of Jameson's *Postmodernism*—then Hutcheon's argument becomes somewhat dated, if not irrelevant.[52] Here Jameson begins to acknowledge a certain utopianism at work in the postmodern, the recognition of which allows him to soften his earlier analysis of postmodern cultural production. This is not to say that Jameson eventually makes the clear distinction that Hutcheon demands; he never posits the possibility of a postmodern mode of cultural production capable of critically separating itself from its own conditions of production. Jameson continues to insist that the cultural production of postmodernism *is* indistinguishable from the socioeconomic event of late-capitalism, while simultaneously suggesting that a certain utopianism[53] necessarily continues to *haunt* that production. What Jameson, as a Marxist critic, ultimately decides to stress—and relocate within postmodernism—is "the political value of the Utopian imagination as a form of praxis" (107). The suggestion is clear: without the persistence of this utopian spirit, the possibility of, or reason for, change atrophies: "if postmodernism is the substitute for the sixties and the compensation for their political failure, the question of utopia would seem to be a crucial test of what is left of our capacity to imagine change at all" (xvi). We need to ask, in other words, why postmodernism *is* at all. If it were as ecstatically nihilistic as many have claimed/lamented, would it not be marked by absolute silence? What compels it to be, to move, to produce *at all*?[54] For Jameson, it would seem, the answer is the inevitable return of a certain repressed utopianism, a type of political, or historical, faith.

Toward the end of this survey of the postmodern debate, then—
or, rather, toward the end of the postmodern debate proper and, thus,
of postmodernism proper[55]—the discussion, once again hinges on the
necessary persistence of a certain spirit of Marxism. And with this (we
might say, unavoidable) return, I can begin to tie things together. This
latent, or spectral, utopianism can be understood, more simply, as the
return of a repressed teleological conception of historical progression. The effects of this inevitable "return of the repressed"—what I
have referred to variously as the specter of utopia, the "incomplete
project of modernity," or a certain teleological aporia—are various.
Hutcheon's own take on postmodernism, including her critique of
Jameson, is, in fact, an interesting example of the way in which Jameson's "repressed" returns.

Like the majority of postmodern critics (working as postmodernists, or *from within postmodernism*), Hutcheon defines the postmodern
as a distinct break with modernism that somehow maintains a certain
modernist impulse. For this reason, Hutcheon's critique of Jameson
ultimately hinges on the fact that he seems unwilling, or unable, to
identify this impulse—an impulse that, for Hutcheon, results in the
most important feature of the postmodern: the activity of "de-doxi-
fication" (or, more simply, "de-naturalization"). That we can identify
this activity—loosely defined as the process of demonstrating that "we
can only know the world through a 'network of socially established
meaning systems, the discourses of our culture' " (*Politics* 7)—speaks
to the reality of a "paradoxical postmodernism of complicity and critique, of reflexivity and historicity, that at once inscribes and subverts
the conventions and ideologies of the dominant cultural and social
forces of the twentieth-century western world" (*Politics* 11). Hutcheon
is critical of Jameson's early work on the postmodern because it fails
to announce the possibility of this paradox, a paradox that allows postmodernism to be *both* the cultural logic of late-capitalism *and* the critique of that logic. Echoing the ironic tone we identified in Habermas
(above), Hutcheon celebrates postmodern cultural artifacts, stressing
the way in which they "both install and subvert the teleology, closure,
and causality of narrative, both historical and fictive" (60). Hutcheon's
postmodern is animated by the critical impulse of modernism, the
need to subvert established assumptions, but it manages simultaneously
to "[call] into question the messianic faith of modernism, the faith
that technical innovation and purity of form can assure social order"
(11). What is interesting about Hutcheon's discussion, though, is that
it ultimately confirms the persistence of the messianic, the specter.
By insisting on the progressive nature of postmodernism's paradoxi-

cal relationship to totalizing assumptions, Hutcheon cannot help but present postmodernism as *a final and true* mode of representation, the end of a linear aesthetic history. Of course, we might say that Derrida (in his discussion of specters and ethico-political responsibility) does a similar thing, but such a suggestion must remain unexplored until the following chapter. What is important here and now is that Hutcheon's definition of postmodernism—and, by implication, her critique of Jameson—ultimately confirms Jameson's identification of a utopianism that necessarily motivates the cultural production of postmodernism. A large portion of Jameson's *Postmodernism* is, in fact, dedicated to uncovering the residual traces of this utopian spirit.

For Jameson, the conventional view of postmodernism as the "end of all ideologies," as the post-ideological, implicitly associates postmodernism with the end of Marxism; and, as Jameson notes, the end of Marxism "went hand in hand with the end of Utopia" (159). What Jameson ultimately suggests, though, is that even the end of utopia requires, necessarily (and paradoxically), the persistence of the possibility of utopia:

> this unforeseeable return of narrative as the narrative of the end of narratives, this return of history in the midst of the prognosis of the demise of historical telos, suggests a second feature of postmodernism theory which requires attention, namely, the way in which virtually any observation about the present can be mobilized in the very search for the present itself and pressed into service as a symptom and an index of the deeper logic of the postmodern. (*Postmodernism* xii)

The sense of a certain spectral logic is hard to miss. That is, Jameson seems to offer us another way of understanding the spectrological conditions of postmodernism. And with the above survey in mind, a survey that has repeatedly encountered the problematic nature of postmodernism's relation to modernism, it seems only reasonable to agree (to a certain extent) with Jameson's claim that "the residual traces of modernism must be seen in another light, less as anachronisms than as necessary failures that inscribe the particular project back into its context, while at the same time reopening the question of the modern itself for reexamination" (*Postmodernism* xvi). Still, it would be misleading to say that Jameson's take on the postmodern is entirely sympathetic to the spectrological position I have been sketching—or, rather, uncovering. The fact that Jameson feels it is possible to "inscribe the particular [postmodern] project back into its context" suggests as much. This is to say, quite simply, that Jameson's is a Marxist argument; mine is not. I am not interested in locating or recovering some sense of a historical trajectory, a progression of the dialectic (Marxist or Hegelian). What Jameson identifies as utopian—and with that identification I agree—I do not associate with a "repressed" persistence of history. In short, I am not interested in Jameson's argument as it functions in its original context. What Jameson sees as repressed, I see as spectral. The spectrology here proposed does not aim to prove the reality of a teleological historical progress that postmodernism can never finally disprove or escape; I am, rather, attempting to highlight the necessity of an implicit (or, at times, explicit) promise of, or faith in, such a teleology. This "promise" has been described as spectral for the various reasons I have explicated above: it compels movement, action, work, if only because we can *never* tolerate its spectrality: its possibility *and* its impossibility, its presence *and* its absence.

By way of a brief summation, I will try to clarify this distinction. Jameson's discussion of the postmodern distinguishes itself from other such discussions in that it views the postmodern as a cultural dominant. By discussing the postmodern in this way, Jameson avoids the restrictive nature of a theory of historic ruptures, while still considering the postmodern as a discrete epistemological unit. Jameson's sense of a dominant allows for the presence, within that dominant, of residual and emergent forms of cultural production. And, certainly, I do not wish to lose Jameson's distinctive take on Raymond Williams' dominant, residual, emergent schema. Without such a schema we cannot account for the persistence of obviously modernist modes (e.g., Hemingway's persistence into the 1960s) and/or the emergence of new cultural modes or styles (e.g., the work of Nicholson Baker, which begins with *The Mezzanine* in 1986) during a distinctly postmodern period. Still, and at the same time, I have attempted to maintain, to a certain extent, the postmodern rhetoric of epochal breaks—or even, of epistemic ruptures. I have, however, tempered this rhetoric (via Burke and Derrida) with a certain concept of repetition. By identifying such breaks as epistemological reconfigurations, my intent has been to highlight a type of spiral movement, a movement that can be defined as a series of shifting spectrological relationships, or ways of dealing with a certain necessarily ineffaceable spectral inheritance. While there is reason to view epistemes such as modernism and postmodernism as being, in Jameson's somewhat disapproving terms, "bounded on either side by inexplicable chronological metamorphoses and punctuation marks" (4), such configurations are inevitably *effected*, or made possible, by a certain persistent specter, a specter that always, that necessarily must, pass on. This specter has been recognized, if not inadvertently encountered, throughout the postmodern debate. In Jameson, as we have seen, this specter is recognized—or, perhaps, mis-recognized—as the persistence of a certain seemingly repressed teleological progress, the emanations of which result in the various teleological affirmations of postmodernist assumptions. While Jameson might argue that these "emanations" are symptomatic of postmodernism's *historical trajectory out of* a still residual modernism, I am suggesting that the possibility of identifying the impulses and assumptions of modernism within the postmodern episteme is an effect of a certain necessarily persistent specter. In other words, what motivates the one carries across to the other; they are, as Derrida would say, "double and unique." And, what carries across, what passes on, neither is nor is not; as a specter, it refuses, as Hamlet might say through the mouth of Derrida, "to be or not to be." It is this impossibly possible nature that, in the end, makes the specter essential and ineffaceable. And if postmodernism has "passed" then it has most certainly passed on this specter. The task, then—the task that will be taken up in the following chapters—is to trace this passing, to locate and then relocate the specter as it moves on heedless of boundaries, epistemic ruptures included. For, as Derrida assures us, "After the end of history, the spirit comes by coming back [revenant] . . ." (*Specters* 10).

CHAPTER TWO

Spectral Circumventions
(of the Specter)

Poststructuralism, Derrida, and the Project Renewed

WALTER: Nihilists! Fuck me. I mean, say what you like about the tenets of National Socialism, Dude, at least it's an ethos.

—Joel and Ethan Coen, *The Big Lebowski*

Without this *non-contemporaneity with itself of the living present*, without that which secretly unhinges it, without this responsibility and this respect for justice concerning those who *are not here*, of those who are no longer or who are not yet *present and living*, what sense would there be to ask the question "where?" "where tomorrow?" "whither?"

—Jacques Derrida, *Specters of Marx*

So Rorty has, as I said, a delicate operation on his hands.

—John D. Caputo, "On Not Circumventing the Quasi-Transcendental"

Poststructuralism and/as Postmodernism

Although many critics view poststructuralism and thus deconstruction as a distinctly postmodern and/or nihilistic form of theoretical discourse, commentators who wish to situate it in a much broader philosophical tradition typically reaffirm poststructuralism as a distinctly French discourse, a discourse that is not entirely sympathetic to the pragmatism of (American) postmodernism. Pointing to the (albeit, latent) remainders of phenomenology and structuralism within poststructuralism, commentators like Tilottama Rajan and Rodolphe

Gasché[1] tend to disrupt the possibility of sustaining a sense of easy parallelism: modernism/structuralism, postmodernism/poststructuralism. Moreover, what North American critics tend to understand as "poststructuralism"—a term, we should note, that is rarely employed in the discourse it describes (i.e., the texts of Barthes, Kristeva, Lacan, Foucault, Derrida, etc.)—typically focuses on a distinctly French "contemporary scene" that is more aligned with the avant-gardist tendencies of high-modernism than with the postmodern confusion of mass and high culture. And when poststructuralists do address (or rather, "celebrate") English cultural production, they almost always focus on modernist texts. Rarely does poststructuralism bother with postmodern works; it's difficult—if not impossible—to say what, exactly, "poststructuralists" know about (American) postmodern cultural production. Did Derrida know his Pynchon? Had Barthes read Philip K. Dick? What does Kristeva think of *Pulp Fiction*? Did Foucault manage to get in a screening of *Stuntman*? Of course, this lack of engagement shouldn't surprise us. During what we might retrospectively view as the height of postmodernism (i.e., the mid-1980s), Andreas Huyssen argued that poststructuralism should be viewed as a "modern" discourse—or rather, as "a theory of modernism" (Huyssen 207). Almost completely forgotten in current discussions of poststructuralism and postmodernism, Huyssen's line of reasoning opens up the possibility that, "rather than offering a *theory of postmodernism* and developing an analysis of contemporary culture, French theory provides us primarily with an *archeology of modernity*, a theory of modernism at the stage of its exhaustion" (209). Poststructuralism is a modernist discourse *because* it tends to privilege modernist texts as objects of study: "Flaubert, Proust and Bataille in Barthes; Nietzsche and Heidegger, Mallarmé in Derrida; Nietzsche, Magritte and Bataille in Foucault; Mallarmé and Lautréamont, Joyce and Artaud in Kristeva; Freud in Lacan; Brecht in Althusser and Macherey, and so on *ad infinitum*" (208–9). By privileging such texts, or so the argument goes, poststructuralism works to reinscribe the rather politically hegemonic "art for art's sake" formalism of high modernism: "the list of 'no longer possibles' (realism, representation, subjectivity, history, etc., etc.) is as long in poststructuralism as it used to be in modernism, and it is very similar indeed" (Huyssen 136).

Admittedly, it is rather hard to contest the claim that, in poststructuralism, "The enemies still are realism and representation, mass culture and standardization, grammar, communication, and the presumably all-powerful homogenizing pressures of the modernist state" (Huyssen 208). Nevertheless, because it highlights the way in which poststructuralism can be read *at the height of postmodern cultural pro-*

duction as implicitly sympathetic to modernism, Huyssen's discussion inadvertently locates the spectral remainder of modernity that is the motivating feature of *both* poststructuralism *and* postmodernism. For this reason, a careful look at Huyssen's perhaps "dated" position will be of some interest. Huyssen wants to argue that poststructuralism continues to resist modernization—and is, for that reason, a remnant (or, better, *a revenant*) of modernism. For Huyssen, though, this resistance paradoxically speaks to a certain complicity *with* the ongoing processes of modernization. In direct contrast to the various and often "leftist" postmodern detractors (Jürgen Habermas, David Harvey, Christopher Norris, etc.),[2] Huyssen attempts to trace a direct line between the negative effects of modernization and modernism's *apparent resistance of modernization.* This collusion of modernism and capital development is, Huyssen argues, most pronounced in poststructuralism's various attempts to reject the traditional notion of the autonomous subject: "Isn't the 'death of the subject/author' position tied by mere reversal to the very ideology that invariably glorifies the artist as genius, whether for marketing purposes or out of conviction and habit?" (213). While this simple reversal links poststructuralism to the modernist exaltation of the author/subject, the fact that the process of modernization has (on its own) dissolved the possibility of the subject makes poststructuralism's "radical" position a simple reaffirmation of the *status quo*:

> It merely duplicates on the level of aesthetics and theory what capitalism as a system of exchange relations produces tendentially in everyday life: the denial of subjectivity in the process of its construction. Poststructuralism thus attacks the appearance of the capitalist culture—individualism writ large—but misses its essence; like modernism, it is always also in sync with rather than opposed to the real processes of modernization. (213)

While poststructuralism is thus a futile continuation of the "good fight" (the "still incomplete project of modernity," as it were), Huyssen's postmodernism (much like, as we will see, Richard Rorty's) seems effectively to resist, or to critique, modernization *because* it views the possibility of a "privileged" position of interpretation, truth claim, or critical response as having passed. In this view, poststructuralism seems to perpetuate a type of post-Kantian idealism, while postmodernism (we might say, pragmatically) abandons teleological assumptions altogether. This apparent divergence of postmodernism and poststructuralism is, perhaps, most obvious in the work of Kristeva. Kristeva's theorizing of the authorless "poetic" *text* seems to privilege one form of textual practice over another. The fact that the privileged text is almost always "modern" only serves to exemplify Huyssen's point. A brief look at Kristeva's understanding of "poetic language" will help to clarify Huyssen's attempts to articulate what we might think of as poststructural "dogmatism."

In *Revolution in Poetic Language*, Kristeva famously articulates the two main features of any language act: the genotext and the phenotext. According to Kristeva, the genotext, which is closely tied to the linguistically anterior *chora*, is the part of the text that is nonlinguistic, but which includes "semiotic processes [as well as] the advent of the symbolic" (86). While it is apprehended—or rather, *sensed*—within linguistic structures, the genotext "is . . . a *process*, which tends to articulate structures that are ephemeral (unstable, threatened by drive charges, 'quanta' rather than 'marks')" (86). Detectable via a text's phonematic and melodic devices, its repetitions, rhymes, and rhythms, the genotext expresses the multiplicity of factors involved in a subject's formation. Distinct from the genotext, though, is the phenotext. If the genotext is "the underlying foundation," the portion of the text that is only ever *sensed* as an ongoing process of subject formation, the phenotext is the portion of the text that obeys the rules of syntactical arrangement, that conveys the plot and characterizations, that "presupposes a subject of enunciation and an addressee" (87). What is of interest here is the fact that, while every "signifying process . . . includes both the genotext and the phenotext . . . , every signifying practice does not encompass the infinite totality of that process" (88). The "infinity" of the signifying process is often halted, or "obliterated," by various sociopolitical factors. By suggesting that these "obliterations" are "conveyed by the phenotext," Kristeva suggests that the phenotext can come to restrict the genotext and, thus, the possibility of "expressing" the infinite process through which the subject is generated. Because such a restriction—or sociopolitical contamination—is possible, some *texts* can be read as infinitely open while certain other works must be rejected as hegemonic, or closed. For Kristeva, then, textual "success" becomes a matter of subverting sociopolitical or ideological restraints. And, not surprisingly, such subversions are most apparent and most effective in the literary works of the modernist avant-garde: "Among the capitalist mode of production's numerous signifying practices only certain literary texts of the avant-garde (Mallarmé, Joyce) manage to cover the infinity of the process, that is, reach the semiotic *chora*, which modifies linguistic structures" (88). The point is that only a "text"—what we can define as the product of poetic language—permits the infinite interaction of the semiotic (*chora*) and the symbolic and, thus, the detectable eruption of the semiotic within the symbolic. With the effect of denying the illusion of stasis as regards subject formation, a *text*'s "rhythmic, lexical, even syntactic changes disturb the transparency of the signifying chain and open it up to the crucible of its production. We can read a Mallarmé or Joyce only by starting from the signifier and moving toward the instinctual, material and social process the text covers" (101). In other words, a *text* announces meaning only to defer it endlessly; because it allows for the detection of the infinite and nonlinguistic process that animates it in the first place, the text refuses, while simultaneously and eternally promising, closure.

Of course, this apparent perpetuation of "modernist idealism" is not limited to Kristeva. Barthes, for instance, privileges "Text" over "work," "writerly" over "readerly," and in doing so, repeatedly finds himself privileging the work of one author over another while simultaneously and paradoxically denying the very concept of "author."[3] As Huyssen puts it, poststructuralists like Barthes (and, I would add, Kristeva) ultimately reintroduce, "through the back door, the same high culture/low culture divide and the same type of evaluations that were constitutive of classical modernism" (212).[4] And, given the above (albeit, cursive) look at Kristeva, we would be hard pressed to simply reject the claim that French, or even American, poststructuralism offers "a theory of modernism not a theory of postmodernism" (214).

Still, can we simply assume that a discourse is wholly complicit with the cultural objects upon which it deploys its theoretical strategies? If so, what does this mean for "poststructuralists" like Baudrillard?[5] In *Simulacra and Simulation*, for example, Baudrillard discusses everything from Francis Ford Coppola's *Apocalypse Now* and J.G. Ballard's *Crash* to the postmodern effect of Disneyland. Is, we might ask Huyssen, Baudrillard postmodern? The answer, I imagine, would have to be "yes"[6]—even though Baudrillard often seems to be lamenting, in a very "modernist" fashion, the loss of the real.[7] However, I would like to suggest that it is as misleading to wholly dissociate poststructuralism and postmodernism as it is to blindly confuse them. On one level, anyway, it seems perfectly logical that poststructuralism rarely addresses postmodern artifacts. As a discourse that is primarily intent on "deconstructing"[8] the basic metaphysical assumptions that have always determined our understanding of language and the world it encodes, poststructuralism and/or deconstruction does not seem quite so radical or effective when applied to a *Gravity's Rainbow* or a *Pulp Fiction*. Indeed, it is hardly surprising that a "poststructuralist" like Derrida was indifferent to texts that were already engaged overtly in the deconstruction of various metaphysical, or logocentric, assumptions; it seems safe to assume that Derrida was far more concerned with deconstruction's possible responses to the dangerous assumptions governing Hegel's dialectic than he was with the possibility that a text like *Gravity's Rainbow* might be engaged in its own form of deconstruction. This is not to say that the various poststructuralist readings of a text like *Gravity's Rainbow* are pointless, or of little value. Such readings are, in fact, extremely important—if only because they demonstrate what I would argue is hardly a coincidental co-development of anti-foundationalist and language-focused sentiments. What I am suggesting, instead, is that there are perfectly good reasons why the principal "poststructuralists" (i.e., Derrida, Lacan, Kristeva, etc.) avoid speaking about postmodern cultural production: (1) they felt it necessary to apply their theoretical strategies to more overtly logocentric, metaphysical and/or onto-theological texts; and (2) discussions of postmodern cultural production do little, if anything, to distinguish poststructural discourse as distinct, or radically new. If anything, the fact that it evades (or, perhaps, has anxiety about) discussing postmodern cultural production speaks to poststructuralism's inherent connection to postmodernism. And, I think, on a certain level at least, Huyssen realizes this.

At one point (and this is, perhaps, what makes him particularly worthy of careful consideration), Huyssen interrupts his discussion of poststructuralism's modernist tendencies to make a rather provocative statement, a statement that he quickly and, for the sake of his argument, necessarily dismisses:

> But, if poststructuralism can be seen as the *revenant* of modernism in the guise of theory, then that would be precisely what makes it postmodern. It is a postmodernism that works itself out not as a rejection of modernism, but rather as a retrospective reading which, in some cases, is fully aware of modernism's limitations and failed political ambitions. (209, my emphasis)

There are several things worth noting here. To begin with, postmodernism is indirectly defined as a type of modern return, an episteme that is ultimately animated by the revenant of that which it succeeds. Moreover, Huyssen entertains the possibility that, even if it is a critique of modernism, poststructuralism must necessarily continue to function in, or *through*, the spirit of modernism. Poststructuralism's rejection of modernism (or, for that matter, "structuralism") is implicitly connected to a certain "return," or remainder, of modernism. Unfortunately, Huyssen quickly drops this more interesting and subtle line of discussion. In the end, Huyssen decides that poststructuralism is to be judged on its ability to avoid hegemonic and elitist politics, politics that he views as complicit with societal modernization and the effect of modernism's insistence on the transformative powers of certain sociopolitically "anterior" types of artistic production. Poststructuralism should free "art and literature from that overload of responsibilities . . . on which the historical avantgarde shipwrecked, and which lived on in France through the 1950s and 1960s embodied in the figure of Jean Paul Sartre" (209–10). Because poststructuralism—especially as it is represented in the work of theorists like Barthes—seems to fall back into such politics, slipping (perhaps, uncomfortably) into the role of contemporary avant-garde, Huyssen concludes that it is simply erroneous to identify it as postmodern. Poststructuralism should thus be viewed as a failed postmodern discourse; it generates new (non)conditions for criteria—or, as Richard Rorty would have it, new "conditions of possibility." Even if these conditions, or grounds, are the paradoxical effect of an absolute denial of all foundationalist, or transcendental, discourses (as with Barthes' deceased author, Kristeva's eternally inaccessible *chora*, or Derrida's differance), they function as a way to recognize "advanced," or progressive, textual practice. Joyce's *Finnegans Wake* is obviously more worthy of praise than, say, Raymond Chandler's *The Big Sleep* because the former, from a poststructuralist perspective, refuses absolute apprehension, pointing to the absence of authorial control and freeing its readers from the constraining illusion of subject-hood and the possibility of stable truth claims. What people like Huyssen fail to see, though, is that postmodern cultural production, from Vonnegut to *The Simpsons*, strives to do the very things that modernists like Joyce are, from a poststructuralist and thus *retrospective* point of view, celebrated as accomplishing: dismantling the traditional subject and representing the illusory nature of both closure and foundationalist truth claims. The difference is that, while poststructuralism tends to view the praiseworthy aspects of modernism as discursively accidental—for even Joyce, I would argue (and I imagine, most poststructuralists would agree), embraced the modernist faith in presence and the *individual* artist's ability to expose, *via* language experiments, certain fundamental structures of reality and human consciousness—postmodernism expresses a self-conscious awareness of its own postmodern/poststructural position. In other words, postmodernism cannot be so easily separated from poststructuralism: both engage in a type of positivist critique—indeed, both function, *if they function at all*, as critique—regardless of their respective objects of study; both necessarily continue to struggle with a certain modern remainder, a certain *specter of modernism.*

Rather than successfully identifying a radical disjunction between poststructuralism and postmodernism, then, an argument like Huyssen's seems to announce (through the "back door," as it were) the spectral contamination that animates both. The fact that Huyssen's critique of poststructuralism inadvertently *implicates* postmodernism *as well* is most obvious in those moments when Huyssen finds it necessary to praise postmodernism for its successful evasion of modernist assumptions. At the very moment he praises postmodernism for managing to "counter" what he views as "the modernist litany of the death of the subject by working toward new theories and practices of speaking, writing and acting subjects" (142), Huyssen indirectly implicates postmodernism, along with poststructuralism, in "the kind of teleological posturing which poststructuralism itself has done so much to criticize" (210).⁹ In these moments Huyssen opens up the possibility that *even* postmodern pragmatism is mobilized by the return of certain post-Kantian, or Enlightenment, assumptions, suggesting that postmodernism is itself necessarily predicated upon the possibility of, and belief in, critique, political intervention, and/or teleological progress. Thus, by positioning postmodernism as progressively distinct from a poststructuralism that is *still* contaminated by a certain specter of modernity—or, rather, a certain specter of the still "incomplete project of modernity"—Huyssen inadvertently and ironically refutes the various critics who, while viewing poststructuralism and postmodernism as virtually synonymous, deride postmodernism for its wholehearted denial of an Enlightenment project.

There are two ways to look at this. If, following Huyssen, the "spectral" assumptions that define modernism (and poststructuralism) make it complicit with the hegemony of societal modernization, then we must view postmodernism as another "complicit" or "failed" episteme. Or, from the other perspective—that is, from the perspective of people like Habermas, Harvey, and Norris—if the assumptions that define modernity make it a viable mode of resisting the processes of modernization, then we need to view postmodernism (and poststructuralism) as another reconfiguration of an always unfinished, or spectral, "project" of societal critique. On whatever side we fall—whether we see the remainder of an Enlightenment project as inherently dangerous or as a necessary element of positive critique—the fact remains that both postmodernism and poststructuralism can be read as parallel reconfigurations of an ongoing spectral problem/project, depending on one's position. Moreover, the reality of these two superficially irreconcilable positions suggests the possibility that, in terms of evading the hegemonic tendencies associated with stringent teleological, or Enlightenment, assumptions—that is, in terms of evading the very tendencies that such a position typically aims to critique—a discourse's success is always contingent (at least partially—or rather, we might say, *spectrally*) on its failure. In fact, this confusion surrounding the question of poststructuralism, postmodernism, and the project of modernity speaks to the aporia of all anti-foundational discourses. All critical attempts to liberate/disassociate postmodernism from the dangerous/positive tendencies of foundationalist or transcendental discourse can be effectively undermined via a relocation *within postmodernism* of the same spectral remainder that animates any such critical attempt in the first place.

This necessary element of failure can be best explicated if we turn, at this point, to a consideration of the Rorty/Norris debate. Concerned with the postmodern/pragmatic sympathies of Derridean deconstruction, this ongoing debate allows us to focus on deconstruction *as postmodern* while simultaneously highlighting the latent specter of modernity, or post-Kantian idealism, which animates postmodern pragmatism in the first place. Before moving on, though, a brief note on terminology. I specify "Derridean deconstruction" because I would like to entertain the possibility that we can view poststructuralism—in a manner that plays on Rajan's recent work—as a postmodern "permutation" of deconstruction, a permutation or reconfiguration,[10] which is defined by its linguistic and stringently anti-foundationalist focus. The implications of such a redefinition are twofold. On the one hand, it encourages us to view the "initial" phase of Derrida's overtly "deconstructive" project as the most representative of poststructuralism generally and, on the other, it allows us to conceive of a deconstruction *after postmodernism* (which is to say, also, *after poststructuralism*).

Private Irony *All the Way Down?*

For most detractors of postmodernism, particularly Christopher Norris, Richard Rorty (along with Stanley Fish and Jean Baudrillard) is the epitome of all that is wrong with the past fifty or so years of theoretical discourse. A self-styled "postmodern bourgeois liberal," Rorty champions hard-line American neo-pragmatism, insisting that the possibility of truth claims and/or meaningful political intervention has long since passed. Following the Lyotardian logic I discussed in the previous chapter, Rorty's postmodern pragmatism is motivated by the assumption that, as Norris puts it, "textual meaning (like the truth claims of science) can only be a product of the codes and conventions that happen to prevail within this or that historically-contingent interpretative community" (*What's Wrong* 6). For the pragmatist, nothing can be located that is anterior to the language games that are continuously played out by a multiplicity of eternally shifting interpretative communities. As Rorty would have it, any attempt at argumentation or public intervention is simply futile, a pointless echo of a now exhausted philosophical tradition that championed logical rigor and the possibility of transcendental revelation(s). In short, we can define postmodernism at this point, via Rorty and while recalling Lyotard, as the denial of any final vocabulary, or "metavocabulary." According to Rorty—or, better, from the perspective of what I will henceforth define "postmodern"[11]—the only thing we can do is explore and/or invent new, and private, vocabularies:

> the realm of possibility expands whenever a new vocabulary is invented, so that to find "conditions of possibility" would require us to envisage all such inventions before their occurrence. The idea that we do have such a metavocabulary at our disposal, one which gives us a "logical space" in which to "place" any-thing which anybody will ever say, seems just one more version of the dream of "presence" from which ironists since Hegel have been trying to wake us. (*Contingency* 125)

While this repudiation of all discourses that assume certain "conditions of possibility" strikes a nerve in any critic who feels ill when reading Kathy Acker, what makes Rorty a real thorn in the side (of people like Norris, Rodolphe Gasché, and Jonathan Culler, people who detest postmodernism but admire Derrida) is his insistence that "later" deconstruction wholeheartedly validates American pragmatism. For Rorty, Derrida has become one of the most successful and innovative "liberal (and *private*) ironists" around. Put differently, and following Rorty's definition of a "liberal ironist," Derrida pragmatically accepts the absolute contingency of his personal belief systems while accepting the irreconcilable division of the public and the private. As Simon Critchley succinctly explains, Rorty's liberal ironist is "someone who is committed to social justice and appalled by cruelty, but who recognizes that there is no metaphysical foundation to her concern for justice" (85). The liberal ironist realizes that any attempt to synthesize individualist quests for autonomy and self-creation with a concern for public justice is a categorical and often dangerous mistake. Those who make this mistake—or rather, those who are unable to rid their thinking of the residual, or "spectral," traces of Enlightenment thought—are, from Rorty's perspective, "metaphysicians"; they cling to the belief that there is some final vocabulary that is applicable to questions both public and private. That being said, it is important to note that, in Rorty's eyes, Derrida is a *private* "ironist"; in fact, Rorty clearly suggests that an "ironist" cannot be a "public" intellectual. Unlike private theorists, those who engage in an "effort to make our institutions and practices more just and less cruel" (*Contingency* xiv) cannot be considered ironists, or what Rorty sometimes refers to as "exemplars";[12] they are, instead, "fellow citizens," writers who can be nominalists or historicists but who fail to escape wholly the confines of social or public categories. The latter category would include people like Orwell, Dewey, Habermas, and Marx, leaving theorists like Nietzsche, Derrida, and Foucault[13] to be classified as distinctly and strategically private, or unconcerned with public discourse. As Critchley puts it, Rorty's "Derrida can only be understood as a private thinker whose work has no public utility and therefore no interesting ethical or political consequences" (84).

Critchley argues that Rorty's "Utopian plan" is to make "metaphysicians" "ironists," and "private ironists" "public ironists." Critchley is wise to focus on Rorty's "Utopian plan" (which ultimately implicates pragmatism in the very idealist discourse it aims to debunk), but he is only partly correct in his description of that plan. Primarily, Critchley is mistaken in his assumption that the "ironist" is only liberal when she[14] is engaged in public discourse. By claiming that Rorty identifies a "non-liberal ironist" as a person who is "concerned with their self-realization, and perhaps the realization of a small group, but have no concern for traditional liberal questions of social justice" (87), Critchley mistakenly suggests that the private ironist is not included amongst Rorty's elite— or, if I can begin to stress the positivist slippages in Rorty's postmodern argument, *enlightened*—"liberal ironists." While it is certainly true that "The critical, Utopian function of *Contingency, Irony and Solidarity* is to persuade liberal metaphysicians to be ironists . . . and non-liberalists to be become liberals" (Critchley 87), Rorty is not interested in making private ironists public. After all, Rorty's liberal ironist is, by definition, "private." Irony is neither possible nor desirable within public discourse: "I cannot go on to claim that there could or ought to be a culture whose public rhetoric is ironist. I cannot imagine a culture which socialized its youth in such a way as to make them continually dubious about there own process of socialization. Irony seems inherently a private matter" (87). What makes a "liberal ironist" liberal is her belief that cruelty is "the worst thing we do"; what makes her an ironist is her refusal to offer, or believe in, a public (i.e., a final, or universal) solution to the problem of cruelty.[15] The liberal ironist demonstrates the possibility of engaging in a process of self-creation that does not cause suffering in others. To miss this is to miss Rorty's rationale for celebrating Derrida.

What makes Derrida important is his usually successful attempts "to create himself by creating his own language game" (*Contingency* 133). For Rorty, Derrida should be celebrated because he is entirely private; by being neither playful nor philosophical, he resists categorization. His work attempts to perform no other function than self-(re)creation; we can either take what we can from it, and apply it to our own *private* attempts at self-construction, or we can ignore it altogether as personal and contingent. Although he recognizes and laments a tendency in Derrida to "sound transcendental," to continue engaging in "the project of finding conditions of possibility" ("Remarks" 13)—to continue taking, in short, the metaphysical tradition seriously—Rorty insists that Derrida is a "liberal ironist" because he consistently avoids making public claims; especially in works like *Glas* and *La carte postale*, he is impenetrably personal. In the end, Rorty's Derrida *is* "a sentimental, hopeful, romantically idealistic writer" ("Remarks" 13) who *does* indeed embrace certain utopian or *liberal* hopes. However, because he repeatedly positions, or expresses, this idealism within the confines of an utterly private discourse, Derrida successfully and pragmatically refuses the possibility of ever identifying some hegemonic final vocabulary, or condition of possibility. Rorty's identification of Derrida as a "liberal ironist" is thus based upon Derrida's apparent refusal to address the public realm—that is, his refusal to claim that his particular utopian ideals are applicable to anyone but himself and the small group that tends to read and understand him. Derrida does not make arguments; he simply explores propositional statements,[16] the validity of which is entirely contingent upon the personal context in which they are uttered and/or received.

This brings me back to Critchley. Although his confusion of public and liberal mars his critique of Rorty's "Utopian plan," the question that drives Critchley's discussion is worth repeating: "if I admit at the outset that deconstruction is allied to pragmatism, then the question is whether *deconstruction is pragmatist all the way down?* That is to say, is deconstruction consistently anti-foundationalist? Or is there a foundationalist claim in deconstruction which cannot be pragmatized: Justice, for example, or responsibility for another's suffering?" (84). Critchley seems to think that this question can be answered in the affirmative if we simply find a way to view Derrida as a "public liberal." As I have already suggested, though, this particular argument ignores the parameters of Rorty's terminology. If we are to engage critically with Rorty's argument, we need to understand that the liberal ironist is always "private." For Rorty, Critchley's "public liberal" would be, at best, a nominalist and/or a historicist; at worst, he would be a metaphysician. Consequently, if we are, as Critchley claims to be, working "in Rorty's vocabulary" (84), then labeling Derrida a "public liberal" is tantamount to saying that he is more of a metaphysician than a pragmatist; and, I imagine, neither Rorty nor Critchley is interested in suggesting this. While I do not disagree with Critchley's affirmative response to the above question, I want to rephrase the reasons for such a response. I agree that there is indeed "a foundationalist claim in deconstruction which cannot be pragmatized," but this foundationalist claim speaks to a similar claim in postmodernism. What I want to suggest (in line with the above discussion of Huyssen) is that deconstruction *isn't* "pragmatist all the way down," but *only insofar as* postmodern pragmatism *isn't* pragmatist all the way down. Calling Derrida a "public liberal" simply confuses the vocabulary that is under investigation and, ultimately, dissolves the possibility that deconstruction is *in any way* "allied" with pragmatism. The question we should be asking is whether or not it is possible to be entirely private—that is, whether or not it is possible to be a "private ironist" *all the way down.* The answer, I am arguing, is quite clearly "no."

However, before we can begin to link the transcendental tendencies of Derridean deconstruction (and, by implication, poststructuralism generally) to those of postmodern pragmatism, we first need to identify those tendencies. We need to return, at least partially, to the line of reasoning I initially associated with Huyssen. Rather than reprising the argument that poststructuralism is a failed critical project, though, I want to consider the position (often taken by critics like Norris, Gasché, and Culler in response to Rorty) that deconstruction perpetuates certain elements of Enlightenment idealism and thus successfully evades the seemingly complicit nihilism of postmodernism.

In terms of insisting upon deconstruction's Enlightenment "ideals"—or, more generally, in terms of insisting upon deconstruction's participation within a decidedly philosophical, or *argumentative*, tradition—Norris is, perhaps, the most adamant. According to Norris, "deconstruction is a Kantian enterprise in ways that few of its commentators have so far been inclined to acknowledge" (*Derrida* 94). In absolute opposition to Rorty, Norris is interested in highlighting the "arguments" of deconstruction, its active participation in discussions of transcendental "conditions of possibility." Norris' Derrida is consciously engaged in a post-Kantian examination of "the inbuilt presuppositions

of . . . *all* cognitive enquiry, the intellectual ground-rules in the absence
of which our thinking would have no sense, no logic or purpose" (*Derrida* 95). Norris puts it like this:

> Derrida's version of this Kantian argument makes writing (or
> "arche-writing") the precondition of all possible knowledge.
> And this is not merely by virtue of the fact—the self evident
> fact—that writing is the form in which ideas are passed down,
> preserved in a constantly expanding archive, and thus made
> available to subsequent debate. His claim is *a priori* in the
> radically Kantian sense: that we cannot *think* the possibility
> of culture, history or knowledge without also thinking the
> prior necessity of writing. (*Derrida* 95)

Norris' argument—especially when put in these terms—tends to make
your typical postmodern pragmatist despair. But, especially in his later
work, Norris tempers his claim that Derrida is ultimately engaged in
a revival of the *a priori* categories he claims, at least outwardly, to be
"deconstructing." While he does indeed disassociate Derrida from the
assumption—an assumption Norris locates in the work of Rorty, as
well as Lyotard, Baudrillard, and Foucault—that "the Enlightenment
is now a thing of the past, a closed chapter in the history of European thought" (*What's Wrong* 30), Norris does not think that Derrida's
engagement with "transcendentals" is ever logocentrically naïve. Even
though his Derrida does not believe that "the only way forward is . . . to
revel in the prospect of a postmodern epoch devoid of all-truth claims,
all standards of valid argumentation or efforts to separate a notional
'real' from the various forms of superinduced fantasy or mass-media
simulation" (30), Norris refuses to label Derrida a "transcendentalist,"
a "metaphysician,' or (even) a "negative theologian."[17]

Following Irene Harvey's discussion of deconstruction's active
participation in a philosophical tradition,[18] Norris argues that, for Derrida, the "quest for first principles must always lead on to a moment of
aporia, or insurmountable paradox, where thought comes up against
the non-availability of any such legitimising grounds" (*What's Wrong*
198). While engaging in "transcendental arguments," Derrida thus
demonstrates that "It is in the nature of transcendental arguments to
push back the process of enquiry from stage to stage and ask at every
point what grounds exist for our claim to know truly what we think
we know" (*What's Wrong* 199).

It is this willingness to *aim at* the transcendental, to posit *the possibility of* a (final) foundational claim that, for Norris, separates deconstruction from postmodernism and saves it from its detractors—in particular Habermas. Of course, Norris agrees with Habermas' basic take on postmodernism; he simply refuses to accept the claim that Derrida is postmodern. In fact, Norris ultimately feels that it is necessary to "save" Derrida and deconstruction from Habermas' attacks.[19] To this end, and in a manner that is quite similar to my own discussion of Lyotard and Habermas, Norris attempts to demonstrate the way in which Derridean deconstruction and Habermasian critique are motivated by very similar "assumptions":[20]

> It seems to me that Habermas goes wrong about Derrida mainly because he takes it for granted that deconstruction is one offshoot—a philosophical offshoot—of this wider postmodernist or counter-enlightenment drift. In what follows I shall point to some of the crucial respects in which Derrida's work not only fails to fit this description but also mounts a resistance to it on terms that Habermas ought to acknowledge, given his intellectual commitments. (*What's Wrong* 52)

From Norris' perspective, Derrida, like Habermas (as we saw in the previous chapter), is motivated by the necessarily impossible ideal of a final and unifying vocabulary—motivated, that is, to draw our attention to the fact that such an ideal is paradoxically threatened by the dissolution of difference that the reality of a "final vocabulary" would effect. More simply, Norris would like to demonstrate that there is "no warrant—prejudice aside—for counting [Derrida] among the postmodern enemies of reason or those who (as Habermas charges) wish to revoke the unfinished project of critical-emancipatory thought" (*Unfinished Project* 51).

Ultimately, then, Norris confirms Rodolphe Gasché's notion that Derridean "conditions of possibility" need to be understood as "infrastructures." For Gasché, "infrastructures"—that is, Derrida's terms for articulating the (we might say, *essential*) characteristics of arche-writing: differance, supplement, trace, and so on—are "quasi-transcendentals"; they are *both* conditions of possibility *and* conditions of impossibility. In opposition to Rorty's various laments that Derrida's early work—with its reliance on *a priori-esque* terms, like trace and differance—needs to be dismissed as still complicit with metaphysical assumptions and a now ineffectual philosophical tradition,[21] Gasché works to expose the manner in which "The law articulated by an infrastructure applies to itself as well" (6–7). An infrastructure thus signifies an essential condition of possibility, an essential condition of writing/thought, but it also always signifies (however paradoxically) the impossibility of its stability as a signifier *of that essential condition*: "It has an identity, that is, a minimal ideality that can be repeated only at the price of a relentless deferral of itself" (Gasché 7). What Gasché (and, to a lesser degree, Norris) repeatedly draws our attention to is Derrida's repeated attempts to undermine, while working within, a transcendental—or better, logocentric—tradition. Unlike Rorty, Norris and Gasché want to stress Derrida's continual acknowledgment of the necessarily inescapable nature of the tradition that he aims to deconstruct. And, certainly, they are not misguided in their apprehension of this acknowledgment. A cursory glance at a text like *Of Grammatology* confirms the fact that Derrida continually attempts to reinscribe differance (or trace, or supplementarity, or whatever) within the very logic of differance (or trace, or supplementarity, etc.). At one point in *Grammatology*, and as he does on numerous occasions, Derrida suggests that a term like "trace" *means* that meaning (or the possibility of bringing meaning *into presence*) is necessarily impossible:

> The trace is in fact the absolute origin of sense in general. Which amounts to saying once again that there is no absolute origin for sense in general. The trace is differance which opens appearance [l'apparaître] and signification. Articulating the living upon of the non-living in general, origin of all repetition, origin of ideality, the trace is not more ideal than real, not more intelligible than sensible, not more a transparent signification than an opaque energy and no concept of metaphysics can describe it. (65)

"[N]o concept of metaphysics can describe it," as both Norris and Gasché would remind us, *because* the very "expression" of trace is caught up in the logic of the trace, the impossibility of presence and of meaning as such. Trace (like differance, or supplementarity, or any other quasi-transcendental infrastructure) is implicated in the conditions of possibility that it permits, which is to say, along with Gasché, that its condition of possibility is its condition of impossibility.

As the articulation of the differences and deferrals (i.e., the "differance") that contaminates and destabilizes all attempts at expression, representation, and so on, trace is never *wholly* articulated; it is never *present* even though it promises presence. Like any other "infrastructure," trace denies the possibility of apprehension, of meaning, of presence, so as to make the possibility of apprehension, of meaning, of presence, possible. Similarly, and functioning within the same logic as the trace, "differance makes the opposition of presence and absence possible. Without the possibility of differance the desire of presence as such would not find its breathing-space. . . . Differance produces what it forbids, makes possible the very thing it makes impossible" (*Grammatology* 143). By "forbidding" presence—or, for that matter, pure absence—differance sustains the possibility of difference, *as well as* differance, of opposition and, thus, of articulation, meaning, presence, truth. The point Gasché and Norris want to make is that these "infrastructures"—like "arche-writing" itself—can only be understood via the conditions of possibility they represent; they are always and necessarily caught up in the logic of supplement that they determine. As origins, or *a priori* "conditions of possibility," they are, like any of the other *a priori* or transcendental concepts that Derrida deconstructs, dependent on a supplementarity that gives them a type of fleeting stability. For this reason, "The graphic of supplementarity is irreducible to logic, primarily because it comprehends logic as one of its cases and may alone produce its origin" (*Grammatology* 259). Nothing can be thought outside the economy of (arche)writing and supplementarity, including (arche)writing, supplementarity, the trace, and differance. "We know this," Derrida would say, "a priori, but only now and with a knowledge that is not a knowledge at all" (*Grammatology* 164).

What this amounts to—for people like Norris and Gasché—is the simple fact that Derrida neither abandons the project of modernity (as it is worked out, particularly, in phenomenology and structuralism) nor accidentally slips into the onto-theological, humanistic, logocentric, and/or metaphysical traps that he aims to expose. Moreover, Derrida's early work should not be read as the failed experiment of a youthful professor, for the "infrastructures" we see so obviously in his early work continue to inform his later work. Even in his most personal, or *private*, texts—for example, *Glas* and *Envois*—Derrida continues to engage in a type of post-Kantian argumentation. In this later work, though, Derrida *performs* his arguments; as Gasché puts it, "the texts themselves become the articulations of [the] infrastructures" (12). In the end, the point is this: given his consistent engagement with(in) the philosophical tradition he critiques—or rather, given his repeated acknowledgment of the necessity of, and his frequent recourse to, some type of metaphysical or logocentric "lure"[22]—Derrida cannot be read as a postmodern pragmatist. Derrida very well may be a "private ironist," but his work is always predicated upon the possibility of a public or universal truth. Derrida, in short, makes nonpropositional, or noncontingent, statements (if only to argue that such statements are logocentric illusions).

Is Rorty simply wrong, then? Perhaps. Certainly, and as we saw in our brief consideration of *Grammatology*, a close reading of Derrida's work seems to confirm the Norris/Gasché position: Derrida never wholly abandons the transcendental tradition that he problematizes, if not simply refutes. There does indeed seem to be, as Critchley would have it, "a transcendental claim" implicitly lodged within the very logic of deconstruction. Furthermore, this "claim" doesn't simply disappear because, as Rorty argues, Derrida's texts become, at least for a time,[23] more performative. In fact, Rorty's analysis of what a text like *Envois* "means"—or rather, the fact that he can make a coherent analysis at all—seems to contradict his claim that Derrida's later work demonstrates that we cannot "touch upon the nature of language without doing it injury," that all we can do is "create a style so different as to make one's books incommensurable with those of one's precursors" (*Contingency* 126). In other words, Rorty finds himself in the paradoxical position of having to explain the argument, or public relevance, of a text that has no argument, or public relevance.[24] The awkwardness of this position is most glaring when Rorty makes claims regarding the absolutely private, or unique, nature of the text. For instance, while offering us a veritable exegesis of the work, Rorty tells us (in a footnote[25]) that *Envois* is too private to have explanatory notes. What Rorty seems to overlook is the way in which his own ability to access the text, to offer an interpretation (of its uninterpretability), speaks quite simply to its accessibility, to its argumentative and public role. After all, as its title suggests, *Envois* is an envoi/envoy, a "conclusive" send-off into the world. And, I would argue, it is the necessity of a desire to "send off"—or rather, to *make known*, to *explain*—that Rorty seems unwilling to recognize in Derrida's work and, as his *public arguments* about Derrida suggest, in his own. Rorty tells us, at one point, that Derrida announces his separation from the metaphysical tradition most clearly when he conflates "the metaphysical urge for a privileged final vocabulary, for general ideas, with the urge to have children" (*Contingency* 128)—that is, the urge to reproduce, to continue a past tradition, to put forth. However, what Rorty fails to address—and, I think, this speaks most clearly to Norris and Gasché's critique of Rorty—is that Derrida *had children* (whether we view "children" as real *or* as metaphorical).

Still, and however contradictory it may sound, I do not think that Rorty is wrong to call Derrida a pragmatist. Instead of simply opposing postmodern pragmatism and deconstruction (or even poststructuralism in general), I would like to suggest that what Norris and Gasché expose in deconstruction is just as evident (albeit, less acknowledged) in postmodern pragmatism. As Jonathan Culler argues, the pragmatist position necessarily gives rise to "a deconstructive moment in which the logic of the argument used to defend a position contradicts the position affirmed" (155). For Culler, and as I have suggested above, the pragmatic "truth" that there is no truth, that "truth is relative," is symptomatic of a "paradoxical situation in which, on the one hand, logocentric positions contain their own undoing and, on the other, the denial of logocentrism is carried out in logocentric terms" (155). While the description of this "paradoxical situation" seems to simply recapitulate Norris and Gasché's take on deconstruction, Culler assures us that deconstruction successfully avoids slipping into this logocentric trap: "Insofar as deconstruction maintains these positions, it might seem to be a dialectical synthesis, a superior and complete theory; but these two movements do not, when combined, yield a coherent position or a higher theory. Deconstruction [unlike pragmatism] has no theory of truth" (155). What I want to suggest, though, is the possibility that what links deconstruction to pragmatism—and, thus, poststructuralism to postmodernism—is the critical necessity of logocentric (or metaphysical, or transcendental, or public) assumptions in any attempt to "deconstruct" those assumptions. On the one hand, then, I completely agree with Culler. Pragmatism, as we have seen, repeatedly and necessarily finds itself essentializing its anti-essentialist claims. Not only does Rorty inevitably end up relying on universal truths—like the "truth" that all humans are bound by their aversion to suffering—his identification, and advocacy, of the "liberal ironist" becomes a very public and thus, following Rorty's own terms of discussion, hardly "ironic" affirmation of the power and necessity of private ironism. To promote his position, Rorty must necessarily fail to sustain it: he cannot be, in short, a "private ironist" *all the way down*. On the other hand, though, I want to suggest that it is naïve to assume that deconstruction somehow manages to accomplish, what amounts to, the impossible. The necessary failure of deconstruction is, in fact, most obvious in those moments when it is identified as a successful critique *and* evasion of the "logocentric trap." When someone like Culler excuses deconstruction from the trap of positivist logocentrism *because* it paradoxically denies, while ironically employing, a logocentric attitude, deconstruction's necessary (and, we might say, *blind*) reaffirmation of certain logocentric (or onto-theological, or metaphysical, or transcendental) assumptions becomes most apparent.

As Rorty suggests, any discourse that assumes it can rigorously critique "something as big as logocentrism" needs to be understood as "one more logocentric hallucination" ("Is Derrida" 139). This is, after all, why Rorty dismisses Derrida's early work. No matter how ironically charged and self-implicating they may be, Derrida's "conditions of possibility" cannot avoid becoming hypostatized. But, as we have seen, Rorty makes the same mistake as Culler when he assumes that Derrida's later—or, from a more contemporary perspective, "middle"—work simply discards these "conditions," or that, moreover, it suddenly manages to completely extricate itself from a type of logocentric complicity, a complicity that Rorty associates with negative theology.[26] Derrida's entire project is, in fact, inflected with moments of anxiety about this complicity, about the threat of becoming what it seeks to expose as both illusory and dangerous: another onto-theological truth claim. And, I would argue, it is the manner in which this anxiety plays out (or, even, *seems to dissipate*) that defines an "early" Derrida from a "late" Derrida—or rather, a poststructural deconstruction *during* postmodernism and a (I will say, if only tentatively at this point, *onto-theologically relaxed*) deconstruction *after* postmodernism.

More specifically, the anxiety we see surrounding Derrida's early discussions *and performances* of the "conditions of possibility"—"infrastructures" that Rorty disregards as symptomatic of a negative theology—speaks to the fact that deconstruction was haunted by the spectral threat that I defined in the previous chapter as the motivating characteristic of postmodernism. Derrida's repeated, and often ostentatious, attempts to distance deconstruction—and, in particular, terms like "differance," "trace," or "supplementarity"—from any onto-theological discourse is indicative of a certain "hostility toward ghosts, a terrified hostility that sometimes fends off terror with a burst of laughter" (*Specters* 47). In fact, this early phase of Derridean deconstruction can be defined—in the same manner that Derrida, in his later work, defines Marxism—as a postmodern discourse that fears ghosts (like the ghost of logocentrism) while, all the while, being unwittingly dependant upon, or haunted by, the very ghost it seeks to exorcise. We must, in other words, ask the same question of deconstruction, whether early *or* late, that Derrida asks of Marxism: "But how to distinguish between the analysis that denounces magic and the counter-magic that it still risks being?" (*Specters* 47).

The *slippage* between an "early" deconstruction and the logocentric discourse, or "magic," it seems to escape via ironic self-reflexivity is most evident in Derrida's utter rejection of a thinker like Sartre. In "The Ends of Man," for instance, Derrida explicitly and, perhaps, "once and for all" distances his own deconstructive project from the positivist, or onto-theological, "humanism" of Sartrean existentialism. Refusing to disassociate Sartre from his metaphysical predecessors, Derrida accuses

Sartre of unifying "man" by announcing the common goal of the *ens causa sui*. While Sartre adamantly refuses the actual possibility of the *ens causa sui*,[27] its privileged position as *lack* is, according to Derrida, a reification of that which ultimately signals the "essential project of human-reality" (116): "This synthetic unity is determined as *lack*: lack of totality in beings, lack of God that is soon transformed into a lack *in* God. Human-reality is a *failed* God" (116n5). From this view, Sartrean existentialism is nothing more than a negative theology, a back-door reinscription of onto-theological claims. However, as critics like Christian Howells and Bruce Baugh have pointed out, the critique of Sartre in "The Ends of Man" needs to be read as symptomatic of Derrida's desire to deny the theological aspects of his own work. As Howells notes, "The vehemence of his rejection of Sartre is perhaps explicable in terms of a similarly close but resisted parallel between his own attempt to undermine Being and that of existential 'nihilism' " ("Hegel's Death Knell" 177).[28] Indeed, in "Differance," Derrida is well aware of, and careful to deny, the apparent similarities between his description of differance and the "sophistical" tactics of negative theology:

> Thus, the detours, phrases, and syntax that I shall often have to resort to will resemble—will sometimes be practically indiscernible from—those of negative theology. . . . And yet what is thus denoted as differance is not theological, not even in the most negative order of negative theology. . . . Not only is differance irreducible to every ontological or theological—onto-theological—reappropriation, but it opens up the very space in which onto-theology—philosophy—produces its system and its history. (134)

Derrida is, of course, walking a fine line. While clearly admitting that differance somehow "encompasses and irrevocably *surpasses* onto-theology or philosophy" (135, my emphasis), Derrida struggles simultaneously to deny the apparent fact that differance is synonymous with "a superessential reality . . . beyond the finite categories of essence and existence" and, therefore, "a superior, inconceivable, and ineffable mode of being" (134). Immediately, in this "pre-emptive" defense of differance, we begin to hear echoes of the accusations Derrida lays against Sartre. After all, he accuses Sartre of participating in the very "theology" that he seriously fears will be mistakenly identified with differance. With this in mind, Howells' claims begin to resonate with particular significance. If differance, as Derrida insists, is a successful evasion of what has previously been a virtually inescapable tradition of onto-theology, and if Sartre's nothingness can be attacked for the same reasons that differance seemingly *needs* to be defended, then we must concede the possibility that the projects of an "onto-theological humanist" like Sartre and a "deconstructionist" like Derrida are far less removed than Derrida would like to believe. Derrida's critique of Sartre—like, more broadly, deconstruction's critique of logocentrism, postmodernism's critique of modernism, and/or poststructuralism's critique of structuralism—thus reaffirms the very "logic" that Derrida identifies in communism's critique of ideology: the logic of opposition always and necessarily positions itself as "the final incarnation, the real presence of the specter, thus the end of the spectral" (*Specters* 103). An effect of this necessary position, this paradoxical promise of the specter as the end of spectrality, is thus the anxiety I described above—that is, deconstruction (or poststructuralism, or postmodernism) seems to be fleeing itself,[29] fearing the specter it senses haunting its own critique of the specter (of teleology, of transcendentalism, of onto-theology, of negative theology, of metaphysics, etc.)—or, more specifically, the utopian specter represented by the teleological aporia of the "still incomplete project of modernity." A brief look at Caputo's insightful essay, "On Not Circumventing the Quasi-Transcendental," will help to clarify this point.

While discussing Rorty's disdain for the Derrida who "[trots] out new metaphysical creatures of his own devising, 'quasi-entities' whose hiddenness reminds us of the hidden God in negative theology" ("Quasi-Transcendental" 154), Caputo makes two noteworthy points. On the one hand, Caputo argues that "Derrida is a transcendental philosopher—*almost*" (157). Highlighting the self-implicating nature of Derrida's "quasi-entities," or "infrastructures," Caputo essentially reasserts Gasché's claim that deconstruction is a "quasi-transcendental" philosophy. As a system of argumentation, deconstruction is dependent upon the "quasi-transcendental," that which is "both necessary and impossible in the system, [and] which makes the system both possible and impossible" (158). That is, "The very thing that is excluded is what makes the system possible and must be included" (161). On the other hand, though (and unlike Norris, Gasché, and Culler), Caputo does not simply oppose this "quasi-transcendentalism" to Rorty's neo-pragmatism. Instead, Caputo argues persuasively that "Rorty *needs* a quasi-transcendental theory of the sort one finds in Derrida, even though he does not feel that need himself" (166). This need is seen most clearly in Rorty's reification of the subject. As Caputo points out, and as I intimated above, Rorty's faith in the possibility of a self-creating ironist, like Derrida, "turns on a freely inventive name-making subject who invents 'vocabularies' " (161). Rather than relying on "an impersonal field [like differance] whose quasistructural laws produce certain temporary nominal entities called 'words' and 'concepts,' " Rorty clings "to a seventeenth and eighteenth-century metaphysics of the subject" (164). Still, Caputo is not interested in condemning Rorty; this is not about pointing out an *avoidable flaw* in Rorty's argument. What Caputo wants to point out—as do I—is the fact that "Rorty [and thus postmodernism] . . . is extremely close to 'Derrida' " (167). Both "Rorty and Derrida have reasons to believe that we will never (that's pretty transcendental talk) attain a metavocabulary within which we can place everything anybody will ever say, which will enable us to envisage what people are going to say before they say it (which is very *un*transcendental)" (168–9). However, and as I have already begun to do, I want to take Caputo's position further, closer to a position Caputo would identify with Norris.[30]

As I suggested in the above discussion of "early-stage" deconstruction, and as I think Caputo's discussion of Rorty's absolute reliance on an autonomous subject reveals, the possibility of sustaining a "quasi-transcendental" attitude is a spectral illusion. I do not want to endorse Derrida and Caputo's ethical appeal to the possibility of sustaining what I referred to in the previous chapter as a non-teleological eschatology. *The transcendental must be absolute* if it is to compel movement, criticism, revolution, deconstruction, or whatever; faith in some type of a *telos* is an absolute necessity. What I am interested in is the way in which the above-mentioned specter, or teleological aporia (for, as I've suggested, this specter continues to compel teleologies rather than non-teleological eschatologies) inevitably animates a given discourse/episteme.

With this separation from Caputo in mind, I would like to turn to the possibility of articulating a "late" period of deconstruction, a period that can be read as the effect of the "passing" of postmodernism and/or poststructuralism. This late period seems to be marked by two overt shifts in Derrida's work: (1) a reappraisal of his previous "conditions of possibility" via an articulation of the spectrological framework I have been employing throughout my discussion of postmodernism, and (2) the explicit turn from theories of language and subjectivity to questions of ethics, justice, and communal responsibility. Moreover, and as with this period of "renewalism" *after postmodernism*, Derrida's late period is marked by an apparent (or, at the very least, more overt) willingness to concede that the specter is a necessary element in the war against spectrality, that the transcendental can never be fully abandoned if we are to deny the possibility of the transcendental. We might in fact begin to identify this period *after postmodernism* and, thus, the most recent phase of deconstruction as a renewed attempt to evade the hegemonic certainties of an Enlightenment project. However, this emergent episteme of *renewalism* attempts to manage its evasion by abandoning the hegemonic imperative that the spectral persistence of an enlightenment project *must be* effaced.

With this in mind, Derrida's late work can be read as an apology for his early work, work that failed to overtly demonstrate that it couldn't really be doing what it *seemed* to be doing—that is, escaping the logocentric, the transcendental, the theological. Not surprisingly, then, this later work is also marked by an explicit interest in religion, and the function of "God" in deconstructive discourse. While Derrida *during postmodernism* is virtually hegemonic in his denial of Enlightenment assumptions, Derrida *after postmodernism* is (if I can borrow Caputo's phrasing) "a man of the Enlightenment, albeit a *new* Enlightenment, one that is enlightened about the Enlightenment and resists letting the spirit of the Enlightenment freeze over into dogma" ("Introduction" 2). Indeed, through the filter of Derrida's later work Caputo has repeatedly argued that deconstruction needs to be viewed as a type of "religion without religion." As I said above, though, I do not think that such a paradoxical position can ever be fully sustained: even a religion without religion must inevitably be a religion *pure and simple*; if it doesn't have faith in itself as a totalizing discourse (as, in short, a religion), it will not have the motivation to articulate itself as a religion *without religion*. What I am suggesting is that deconstruction after postmodernism (like/as this emerging epoch of renewalism that seems to be arriving "late to the end of history") is troubled by the very specter with which it claims to have come to terms. This will make more sense as we turn, at last, to a close reading of Derrida. In particular, I would like to focus on what we might consider as one of the first texts of a "late Derrida": *Force of Law*. By examining this text in some detail I hope to achieve two basic goals. On the one hand, I want to explicate further the spectrological argument I have been employing since the beginning. That is, I would like to examine the way in which the concept of the specter is, for Derrida, intimately connected to theological discourse, the possible impossibility of the messianic, or the "quasi-transcendental," and the necessity of the "gamble" in the process of ethical decision making. On the other hand, I want to begin considering, via this shift in deconstruction, the way in which this epoch after postmodernism continues to struggle with the very specter, or teleological aporia, with which it claims to have come to terms.

The Force of Derrida's Indecision

Following Caputo, it would be (in)accurate to say that Derrida is an atheist.[31] Of course, such a statement—it is (in)accurate to say that Derrida is an atheist—is probably misleading; or rather, it doesn't seem to lead anywhere. Whether or not Derrida believes in God is hardly addressed; because of the parenthetical prefix, this statement fails to embrace fully a particular position. It is not decisive in the sense that it is not without doubt. Yet, at the same time (and this is in fact the point), this statement leaves open, or opens up, the *possibility* that Derrida—and, by implication, deconstruction—is not, as seems only logical, atheistic. If it does anything, this statement gambles with its fingers crossed on the uncertainty that necessarily surrounds the question (if it has even been at any time a serious question) of deconstruction's atheistic position. This statement speaks to the indecisiveness that should, that *must* (if we are to believe, if we are to *have faith in*, Derrida) haunt any decision concerning the function of God in deconstructive discourse—indeed, that *must* haunt *any* "just" decision.

I begin with these issues—of (a)theism, of indecision and "just" decisions, of gambles, of haunting—simply as a point of departure for a discussion of the position of "late" deconstruction. These issues are of paramount importance in Derrida's more recent work on ethical responsibility, the possibility of justice and the necessity of the messianic in the work of deconstruction. They are also, then, as I've suggested previously, a point of departure for a discussion of deconstruction's commitment, or sense of responsibility, to Marx—or rather, a certain specter of Marx, or Marxism. Throughout his later work, as we saw in the previous chapter, the "emancipatory and *messianic* affirmation" (*Specters* 89) that Derrida locates in Marxism, the promise of something "to come," the transcendent, is identified as the animating feature of deconstruction. However, and at the same time, Derrida repeatedly cautions us. While the possibility that the promise will be fulfilled, that the future will become *present*, encourages the movement of deconstruction (as it does the utopian impulse of Marxism and, I would add, postmodernism), such a promise *must* be understood as impossible, as only ever the promise of what can never arrive—what can never be effaced as the other, as the still "to come," as, simply, the promise. By employing the metaphor of the specter, the later Derrida explicitly points to the fact that deconstruction, like Marxism, must *always* be haunted by the specter of the promise (of the messianic, of the transcendent, of God), haunted in the sense that what haunts it (a ghost) is never wholly spirit (i.e., ideal), nor is it ever wholly realized, or made present *in the flesh*. Faith in the messianic, or the promise, gives us the reason (or perhaps, the *right*) to decide, to deconstruct, or even to revolt, but the impossibility of the messiah, or messianism, *allows us to* decide. The impossibility of the future present,[32] of the messiah, of God, is the very condition of uncertainty and, thus, of decisions. A decision is, and must always be, a gamble on an impossible future, an impossible messiah. Were the messiah finally "to have arrived," no decision would be necessary—indeed, no decision (and, for that matter, no deconstruction) would be possible.

This ironic positioning, this faith without belief, is the "quasi-transcendental" ground of, what we might call, late-Derridean ethics—what Caputo understands as "the first movements of the first covenant in a religion without religion" (*Prayers and Tears* xxi). However, as I pointed out above, I want to consider the possibility that Derrida's arguments concerning the need to respect the spectrality of the specter, the possibility *and* the impossibility of the Kantian transcendental, of the future "to come," is necessarily contingent upon the very thing it is intent on endlessly circumventing: teleology, positivism, absolute faith, and the effacement of the specter's spectrality. The late Derridean (or perhaps "renewalist") imperative to respect the specter—"the specter *must* be respected" (*Politics* 288, my emphasis)—is, itself, an imposition on the specter; it is tantamount to what Derrida condemns as a "conjuration" of the specter's spectrality. The inherent positivism of Derrida's call for respect speaks to the impossibility of such respect: our faith in the truth and necessity of "the messianic without messianism" (*Specters* 73) is necessarily contingent upon an implicit, yet absolute, faith in messianism, teleology, onto-theology, logos, and so on. After all, this discourse without messianism, this "revised" deconstruction, is offered to us as the final answer, the *final solution* to the problem of teleological traps, humanistic imperatives, or whatever. The gamble that Derridean ethics requires we endlessly perform is never really a gamble, for its performance is contingent upon the belief that a gamble is the only way to win. Let me explain.

Gayatri Chakravorty Spivak has argued that it was "good that Derrida wrote *Specters*" (his most prolonged consideration of Marx and Marxism to date) because "Deconstruction has been so long associated with political irresponsibility by those who practice criticism by hearsay that it was significant for its inventor to give his imprimatur to rereading Marx" (66). The suggestion is that deconstruction's entry into the realm of "ethico-political responsibility"—or, at the very least, its willingness to recognize and announce its already significant role in the realm of ethico-political responsibility—is inextricably linked to its engagement, or association, with some type of, or some specter of, Marxism.

In other words, this engagement, or "rereading," can be thought of as a response to the apparently polemic issue of deconstruction's pertinence to the more "public" realm of ethics, politics and justice. For a long time, as Thomas Keenan notes, "Deconstruction's ethico-political pertinence [has been] *either* (1) taken for granted (often but by no means always presumed to be 'progressive') . . . *or* (2) condemned (as nefariously antipolitical or paralyzing)" (236, my emphasis). While the advocates of deconstruction tend to argue that deconstruction is and has always been fundamentally concerned with ethico-political issues, its enemies—or, at the very least, its staunchest critics (e.g., Harvey, Habermas)—suggest that deconstruction destroys the very foundations upon which ethics, or moral and political responsibility, are based. As Keenan puts it, and as we have seen, "[deconstruction] appears to ruin the categories on which political discourse has tried to found itself for as long as anyone can remember: subjectivity and agency, and the reliable knowledge . . . that allows it to act" (263).

Speaking specifically on the possibility of justice, which is the specific ethico-political issue upon which I'd like to focus, Derrida describes the debate over deconstruction's ethical position in this way:

> Do "deconstructionists" have anything to say about justice, anything to do with it? Why, basically, do they speak of it so little? Does it interest them, finally? Is it not, as some suspect, because deconstruction does not in itself permit any just action, any valid discourse on justice but rather constitutes a threat to law, and ruins the condition of possibility of justice? Yes, some would reply; no, replies the adversary. (*Force of Law* 231)

This sense of either/or, noted by both Keenan and Derrida, is worth highlighting. It is, in fact, the issue around which I want to move—that is, the issue of decisiveness and, thus, indecisiveness, the issue of taking sides. What seems to be at stake here—both in terms of the possibility of justice, or ethico-political responsibility, and deconstruction's relationship to that possibility—is the possibility of determining, or deciding upon, a "just" decision. It is in fact, for this reason, that I would like to focus at this point on deconstruction's commitment to justice—which is, necessarily, a commitment to decisiveness, a commitment that is (moreover) predicated on the possibility of what Critchley calls a foundational claim.

According to the later Derrida, deconstruction has *always* been concerned with justice; he suggests, in fact, that it would probably be inaccurate to say that deconstruction is distinct from justice. This is a provocative suggestion, a suggestion that speaks directly to the above discussion of deconstructive transcendentalism and the (im)possibility of being pragmatic *all the way down*. Before we can fully address such a suggestion, it is necessary to explore in some detail the ways in which Derrida has attempted to bring the issue of justice (and, in turn, ethico-political responsibility and the possibility of a transcendental truth claim) to the forefront of his thinking. In the first part of *Force of Law*, "Of the Right to Justice / From Law to Justice,"[33] Derrida begins, before addressing the issue of justice and ethical responsibility directly, by pointing out that the term "force"—for he introduces the topic of justice by highlighting the fact that "justice as law" (233) is *enforced*—has often been employed in "deconstructive" texts. In many of his own texts, Derrida is quick to point out, "recourse to the word 'force' is both very frequent and, in strategic places . . . decisive, but at the same time always or almost always accompanied by an explicit reserve, a warning" (*Force of Law* 234). But Derrida does not list the particular texts that he has mind, stating that such a list "would be self-indulgent and . . . would waste time" (234). Instead, he asks us to take his word *on faith*: "I ask you to trust me" (234). This request is significant.

There are two things worth mentioning. On the one hand, there is a request for trust—Derrida implores us to trust him *as an authority*. And, on the other, he asks us to trust him because he does not want to list "self-indulgently" all of his various texts that deal with the issue of force and, therefore (however obliquely), with the issue of justice, law and ethical responsibility. Yet, on the next page—or, rather, at the end of the very paragraph from which the above portion is drawn— Derrida again addresses the fact that deconstruction has seemed to be unconcerned with ethico-political issues, noting that "There are no doubt many reasons why the majority of texts hastily identified as 'deconstructionist' seem . . . not to foreground the theme of justice (as theme, precisely), nor even the theme of ethics or politics" (235). Although he never specifies what, precisely, these reasons might be, Derrida assures us that what *seems* to be a lack of interest in ethico-political responsibility "is only *apparently* so" (235). Presumably to prove his point (now made twice, in two different ways), he promptly follows this statement with an almost comprehensive list of texts by Derrida that deal, in one way or another, with ethico-political issues:

> for example (I will only mention these) the many texts
> devoted to Levinas and to the relations between "violence
> and metaphysics," or to the philosophy of right, that of

> Hegel's, with all its posterity in *Glas*, of which it is the prin-
> cipal motif, or the texts devoted to the drive for power and
> to the paradoxes of power in "To Speculate—on Freud," to
> the law, in "Before the Law" (on Kafka's *Vor dem Gesetz*) or
> in "Declarations of Independence," in "The Laws of Reflec-
> tion: Nelson Mandela, In Admiration," and in many other
> texts. (235)

There is here, it would *seem*, a certain amount of irony. If self-indul-
gence was a concern twenty-or-so lines previous, it certainly isn't anymore. There is, in fact, a certain sense that Derrida has now betrayed
the trust that he asked us to grant—as if he decided in the end that
we wouldn't (perhaps, *shouldn't*) trust him. The question is, then: is this
sort of subtle self-contradiction, or rhetorical flip-flopping, a sign that
we should *not* trust him—that our trust is in some way *unfounded*, that
it is *without foundation*? Of course, we cannot answer this question with
any certainty. Nevertheless, this irony, or contradictory self-positioning,
seems hardly coincidental in a paper that is interested in dismantling
the distinction, and hierarchical relationship, between two types of violence: the violence that founds law and the violence that preserves law.
Such irony may be understood as a strategic device in a paper that is
interested in frustrating the possibility of *deciding*, with any certainty,
between *either* this *or* that. But if this is an attempt on Derrida's part
to create an "ordeal of indecision" as regards our faith in him, is it, or
can it be, successful? I would say—if only tentatively at this point—that
the answer is "no." For, as I have already suggested, our willingness
to embrace the necessity of indecision—or, more bluntly, Derridean
"quasi-transcendentalism"—seems to be the effect of a decision that is
necessarily anterior to what Derrida calls "the test and ordeal of the
undecidable" (*Force of Law* 253).

   In the second portion of *Force of Law*, "First Name of Benjamin,"
Derrida engages in a reading of Benjamin's 1921 essay, "Critique
of Violence." More specifically, Derrida concentrates on Benjamin's
desire to distinguish—or, we might cautiously say, *decide between*—two
types of violence: "There is, first, the distinction between two kinds
of violence of law, in relation to law: the founding violence, the one
that institutes and posits law . . . and the violence that preserves, the
one that maintains, confirms, insures the permanence and enforce-
ability of law" (265). Derrida is interested in the way in which these
two forms of violence become indistinguishable, or indeterminable,
from each other: "For beyond Benjamin's explicit purpose, [Derrida
proposes an] interpretation according to which the very violence of

the foundation or *positing of law* . . . must envelop the violence of the *preservation of law* . . . and cannot break with it" (272). In other words, Derrida argues, the distinction between these two types of violence is dissolved, or "threatened," by the "paradox of iterability." According to Derrida, "Iterability makes it so that the origin must repeat itself originarily, must alter itself to count itself *as origin*, that is to say, to preserve itself" (278). And, for this reason, it would seem, "The law is both threatening and threatened by itself" (275). Or, put another way, "Law preserving violence . . . is a threat of law" (276). This is, as Derrida hastens to note, a "Double genitive: it both comes from and threatens law" (276). The "foundational claim," or the authority upon which the preservation of the law is based, is a type of prosthetic origin; it is determined by its own preservation. The preservation of the law is always based on the founded law but, paradoxically, the preservation determines that founding by positing it as the condition of its own preserving violence. For this reason, "All revolutionary situations, all revolutionary discourses, on the left or the right . . . justify the recourse to violence by alleging the founding, in progress or to come, of a new law, of a new state. As this law to come will in return legitimate, retrospectively, the violence that may offend the sense of justice, its future anterior already justifies it" (269).

The law (as posited and as preserved, for the two are indistinguishable) is *haunted* by the specter of justice—the "to come," the messianic. The law carries with it the promise of justice (never to be fulfilled): "The law is transcendent and theological, and so always to come, always promised, because it is immanent, finite, and thus already past" (*Force of Law* 270). It is haunted, that is to say, in the sense of Derridean spectrality, "which has to do with the fact that a body is never present for itself, for what it is. It appears by disappearing or by making disappear what it represents" (*Force of Law* 276). And it is, as we've seen already, this specter of the messianic, of the promise "to come," that links justice to deconstruction, deconstruction to Marxism and, indeed, Marxism to religion. We need to remember, though, that Derrida is very careful to distinguish the *specter of the messianic* from the teleological tendencies of Marxist and religious discourses: "what remains irreducible to any deconstruction, what remains as undeconstructable as the possibility itself of deconstruction is, perhaps, a certain experience of the emancipatory promise; it is perhaps even the formality of a structural messianism, a messianism without religion, even a messianic without messianism, an idea of justice" (*Specters* 59). As Ernesto Laclau suggests, "This does not mean this or that particular promise, but the promise implicit in an originary opening to the 'other,' to the unforeseeable, to the pure event which cannot be mastered by aprioristic discourse" (90). This is worth stressing.

So as to ensure that we understand "the messianic without messianism" as a type of non-teleological eschatology, the later Derrida often struggles to distinguish between "teleology" and "messianic eschatology." The messianic without messianism does not have a programmatic or systematic code (i.e., no messiah) that could link us, or definitively guide us, to the future *as present.* As Werner Hamacher points out, "There is no preestablished telos for the 'messianic without messianism' which could be recognizable now, programmatically striven for, and ultimately achieved in some particular organization of social life" (168). It is, after all, the very absence of a telos that defines "this strange concept of messianism without content, of the messianic without messianism, that guides us here like the blind" (*Specters* 65). Still, we must consider the possibility that this "strange concept" is necessarily a failure, that it is caught within the very teleological trap it seems to be guiding us safely past. While this faithless faith appears to function effectively as a way to move without movement, to be goal-oriented without the possibility of goal fulfillment, it necessarily must exclude itself from the ironic position it demands. It would seem that our faith in this "religion without religion" must be absolute or final if we are to successfully employ it as a way to avoid the dangers of all other teleological assumptions.

Ultimately, Derrida's concept of the messianic without messianism suggests that the promise is always "at a distance" and paradoxically conditioned, or determined, by the entity that stands before it. In a very Rortian, or "privately ironic" fashion, the promise, like the law—or, rather, *in the form of the law* (for the law *promises* justice)[34]—"only appears infinitely transcendent and thus theological to the extent that, nearest to him, it depends only on him, . . . on who is before it (and so prior to it), on who produces it, founds it, authorizes it in an absolute performative whose presence always escapes him" (*Force of Law* 270). Caught up in a type of circular or paradoxical logic, the possibility of the promise can be understood as the possibility of repetition. As a type of quasi-transcendental possibility, the messianic leads us in a circular fashion, but we never finally return to it (to the starting point—which is, also, our final destination).[35] This circle, within which the messianic is located, never closes in on itself; the "to come" never arrives. In this sense, the movement toward the messianic is more spiral than circular, for in attempting to return to an origin and/or future destination, law (like Marxism or even deconstruction) refounds—and, in this sense, destroys—the origin/future that it seeks to preserve. If the promise were ever fulfillable, if the future were ever accessible, then it would already be known, or realized—that is, it would already be *here and now*. At the same time, though, the possibility of the promise *must be* the possibility that its fulfillment *is possible*, that the circle will close on itself, repeat, and thus dissolve. The messianic promises what cannot be deconstructed, what is justice (or friendship, or forgiveness, or arche-writing) itself and, therefore, the very absence or annulment of justice, or friendship.

While "Justice in itself, if such a thing exists, outside or beyond law, is not deconstructable" (*Force of Law* 243) it is (nevertheless) always, and must remain, still "to come." The same goes for deconstruction itself, "if such a thing exists" (*Force of Law* 243). In this sense, as Derrida puts it, "*Deconstruction is justice*" (*Force of Law* 243). These undeconstructables—these messianic promises—however impossible or unreal they may be, *condition*, or are the very ground of possibility for, deconstruction, or justice, or writing, or whatever. They are, as Derrida seems to suggest, what " 'keeps us moving . . . ' stronger and faster" (*Force of Law* 255).[36] Put differently, a Derridean promise can be understood as a type of "horizon," a concept that for Derrida connotes two contradictory things. On the one hand, "horizon," particularly in *Force of Law*, stands in for an impossible destination that is ultimately determined by the position of the entity that moves toward it. On the other, "horizon," as it is often employed in *Specters*, represents a determinate end; for this reason, Derrida's messianic must be understood as "a waiting without horizon of expectation" (*Specters* 168).[37] But these two seemingly contradictory usages only serve to highlight the way in which the horizon functions as an apt metaphor for the messianic. By moving toward the horizon we change the position of, or we "refound," what we are moving toward, as if we were a donkey to which Derrida had tied a dangling carrot. It is, that is to say, both a determinate end and an infinite opening, a final destination "yet to come" that is always determined by that which precedes it.[38] The horizon is thus representative of the messianic end, or *a priori* "condition of possibility," an end for which we will always be waiting. In this way, as Richard Kearney suggests, "Deconstruction is like waiting for Godot—not just in two acts but forever (*go deo*)" (124). Nevertheless—and this brings me at last and full-on to the issue of decision making—"justice, however unpresentable it remains, does not wait" (255). We are every day called upon to make "just" decisions. Such decisions, according to Derrida, demand our attention. They demand our decisiveness.

Because the just decision is required "as quickly as possible . . . [, i]t cannot provide itself with the infinite information and unlimited knowledge that could justify it." Consequently, "the decision always marks the interruption of the jurdico-, ethico-, or politic-cognitive deliberation that precedes it, that *must . . .* precede it" (255). As it is always based on incomplete knowledge, a decision must always gamble on the future. A decision is possible—it is, in fact, made *at all*—because of the (im)possibility of justice that it anticipates on or at the horizon. However, and necessarily, the decision (or we might say, the law) always misses its mark—that is, justice always exceeds the decision, or the law. For this reason, justice, like deconstruction, is always giving itself in that it is always still "to come"; it is always *arriving* as the other—indeed, as the wholly other. Moreover, as we have seen, this "to come" is always in a state of flux, as its very condition is also and paradoxically conditioned by the decisions or laws that are themselves precipitated by the possibility of its *arrival.* In order to touch on[39] this idea of the "just" decision fully, though, we need to look again at Benjamin's attempts to distinguish between forms of violence.

In addition to, or perhaps as a modification of, the other two forms of violence that he attempts to maintain as distinct, Benjamin distinguishes between mythic and divine violence. Mythic violence, which includes the founding and the preserving violence of the law, comes as fate. In the sense that it is fated, it is not mediated and it is always new; it is determined (found and preserved) in the instant that it is dispensed. Mythic violence, then, leaves us in a state of indecision. It leaves us without a decision to make: no choice and thus no responsibility. Divine or Judaic violence, on the other hand, destroys law. It commands an imperative—"Thou shalt not kill," for example—but it offers no judgment: "one could not find in it the authority to automatically condemn any putting to death. The individual or the community must keep the 'responsibility' (the condition of which being the absence of general criteria and automatic rules)" (*Force of Law* 288). Divine violence, unlike mythic violence, *forces us* to decide. It leaves us with the possibility of decision. Accordingly, "All decidability is situated, blocked in, accumulated on the side of law, of mythological violence that founds and preserves law. But on the other hand all decidability stands on the side of the divine violence that destroys the law, we could even venture to say, that deconstructs the law" (*Force of Law* 289–90). What is important here—and what, in a fashion, dissolves the distinction between divine and mythic violence—is the fact that the "just" decision is only possible given both the possibility *and* the impossibility[40] of a decision. Simply—and I can, at this point, begin to tie things together—the decision must always be *haunted* by indecision. Otherwise it is not a decision. And, as Derrida assures us, "only a decision is just" (*Force of Law* 253).

By indecision, Derrida means two contradictory, or ironic, things. On the one hand, indecision is the impossibility of decision—that is, *no* decision—in the sense of mythic violence, or fate: I must go to war and spread democracy because I have no choice but to go to war and spread democracy. Indecision, in this sense, is the effect of the divine dispensation (in both senses of the word, "a distribution" and "a rendering useless") of justice. On the other hand, though, indecision is the burden of uncertainty and, therefore, of responsibility. It is the hesitancy that is the effect of the impossibility of justice (or indecision, in the former sense) and yet it makes a "just" decision possible. The former being messianism, the transcendent, justice itself; the other, its impossibility. And it is indecision *in both senses* that haunts, that, according to Derrida, *must* haunt the "just" decision. While a belief in, or even a desire for, the possibility of indecision in the former sense—or, rather, the possibility of a transcendental truth claim—prevents paralysis, giving us a reason to move, indecision in the latter sense—or rather, the impossibility of a transcendental truth claim—is what makes a decision necessary in the first place. For this reason, "the test and ordeal of the undecidable, of which I have just said it *must be gone through* by any decision worthy of its name, is never past or passed" (*Force of Law* 253, my emphasis). This "test and ordeal" is ultimately a matter of respecting the spectrality of the undecidable—that is, the possibility *and* the impossibility of the just decision: "The undecidable remains caught, lodged, as a ghost at least, but an essential ghost, in every decision, in every event of decision. Its ghostliness . . . deconstructs from within all assurance of presence, all certainty or all alleged criteriology assuring us of the justice of the decision" (*Force of Law* 253). This is the imperative of Derridean ethics; this is the decision we *must* make, yet the decision to make such a decision is necessarily anterior to the ironic ordeal of indecision. In fact, the decision to make a *just decision*, the decision to follow Derrida—to *believe in him*—is, it would seem, solely an effect of indecision in the single sense of "no decision." Such a decision (or such faith) is, I am suggesting, necessarily aligned with what Derrida via Benjamin refers to as mythic violence, or what Rorty understands as hegemonic *a priori* conditions of possibility. It is the *only way* to make a just decision. The call to respect, to endure, the spectrality of the specter—the possibility *and* the impossibility of the promise, the possibility *and* the impossibility of the transcendent, of the "just" decision—necessarily conjures/exorcises that spectrality. Only through such an exorcism can we claim to know that such an exorcism is impossible—or, at the very least, unethical. Put differently, and in a manner that will make more sense if we consider the way in which the Derridean decision is associated with the gamble, the decision to gamble on a decision is never, itself, a gamble.

Haunted by indecision in both senses, the Derridean decision—or, if I can continue stressing the inherent positivism of this argument,[41] the *truly* ethical decision—is always a type of wager, or gamble. And, as Jean-Michel Rabaté notes, "The word wager, for its part, implies a calculation combining the plural and the future: it yields a plural 'futures' that has to do with debt and risk, all thrown in a balance whose equilibrium depends upon a measurement capable of calculating 'times to come' " (182). A wager is infused with a sense of hope, belief, or faith in the "to come," the messianic, the utopian. But that hope or faith must always be unfounded. There is never any certainty; there is never, Derrida assures us, a messiah, a stable and transcendental foundation. If we are to decide—and by deciding we are to make Derrida proud—a wager must be placed on a race that isn't fixed. The wager is, simply, the result of the just decision, the decision haunted by indecision. As Peggy Kamuf suggests in her examination of *Specters*, the wager stresses the necessity of taking sides in the absence of certainty: "This wager . . . sums up the principal gesture or act of the book, the taking of sides that Derrida constantly assumes throughout" (280). And, indeed, *Specters* is filled with decisions. Derrida *chooses* to embrace one specter of Marx over others; he *decides* on the "ten current plaques of humanity." With each decision, though, Derrida reminds us (or perhaps, he reminds himself) that he is gambling, that his decisions are necessarily haunted by indecision. He relentlessly reminds us that the impossibility of the *certainly right* decision is what makes the *just* decision possible, the decision that must bear the mark, must be haunted by what it could have been and by what it can never be. The possibility of the "just" decision is, in short, wholly contingent on the impossibility of certainty. Justice—like, say, the transcendental signified—is only possible because it is impossible.

This brings me back, at last, to the issue of the either/or, and Derrida's ironic self-positioning in *Force of Law*. For Derrida, the either/or must, in some fashion, remain (in terms of deconstruction's relationship to the possibility of justice, in terms of founding and positing violence, in terms of decidability and undecidability, in terms of the possibility and impossibility of the Kantian transcendental). However, and at the same time, the "to come" must also remain a possibility, if only as the promise of choosing the right side *with certainty*: justice, deconstruction itself, God. As I have already stated, this becomes a type of imperative: it is absolutely necessary to ironically maintain these two contradictory things. Derrida is essentially imploring us to continue attempting to exorcise the ghost of the messianic (which haunted Marx, and which continues to haunt deconstruction) while simultaneously and paradoxically allowing it to remain a revenant, to return, to continue coming. Derrida seems to be arguing that, if all gods are dead, then their ghosts continue, and *must continue*, to haunt us. While deconstruction, like Marxism, can be understood as a relentless attempt to exorcise these ghosts, each moment of deconstruction, like each revolution, *must be*, itself, haunted. Consequently, Derrida's ironic self-positioning, his attempt to frustrate our ability to make a decision as regards our faith in him, as regards the finality of his argument(s), can be read as a necessarily unsuccessful attempt to evade the absolute decisiveness he would like us to abandon.[42] For, as I am suggesting, the imperative of Derridean indecision, the ethic of the possibility and the impossibility of the just decision, the identification of any condition of possibility or final vocabulary, is absolutely and necessarily contingent upon a decision that is not subject to "the ordeal of the undecidable." By way of conclusion, I will attempt to clarify this point by turning somewhat abruptly, and in a rather platonic fashion, to a particularly applicable myth.

Toward the end of *Exodus*, after he has shattered the tablets of the law and after he has begun to doubt his own authority, Moses goes into the tabernacle to talk with God. Once in the tabernacle, Moses asks God to confirm his presence amongst the Israelites: "I pray thee, if I have found grace in thy sight, shew me now thy way, that I may know thee, that I may find grace in thy sight" (Ex 33:13). We might say that Moses here asks God to arrive *finally* so that the law can be *dispensed with*, at last. But God (perhaps, I might add, necessarily) denies this request—or rather, grants it in a very unfulfilling fashion. God tells Moses that he will place him in the cleft of a rock and that he will cover Moses' eyes with his hand: "And I will take away mine hand, and thou shalt see my back parts: but my face shall not be seen" (Ex 33:23). This is, it would seem, the experience that, according to the later Derrida, any law maker/preserver—or, for that matter, any decision maker, any philosopher, any interpreter—must endure. It is the experience of *believing* (a word that is used repeatedly by Derrida throughout *Force of Law*) in, and desiring to have, the authority to dispense (with) justice, truth, while knowing, or at least discovering, that that belief is unfounded, that it is only passing, out of reach and still "yet to come."

Yet Moses, even though he is never permitted to see God face to face, does not consider his faith to be unfounded. It seems reasonable to suggest that, were he to have any doubts, even ironic ones, he would cease to be active/mobile. With this in mind, I would argue that Derrida (and, indeed, Rorty) needs to be viewed as a type of modern-day Moses, a type of prophet. Or rather, from another angle—that is, if we consider all those who read and quote and *believe in* them—both Derrida and Rorty continually and necessarily *slip*, however uncomfortably, into the role of Messiah, the role of God (if only because they resist exposing their "private" faces to the public). This unavoidable "slippage" is the very thing I have attempted to expose throughout the above discussion of *late* deconstruction. If we believe in this *late* Derrida—if we *believe*, in short, that we *must* respect the spectrality of the specter, its impossible possibility—then we are left in a state of indecision, but indecision in the mythic or hegemonic sense of "no decision." And it is this *particular* state of indecision that is the defining characteristic of this emergent epoch after postmodernism. Indeed, one of the things I have been attempting to highlight through this examination of "late-phase" deconstruction is the way in which this current epistemological reconfiguration, this *episteme of renewalism*, is marked by a distinct manner of representing, or understanding, the history of knowledge. It is marked, that is, by its view that all previous epistemic configurations can be understood via their paradoxical and hostile relationships to a certain spectral remainder, or teleological aporia[43]—relationships that have inevitably resulted in violently hegemonic claims. My point, though, is that this spectral relationship does not cease to be a problem—that is, a source of teleological assumptions—simply because we claim to recognize it, to accept it. It is, I am arguing, impossible to respect the specter. This seems to be implicit in the teleological imperative that we *must* respect the specter. After all, if we *must* do it, it's hardly a gamble. Or, as I stated above, a gamble is hardly a gamble if it is animated by the absolute conviction that to gamble is to *always win*. So, I'll end (almost, but not quite) where this final section on Derrida began: It is inaccurate to say that Derrida is an atheist—or rather, it is inaccurate to say that any discourse, or episteme, *can ever be atheistic.*

CHAPTER THREE

Writing of the Ghost (Again)

The Failure of Postmodern Metafiction and the Narrative of Renewalism

Once again I tried committing suicide—this time by wetting my nose and inserting it into the light socket. Unfortunately, there was a short in the wiring, and I merely caromed off the icebox.

—Woody Allen, *Without Feathers*

Baby Suggs died shortly after the brothers left, with no interest whatsoever in their leave-taking or hers, and right afterward Sethe and Denver decided to end the persecution by calling forth the ghost that tried them so. Perhaps a conversation, they thought, an exchange of views or something would help. So they held hands and said, "Come on. Come on. You may as well just come on."

—Toni Morrison, *Beloved*

So why do I do it then? Why do I sit here like this?
    Because if writing this book—which, according to several people who are knowledgeable about literature, is the first tetherball novel *ever*—can help just one kid who's gone through a similar experience, i.e., having a dad who survived an attempted execution by lethal injection and is resentenced to NJSDE, and losing your virginity to a 36–year-old warden, then it will have been worth it.

—Mark Leyner, The Tetherballs of Bougainville

Neither Logocentric nor Logo Centric

In the preface to *The Tetherballs of Bougainville*, Mark Leyner reminds us that "When an astronomer observes a galaxy in some distant realm of the universe, . . . [h]e is quite literally looking at the past" (9). This is, of course, as Leyner goes on to point out, an effect of light; by the time the light of a distant galaxy reaches us, here on Earth and in the "present," the galaxy itself "may no longer even exist" (9). So, Leyner goes on to suggest, "if we could travel to a point many light-years from the earth and somehow view the light emanating from our planet with the resolution of, say, a spy satellite—advanced photoreconnaissance spacecraft are capable of reading the washing instructions on a black silk chemisette from 22,300 miles in geosynchronous orbit—we could actually observe ourselves in the past" (9). However, because we cannot yet "outrace light," Leyner admits that "we must make due with our memories, our diaries and notebooks, our videotapes, microcassettes, floppy disks, our photo albums, our evocative souvenirs and bric-a-brac—all the various and sundry madeleines we use to goad our hippocampi into reverse-scan" (9). By highlighting this inevitable "limitation," Leyner's preface works to stress the problems associated with any historical account. The preface thus prepares us for the text that follows: an "autobiographical account" written from the perspective of a thirteen-year-old Mark Leyner. This "autobiography" recounts a single day in Mark's[1] life. On the day in question, Mark's father—a relatively good man who "just can't do PCP socially" (22)—is scheduled to be executed for murdering a security guard with "a Cuisinart variable-speed hand blender and a Teflon-coated ice-cream scooper from a vendor's kiosk at an outlet in Secaucus" (23). Minutes before the execution, Mark gets a phone call from his "agent" who tells him that he's "going to win the Vincent and Lenore DiGiacomo/Oshimitsu Polymers America Award" (17), an award worth $250,000 a year (for life), which Mark's high school gives out annually for the best screenplay written by a student. The problem, though, is that Mark hasn't yet written his "winning" screenplay, which is due the following day. In brief, then, the first half of the text, or "autobiography," recounts the various experiences Mark has as a result of his father's execution (which is unsuccessful), his attempt to have sex with the thirty-six year-old warden of the prison (which is successful), and his struggle to produce a screenplay before the end of the day (which is also, apparently, successful).

What is important to note here is the apparently incongruous nature of the preface of Leyner's text and the text proper. In the preface, Leyner seems to address the problem of historical accuracy "sincerely" (albeit, in a comedic manner that is ultimately or simultaneously a type of imitation, or exaggeration, of the most obvious signs of sincerity and/or seriousness[2]). In doing so, he highlights his apparent desire to be as "honest" as possible. After all, Leyner repeatedly intimates that he is intent on accuracy: "I have tried my best—in the following capsules—to provide an accurate chronicle of the past" (10). For Leyner, it would seem such accuracy, or "realism," is a vehicle for shared understanding, the best and perhaps *only* mode of accurate communication. According to the preface, the text proper functions—or, at the very least, *is meant to function*—as a tool for relocating certain human constants; it is meant to produce an effect of shared, or communal, recognition:

> As you read on, some of you may experience an eerie shock of recognition. You may bolt upright in bed, murmuring to yourself, "I think I actually *know* this guy." Some of you may even say, "Hey, I think I *dated* this guy." (For female readers who lived in the Dallas-Fort Worth metropolitan area in the mid-eighties—if the droll conversational icebreaker "I'd like to get real high and eat your pussy for an afternoon" sounds familiar—yes, that was me.) (11)

Not only does Leyner aim to connect his readers via their recognition of the subject in question (i.e., the author himself), he suggests that the text may also give us the impression that we are reading our own autobiography, as if we are "peeping through the window of [our] own doppelgänger" (11). Leyner goes so far as to insist that "each page is like a mirror, and you've literally never seen yourself so closely and the pores of your nose have never seemed so gaping" (11). Leyner's story is, in short, *our story*. As parodic as it might seem, the preface—and, I would argue, the text as a whole—is earnestly engaged in an outright rejection of what is typically understood as the postmodern impulse toward narrative paralysis, or authorial suicide. The preface, it would seem, refuses to reject the possibility of communication with the other; it refuses, that is, to abandon the impossible *as impossible*. Leyner (like, we might say at this point, a late-Derrida) actively resists the apparent nihilism of postmodernism by identifying the impossibility of certain spectral lures as impossible. While the preface and, indeed, the text as a whole seems to accept the postmodern lesson that certain teleological ideals—communication, mimesis, shared understanding—are illusions of a now defunct project of modernity, it simultaneously embraces the possibility, or promise, of such ideals. Of course, I do not want to suggest that postmodernism was simply and utterly ignorant of, or blind to, the fact that such illusions are essential animating factors, but I would like to highlight the way in which a text like Leyner's distances itself from postmodernism proper by overtly embracing the impossible possibility of certain teleological promises. Ultimately, though, the only difference between a text like Leyner's—which, I would like to suggest, is representative of a newly emergent period of cultural production—and a work of high postmodern metafiction is a difference in emphasis. Rather than focusing exclusively on the need to expose as illusory the teleologies associated with a distinctly modern project, a text like Leyner's acknowledges the impossibility of such lures while simultaneously and emphatically articulating the ways in which they remain necessary to any critical and/or aesthetic enterprise.

In short, and as his initial claim concerning the possibility of seeing the past accurately projected via light suggests, Leyner outwardly embraces the impossibilities—that is, the impossibility of communication, of shared understanding, of essential human connections—that the historiographic metafiction of postmodernism worked to expose as dangerous ideological lures. Leyner's *Tetherballs*, or so the preface suggests, reembraces the impulse toward mimesis that defined the realist mode of the nineteenth century as well as the experimental imperatives of the early-twentieth. Narrative, Leyner seems to be claiming, can be a productive form of social, or public, exchange. Still, as I pointed out above, the text proper, if not the comedic tone of the entire novel, seems to wholly abandon the mimetic project set out in the preface. As my brief plot summation (above) suggests, the text is almost decadent in terms of its "postmodern" attributes. Not only is the basic plot utterly improbable, if not simply impossible, the text is filled with digressions, satirical attacks on mass culture, corrosively self-reflexive statements, absurd dialogue, and temporal incongruities.

That the text shares certain undeniable affinities with a decidedly postmodern aesthetic is, perhaps, most obvious in the screenplay that constitutes the last half of the text. This screenplay recounts Mark's affair with the prison warden in the hours following the failed attempt to execute his father. By the end of the first half of the text, Mark realizes that, because of the hours he has spent with the warden, he will hardly have the time to plagiarize a script (never mind produce an original work). After being told of his dilemma, the warden suggests that (to save time) he write about the events that just happened: "And she says, 'Yeah, this,' indicating, with a panoramic gesture, the whole drug-addled liaison we're presently engaged in. And she says, 'Do a screenplay that appears to be *faux* autobiographical documentary, but that's actually—here's the irony—completely factual. *Faux* irony' " (107). What follows is thus a screenplay depicting Mark's "drug-addled liaison" with the warden—which is, from a reader's perspective, a fictional screenplay *pretending to be* a *faux* autobiographical documentary that is really completely factual. The sense we get initially is that Leyner, in an ostentatiously metafictional manner, is attempting to frustrate the line separating fact and fiction and thus highlight the illusory nature of any seemingly stable referent. However, the attempt—if such an attempt is actually being made—ends, quite obviously, in failure; the screenplay is simply *too* improbable. Along with unbelievably excessive drug use, the screenplay includes "the notorious and achingly beautiful CUNNILINGUS SCENE"—which is "over three and a half hours" (171)—as well as a reading (by Mark) of an imaginary movie review Mark wrote for a film he never made. Although the "review," which takes up almost half of the screenplay, was written before the events detailed in Mark's "autobiography," it describes an autobiographical film based on the years following the failed attempt to execute Mark's father. In short, the review refers to a film that recounts events that occurred *after* Mark wrote the review.

If anything, then, Leyner's confusion of the factual and the fictional works to reaffirm the fictional *as fictional*. For this reason alone *Tetherballs* is not postmodern in the way that a text like Pynchon's *Gravity's Rainbow* or Vonnegut's *Slaughterhouse Five* is postmodern. While the latter two texts carefully blur the boundaries between the real and the imaginary, between history and narrative—that is, both texts are focused almost exclusively on the way in which the traumatic "reality" of World War II is contingent upon narrative filtration, that it exists only as the unstable effect of an eternally shifting chain of signifiers—*Tetherballs* seems to do exactly what its preface claims it will do: it offers us the possibility of shared recognition, even if what we *recognize* is the impossibility of recognition. Leyner seemingly embraces the impossibility of mimesis as a portrayable reality in itself, as a way of returning to a type of realist mode of representation. In a manner that speaks to a discernable shift in narrative production—a shift that seems to mark the end of the postmodern metafictional imperative and that is often associated with the emergence of a type of "neo-realism" (discussed below)—Leyner reembraces a certain faith in the possibility of the impossible referent, of the transcendental signified. Leyner's autobiographical account, while absolutely incongruous with anyone else's "reality," highlights the absolutely contingent nature of existence *so as* to reestablish the possibility of a common ground, a stable point of reference. Leyner suggests that the one thing we *can* communicate is the impossibility of communication, the impossibility of finally articulating our "true" selves. Leyner thus articulates the possibility of communication by stressing the fact that it is an impossibility; he works to communicate *the impossibility of communication* by continually failing to communicate. For this reason, Leyner's story is indeed, as the preface claims, our story; it is an impossible and/or necessarily failed articulation of the self. Put differently, and in a manner that recalls Derrida's claim[3] that a decision is only possible if it embraces *both* the impossibility *and* the possibility of the certainly right decision, Leyner's text speaks to the way in which the recent narrative shift is defined by the conviction that the narrative act—or rather, the decision to write—*must* endure the "ordeal of indecision." In brief, then (and as I explain more fully below), a text like Leyner's can be read as representative of a still emergent period of "renewalism" because it works to embrace a certain spectral paradox: the paralyzing knowledge that there can never be an absolutely correct narrative act *and* the animating faith that the certainly right narrative act is, in fact, possible. And, of course, Leyner's main vehicle for articulating this "impossible possibility" is humor.

Like the traditional male stand-up comedian, Leyner employs humor that (from the naïve perspective of the narrator, "Mark" and, perhaps, Leyner himself) is meant to prey on an individual's desire to recognize her- or himself *once and for all*.[4] More specifically, Leyner's humor is an ostentatious exaggeration of the distinctly phallic and politically incorrect routines that male comedians tend to perform. However, while seemingly replicating essentialist and oversimplified jokes that crudely reaffirm illusory categories of gender and race, Mark ultimately establishes what a late-Derrida would celebrate as a type of "relation without relation." This simultaneous affirmation and deferral of recognition is, quite simply, accomplished via Mark's various attempts to share events no one would recognize as *common experience*.

For example, in one of many digressive interruptions of the basic plot, Mark pastes an article from *People* into his autobiographical account. The article, which Mark is "perusing" while waiting for the prison doctor to explain why his father's execution was unsuccessful, tells of a recent diplomatic party at which several of the high-profile female guests were hypnotized. After being put in a trance, all of the women "immediately disrobed, rending garments from their bodies as if they were aflame, and then, like deranged children, spreading caviar and blintz filling over each other's naked flesh" (56). Eventually, or so the article explains, the women "overpowered a chosen male guest, shackled his legs, cuffed his hands behind his back, and took turns sitting on his face as they swigged caraway and jimsonweed-infused vodka from crystal decanters" (56). After being interrupted in mid-sentence by a nurse who informs him that the doctor is now ready to see him, Mark returns to his own story, asking us (in standard comedic form) if we have ever had an experience like he just had: "Have you ever read an article in *People* that was so perfectly suited to your interests that it seemed as if the writer had intended it exclusively for you, so that you could . . . perhaps derive some subliminal or encrypted communication or some secret gnostic insight? That's how I felt about this particular article" (57). While the question itself seems to open up the possibility that Mark's autobiographical experiences are being communicated with a certain amount of mimetic success[5]—after all, haven't we *all* found an article in a magazine (while waiting for a doctor) that was surprisingly attuned to our personal interests?—Mark's reason for enjoying the article in question simultaneously frustrates that possibility:

> I can't tell you how many afternoons I've fritted away contemplating what it would be like to be held captive and abused by various groups of fanatical and/or unbalanced and/or unwashed women. For a while it's *all* I talked about, which I realized became rather tedious for my parents. (57)

In the end, then, Mark's various attempts *to share* his ostentatiously unique experiences and personality simultaneously and paradoxically holds out the promise and/or possibility of mimetic accuracy—of shared experience, of "subliminal or encrypted communication or secret gnostic insight," and so on—while incessantly deferring that promise and/or possibility. The deferral, or impossibility, of a type of communal recognition is thus continually reasserted as the very ground for its possibility.

In "Figuring Out Mark Leyner: A Waste of Time," William G. Little makes a similar observation about Leyner's work. Focusing on Leyner's earlier texts—in particular, *Et Tu, Babe* and *My Cousin, My Gastroenterologist*—Little argues that Leyner successfully evades the positivism of modernism, while simultaneously rejecting what Little articulates as the postmodern insistence on negation. Significantly, Little bases his argument on Mark C. Taylor's suggestion that postmodernism endorses a type of "logo centrism" that simply inverts (and thus falls prey to) the blind idealism typically associated with the logocentrism of modernism. For Taylor, logocentrism struggles to dismantle the veil of signifiers and finally exposes the transcendental signified; logo centrism, on the other hand, struggles to deny (absolutely, or *once and for all*) the possibility of the signified. In the latter, the signifier—that is, the logo, the sign, the symbol—is privileged absolutely. Affirming that nothing exists beyond or beneath the signifying chain, the logo

centric impulse abandons, in reaction to the hegemony of logocentrism, the possibility of a "positive" claim, a claim that can escape the
contingent "nature" of signification. What Taylor suggests, though, is
that the negation we see in logo centrism—or, we might say, more
simply, postmodernism—ultimately becomes a type of backdoor positivism, or negative theology. In a passage to which Little refers, Taylor
puts it like this:

> Postmodern logo centrism appears to involve the rejection
> or negation of the logocentrism that informs the theoes-
> thetic of modernism. But any simple opposition between
> logo centrism and logocentrism is misleading, for they are
> really contrasting expressions of a single impulse. Both logo
> centrism and logocentrism seek immediate union with the
> real. Within this similarity, an important difference emerges:
> contrasting interpretations of reality lead to alternative
> aesthetic strategies. While logocentrism struggles to erase
> signifiers in order to arrive at the pure transcendental signi-
> fied, logo centrism attempts to extend the sign to infinity
> by collapsing the signified in the signifier. Union with the
> real[6]—regardless of how the real is understood—holds out
> the promise of overcoming alienation and achieving recon-
> ciliation. (222–23)

In this sense, the paradox of logo centrism can be compared to the
reification of nothingness that Derrida identifies in the work of Sartre—a type of reification that theorists like Rorty see played out again
in Derrida's own early, or "postmodern," work (particularly in his initial
discussions of trace and differance). Still, we need to remember that
Rorty's reading of Derrida's early work (like, I would add, Derrida's
reading of Sartre in "The Ends of Man") is, to a large extent, a mis-
reading. Rorty seems to miss the fact that Derrida subtly, but continually, points to the fact that his project can never escape the "lures"
that he aims to deconstruct. And, as I've suggested throughout, we
can say something similar about postmodernism generally. Indeed,
a "black/white" (or, rather, a logocentric/logo centric) reading like
Taylor's misses much of the subtlety at work in the broad spectrum
of postmodern cultural production. Hutcheon, in fact, makes this very
point when she addresses the work of Terry Eagleton: "absolutist binary
thinking—which makes postmodernism into the negative and opposite
of modernism—denies much of the complexity of that art" (*Poetics* 18).
As a result, such thinking also fails to take into account the overlap that
seems to define this period of renewalism as a rejection *and* a continu-

ation of a distinctly postmodern project. Like Eagleton's, then, Taylor's position, if embraced too rigidly, can blind us to fact that postmodernism—like an early-Derrida—was largely cognizant of the ultimately untenable nature of its seemingly logo centric position. By identifying all postmodern cultural production as simply logo centric, we risk overlooking the fact that the postmodern "problem"—that is, the problem that seems to be addressed in this most recent epistemological reconfiguration—was, or *became*, a problem of emphasis. Because it was, for the most part, a reaction to the dangers of logocentrism, to an increasingly hegemonic project of modernity, postmodernism was far more interested in exposing the absence of the real (or the signified, or the subject, or whatever) than it was in highlighting the need to identify such illusions as ineffaceable and essential animating lures/possibilities. To a certain extant, then, we should read this current shift away from postmodernism in the same way we might read the shift from an early-Derrida to a late-Derrida: this shift is not so much a "rejection" as it is a reassessment of/in emphasis, a radical recuperation of something (i.e., a certain understanding of the spectral lure) that was present from the beginning.

That said, we should not simply abandon Taylor's understanding of the logo centric impulse. For even if postmodernism was, to a degree, aware of the impossibility of completely rejecting all idealistic lures, it was primarily motivated by a desire to expose all such lures as illusory, as false. Regardless of its subtleties, postmodernism can be accurately defined by its willingness to endorse some form of logo centrism. Consequently, it is worth exploring Taylor's claim further, particularly his claim that logo centrism is animated by the very "theoesthetic" program that so obviously defined the modernist, or logocentric, aesthetic. For Taylor, this strange inversion is the effect of an ongoing process of "dis-figuration." In a manner that recalls Kenneth Burke's terministic screens,[7] Taylor understands this process of disfiguring as simultaneously both revealing and repressing, both demystifying and mystifying. For example, the formalist and the realist designs of the modernist/logocentric enterprise are meant to *dis*figure—that is, to expose the "real" beneath figuration—and thus liberate the referent from the contingency of the signifying chain: "Modern art and architecture dis-figure by removing figure from the work of art. Abstract or nonobjective art and formalist architecture seek to uncover the transcendental signified by erasing signifiers and to discover pure form by eliminating all ornamentation" (189).

Postmodernism, argues Taylor, comes to understand this effort to disfigure as just another delusion of the enlightenment, another inevitable process of figuration. Ultimately, then, Taylor would like to view

all postmodern production as an utter rejection of the theoesthetic
or "spiritual" enterprise of the Enlightenment project, an utter rejection that, "By inverting logocentrism, . . . not only allows but actually
solicits the return of the repressed" (189). And certainly, the modernist project does attempt to withdraw from consumer culture and the
impurity of the signifier (which the process of modernization increasingly fetishizes) while postmodernism, as seen in the work of a pop
artist like Warhol, rejects the possibility of an aneconomical space of
production and self-consciously flaunts its contingent position in an
inescapable exchange of signifiers. However, as I suggested above, postmodernism rarely abandons (without, at the very least, some latent
sense of nostalgia) *all* logocentric lures. As an epistemological response
to—or, perhaps, as an epistemological reconfiguration of—the idealism of modernity, postmodernism worked to expose the dangerous
and illusory nature of the prevailing logocentric illusions; but (as I
demonstrate below) postmodernism often seems to suggest, if only
subtly, that such illusions are impossible to abandon. I do not want to
suggest via Taylor that postmodernism *is* logo centric; rather, I would
like to argue that postmodernism *employed* a logo centric mode of critique—albeit, in an increasingly ostentatious and unsustainable manner—as a way of deconstructing the logocentrism of modernity. To a
degree, then, Taylor's critique of logo centrism and, thus, postmodernism speaks to my own understanding of a certain spectral return,
a certain inevitable return of the repressed. In fact, Taylor's reading
of postmodernism—while limited by an overly strict logo centric/logo-
centric binary—stresses the ways in which the logo centric aspects of
postmodernism were necessarily haunted by the very spectral impulses
they were expected to exorcise.

Although he cites various examples, Taylor's reading of postmodern cultural production is most succinct when he discusses two
well-known buildings: Le Corbusier's overtly modernist *Villa Savoye* and
Philip Johnson's distinctly postmodern *AT&T Corporate Headquarters*. In
the case of the former, all figurations or ornamentations are *de-formed*.
The building is thus an architectural continuation of a type of cub-
ist aesthetic; it is stark, monochromatic and simplistically geometric,
a structure that epitomizes purity, transparency, levity. As Taylor suggests, "The use of empty space and the interruption of the outer walls
creates a liberating feeling of openness. The ethereality of the villa
is accentuated by its elevation above ground. The pilotis, or slender
pillars, supporting the structure give the sense of a building about to
ascend to higher spheres" (110). The building is presented, in other
words, as completely self-referential, as the referent itself. As I briefly

suggested in chapter 1, this distinctly modern sense of "elevation," or purity, is meant to have a revolutionary function; it is meant to draw the still ignorant masses toward the utopian state represented by its very *deformed form*. Johnson's building, on the other hand, stresses the impossibility of getting beneath or beyond form. A work of obvious pastiche—that is, it employs, as Taylor puts it, "a classical three part structure" as well as a "Romanesque lobby" and "a cathedral-like base" (204)—Johnson's structure revels in the fact that its "reality" is purely "simulation." The *AT&T Headquarters* combines both real and false masonry work, and the circular openings give the illusion of incredibly thick stone walls. In the end, as Taylor puts it, the building flaunts its artificiality, repeatedly stressing the fact that "apparent depth is really superficial" (204). In terms of the spectrological argument I have been articulating throughout, we might say that Johnson's building speaks to the way in which the postmodern desire to exorcise the specter of a distinctly modern utopianism is necessarily animated by the very specter it aims to conjure away—that is, the specter, or "utopian" promise, of a *finally* "non-utopian" mode of production, one that is *finally* uncontaminated by all such ghostly promises. Not surprisingly, Taylor's point is similar, stressing the way in which this distinctly postmodern act of disfiguration is ultimately, if ironically, effected by the very same "theoesthetic" impulse that animated Corbusier's construction of the *Villa Savoye*. What Taylor usefully demonstrates, then, is the fact that, in its extremity, postmodernism's logo centric critique of logocentrism seems to risks becoming a type of reified negation, a form of inverted logocentrism, for ultimately "logo centrism is logocentric" (189).

Put differently: a work like Warhol's *192 One-Dollar Bills*—a work that ostentatiously confuses the distinction between the "real" value of a dollar, the value of the material object or "sign" that designates that value, and the value of Warhol's own piece (which is ultimately caught up in the illusory system of valuation represented by the economic signifier Warhol reproduces)—seems to eviscerate the sign utterly, repositioning the "image" as the "real." What is obscured in a process like this, Taylor argues, is the inevitable return of repressed. Taylor's point is this: the postmodern aesthetic (or perhaps, theoesthetic) is, in the end, "idealist—it is the *idealism of the image*. Since there is nothing outside the image, the image is (the) 'real.' Within the secular economy, the 'real' is ideal and the ideal is 'real' " (181). Of course, I would modify this claim somewhat; rather than stating that postmodernism was simply, always and inadvertently idealist, I would argue that the more it insisted on a type of logo centric critique the more *it came to be viewed* as little more than a simple and increasingly hegemonic inversion of the utopianism it aimed to disrupt *once and for all*. The problem needs to be understood as a problem of emphasis; postmodernism's overt demystification of logocentrism does eventually *seem* hegemonic, and few now associate postmodernism with little else. Nevertheless, this does not mean that postmodernism (in all its complexity) *is* logo centric.

Still, from a certain perspective, as Little argues, both modernism and postmodernism can be understood as "puritanical regimens undertaken in the hope of realizing whole-some identity" (Little 152). What this means for both Taylor and Little is that postmodernism, as most typically define it, is not *really* POSTmodern. Indeed, given the inevitable confluence of the logocentric and logo centric impulses, Taylor distinguishes between a "modernist" postmodernism (i.e., a logo centric postmodernism) and a POSTmodernism proper. And, of course, according to Taylor, "postmodernism *sensu strictissimo* subverts both modernism and 'modernist' postmodernism as if from within" (6). At this point, then, we might transpose Taylor's framework onto a more obviously spectrological one. As I've already suggested, Taylor's understanding of logocentric modernism echoes the claim, discussed in chapter 1, that modernism attempted to deal with the specter of the Real by "ontologizing" the spectrality of the ghost (i.e., by falsifying all things immaterial). Likewise, Taylor's identification of postmodernism's logo centric impulse suggests yet again that postmodernism tried to "conjure" its spectral inheritance by emphasizing the illusory nature of all things material, or real, by identifying *as false* all seemingly stable distinctions. Modernism, in other words, works to deny absolutely the specter's immateriality while postmodernism, at its extreme (or in its now canonized form), seems to deny absolutely the specter's materiality. In both cases, though, the ghost's ironic spectrality—its presence *and* its absence, its possibility *and* its impossibility—is challenged and seemingly effaced altogether. Both poles thus become—because, I am arguing, they are spectrally compelled to do so—hegemonic, or logocentric, ideologies. However, in Taylor's third "epoch"—that is, within the period that Taylor associates with *true* postmodernism—logos is neither denied as an impossible illusion nor privileged as the ultimate origin/end. This third period is, for Taylor, another period of "disfiguring," but it is also a period that paradoxically promises the end of figuration while simultaneously and incessantly drawing our attention to the impossibility of such an end:

> In its third guise, disfiguring neither erases nor absolu-
> tizes figure but enacts what Freud describes as a process

of "denegation," through which the repressed or refused
returns. . . . When interpreted in terms of denegation, disfiguring figures the impossibility of figuring in such a way that
the unfigurable "appears" as a disappearing in and through
the faults, fissures, cracks, and tears of figures. (230)

In other words, and in terms of my own spectrological argument, Taylor's third epoch, or epistemological reconfiguration, is defined by a
willingness, as Derrida would put it, to respect the spectrality of the
specter—that is, the impossible possibility of the logos, of the certainly
right decision, of an end, of meaning, and so on. This brings me back
to Leyner. It is, after all, within Taylor's third "epoch" that a critic like
Little positions Leyner's work.

According to Little, Leyner's work is characteristic of Taylor's
late, or "successful," postmodernism *because* it overtly undercuts "both
modernism's positive negation of figure and modernist postmodernism's positive negation of ground" (157).Leyner manages to expose
both the presence *and* the absence of the trace, or deferred signified,
simultaneously; in so doing, he evades the process of reification that
inevitably occurs when either extreme is privileged. Along with a writer
like Pynchon, Leyner (in Little's opinion) produces texts that carefully
occupy, and thus endorse the reality of, Derridean differance[8]—a space
that is neither present nor absent, a space in which meaning endlessly
proliferates. Although Little is primarily interested in demonstrating
the way in which a text like *Et Tu, Babe* performs this evasion via
a satirical look at mass culture and the idealism of pop art, we can
locate this same effort to avoid hypostatization in *Tetherballs*. However,
in *Tetherballs*, Leyner's attempt to respect both the materiality and the
immateriality of the sign—that is, his desire to "respect the specter"—is
seen less as a comedic negotiation of consumer culture and more as a
concern for the possibility of communication and shared understanding. Nevertheless, it seems evident—given the cursive analysis of the
text above—that *Tetherballs*, like *Et Tu, Babe*, can be read as *both* "a pop
critique of modernism's vacuous attempts to re-present presence by
making figure absent [*and*] a critique of modernist postmodernism's
attempt to re-present presence by making figure all there is" (158).
What we see in Leyner's work, then, is a satirical repudiation of postmodernism[9] that continues to reject the modernist impulses that postmodernism struggled to reject. Quite simply, Leyner's work privileges
neither the logocentric nor the logo centric.

That said, I'd like to complicate things somewhat. As I pointed out
above, and as I explain in detail in chapter 2, Derrida's conception of

differance changes subtly over time; in an apparent attempt to account more obviously for the reification, or transcendental impulse, critics like Rorty sees contaminating his original theorizations of differance as a fundamental non-ground for all processes of signification and representation, Derrida turns in his later more ethics-oriented works to the model of the specter. This later model functions as a way of more overtly identifying and embracing the latent idealism that necessarily "haunted" concepts like differance, trace, and the supplement while reaffirming them paradoxically as articulations of the illusory nature of any idealist impulse. Because they fail to embrace this spectral contamination outwardly, Derrida's early conceptions of differance are often viewed as still complicit with, what Taylor understands as, "modernist postmodernism." However, Derrida's shift from a theory of differance to a theory of the specter is, like the current shift in narrative production, a shift in emphasis. While the early Derrida is primarily intent on exposing the problems and dangers of logocentric assumptions, the later Derrida is far more willing to announce *overtly* that the "lure," or spectral promise, is necessarily the animating factor in all critical discussions (his own included).

With this in mind, I would argue that what Taylor and Little identify as "modernist postmodernism" can be more correctly and *more usefully* understood if we continue to identify it as postmodernism proper.[10] And, while it is not entirely incorrect to argue that a concept like differance is being worked out in Leyner's texts, it is more accurate to say that Leyner's work aligns with Derrida's later work on specters—which cannot be disassociated from his earlier discussions of differance and trace. And as I suggest in chapter 2, Derrida's "ethical turn" in the late-1980s marks a larger cultural transition from a postmodern episteme to a period of renewalism, a period in which the "still incomplete project of modernity" is renewed and reassessed in the wake of a postmodern "failure."[11] By reading Derrida (along with the entire shift away from postmodernism) through Derrida's own spectrological framework, it is possible to see that the teleological impulse, or "specter," that animated the Enlightenment project—that animated modernity's desire for meaning, truth, historical progress, and so on—inevitably *passed on* to postmodernism in the form of a hegemonic mode of logo centric critique that became increasingly hegemonic. The paradox of a "modernist postmodernism" makes sense, then, if we understand it as the effect of this spectral persistence. What Taylor, and thus Little, see as a type of inverted modernism—that is, a rejection of depth that ultimately reaffirms *depth as surface*—speaks to the way in which the postmodern mode of critique was *necessarily* animated by the very teleological promise, or spectral possibility, that it sought to undermine *finally*, that it sought to expose as absolutely immaterial. Like Derrida's later work—which attempts to account for the inevitability of a certain spectral compulsion, which seeks to embrace the specter by denying neither its immateriality (as modernism did) nor its materiality (as postmodernism ultimately seemed to do)—Leyner's work stresses and embraces the necessity of the spectral promise; it reaffirms a certain faith in the possibility of the impossible. In this sense, Leyner's work is less an example of "late postmodernism" than it is a literary mani-festation of "renewalism." What I'm suggesting is that Leyner's work—particularly as it is exemplified in *Tetherballs*—speaks to an emergent narrative strategy, a strategy that abandons the increasingly nihilistic (or, we might say, suicidal) trajectory of postmodern metafiction while simultaneously and perhaps paradoxically embracing the postmodern rejection of a distinctly modernist form of idealism. We might then say that a "renewalist" work like Leyner's rejects what Slavoj Žižek critiques as the celebration of absolute "perversity"—which is to say, tentatively and somewhat crudely, that renewalist forms of narrative can be read as, what Žižek has termed, the "art of the ridiculous sublime."

From an Ethics of Perversity to an Ethics of Indecision

In his extended discussion of David Lynch's *Lost Highway*, Žižek argues that "the art of the ridiculous sublime," as exemplified in Lynch's films, is neither a "cold postmodern exercise" nor a "New Age" affirmation of "a subconscious Life Energy" uniting all events and experiences. High-lighting the fact that Lynch is associated with both positions—that is, some view him as "the ultimate deconstructionist ironist" while others insist that his work seriously exposes "a Jungian universal subconscious spiritualized libido" (3)—Žižek exposes the way in which a film like *Lost Highway* can be taken seriously *if* we understand that its " 'seri-ousness' does not signal a deeper spiritual level underlying superficial clichés, but rather a crazy assertion of the redemptive value of naïve clichés as such" (3). As Žižek suggests, "The enigma of this coincidence of opposites is . . . the enigma of 'postmodernity' itself" (3). But, for Žižek, this is the enigma of *a* "postmodernity" that, if we borrow a line from Žižek's *The Sublime Object of Ideology*, does not "fall prey to any kind of 'post-modernist' traps" (7). One of these postmodern-ist traps, it would seem, is the trap of textual "perversity." Associated specifically with the absolute contingency of a "cyberspace notion of hypertext" (36), Žižek's "perversity" can be understood as unchecked textual play: "the pervert's universe is the universe of the pure symbolic order, the signifier's game running its course, unencumbered by the Real of human finitude . . . a universe without closure, unencumbered by the inertia of the Real" (36). In a manner that recalls the logo centrism identified by Taylor, the perverse text refuses closure absolutely only to inadvertently "enact a proto-ideological denial" (36). Through the filter of Lacan, Žižek explains the paradox of the "perverse" postmodern text like this:

> The paradox is that this ultimately helpless confusion, this lack of final orientation, far from causing an unbearable anxiety, is oddly reassuring: the very lack of a final point of closure serves as a kind of denial which protects us from confronting the trauma of our finitude, of the fact that our story has to come to an end at some point. (37)

The answer, or "cure," for these false acts of subversion is, Žižek insists, the type of textual negotiation we see in the work of a director like Lynch. Instead of texts that simply abandon the Real as impossible—as nothing more than the effect of an always contingent symbolic order—Žižek thus endorses a type of enigmatic postmodernism that refuses closure within the horizon of the impossible Real, which Žižek repeatedly associates with the unspeakable nature of certain traumatic events. According to Žižek, such texts, in typical postmodern fashion, endorse the "reality" of an infinite number of discursive perspectives (or, as Kenneth Burke might put it, "terministic screens") while simultaneously highlighting the fact that each of those perspectives is confined by, or faced with, an ultimately unrepresentable truth or end: "the endlessly repeated reenactments refer to the trauma of some impossible Real which forever resists its symbolization (all these different narratives are ultimately just so many failures to cope with this trauma, with the contingent abyssal occurrence of some catastrophic Real, like suicide, apropos of which no 'why' can ever serve as its sufficient explanation)" (38). This is not to say that such texts simply incorporate multiple versions of a single event, although that certainly could be the case. The point is that postmodern texts—successfully "enigmatic" or not—stress the semantic slippage that necessarily prohibits the possibility of any conclusive narrative, or representational, act. While Žižek seems to suggest that the intended representations are always representations of some unspeakable trauma, it seems obvious, if we follow Žižek's logic, that all events are necessarily—and, to some extent, *traumatically*—inexplicable from the perspective of a distinctly postmodern text.

In Žižek's opinion, though, films like *Lost Highway* and *Blue Velvet* repeatedly and successfully point to the "fantasmatic" and contingent nature of any given "reality" while simultaneously highlighting the ineffaceable determining factor of the unspeakable and/or impossible Real. While portraying "reality" and, indeed, the "subject" as the fragmentary effect of innumerable layers of discursive "screens"—from popular cultural clichés to bizarre ritual and mundane tradition—Lynch manages to incorporate bursts of the incomprehensible or "unspeakable." Like any good Lacanian symptom, these "bursts" evade full reintegration into the signifying chain (or, we might say, the "plot"); they thus repeat throughout a Lynch film, appearing in any number of "dream-like" images and/or phrases. Žižek's Lynch puts "the two dimensions—reality and its fantasmatic supplement, surface and its 'repressed'—on the same surface" (*Ridiculous Sublime* 35). By doing so, Lynch successfully highlights the persistent influence of the impossible Real while maintaining the standard postmodern acceptance and celebration of an inescapable economy of contingent signifying acts. In Lynch's films the "traumatic kernel," or impossible Real, can only be recognized via a contingent symbolic order. Understood by Žižek in terms of its manifestation as a symptom, or disruption of the signifying chain, the Real both threatens and entices. Only once it is spoken, only once it appears sensical—and is thus reincorporated into the symbolic order—is it once again satisfactorily alleviated *as symptom*. To know, or actualize, the Real is always portrayed as impossible; like the Sartrean desire for the *ens causa sui*, or the "self-identical subject," the desire for the Real is the desire for the impossible, the desire for death. Consequently, a film like *Lost Highway* is "based on the impossibility of the hero encountering himself" (18). This is, as with the Leyner text discussed above, a question of self-recognition. Beginning with the main character, Fred Madison (played by Bill Pullman), hearing a strange message coming through his home intercom system—"Dick Laurent is dead"—the film depicts Fred's futile attempts to make sense of a series of increasingly bizarre events: his eventual transformation into a young man named Pete (played by Balthazar Getty), his change back into "Fred" (or Bill Pullman), and his final act of speaking the very message he heard at the beginning into his own intercom system and paradoxically positioning himself as the very catalyst for the events leading to this final utterance. Instead of a final answer, or stable representation of the Real—in this case, an explanation of the significance of the motivating message—we get a type of circular pattern that works to repeatedly reintegrate the unrepresentable Real into some contingent yet sensical "reality," or mode of representation. Fred's repetitive attempts to apprehend his "impossible-real object of desire" (i.e., himself) is necessarily prevented by a corresponding series of repressive fantasmatic constructions, or filters, that ultimately protect the subject from the incomprehensible trauma of the Real.[12] What we get, then, is a type of "temporal loop" that highlights the infinite process of apprehending the Real. And, for Žižek, this "temporal loop" is "the very loop of the psychoanalytic treatment in which, after a long detour, we return to our starting point from another perspective" (18).

Although Žižek's Lacan-inflected criteria for a successfully "enigmatic" text is far too limiting to be applied to an entire epistemological transition, his separation of "perversity" and the "art of the ridiculous sublime" can be usefully employed to further explain and modify Little's reading of Leyner and what I have been calling a renewalist narrative strategy. As I suggested above, a work like Leyner's—or, more broadly, recent works of renewalism—can be read as a reaction to the hegemonic endorsement of a type of Žižekean perversion. From a spectrological perspective, this perversion can be seen in any text that is focused almost exclusively on exposing as illusory the promise of the impossible end, or the "impossible-real object of desire"—that is, the promise of the specter's impossible materiality, or presence. Any number of postmodern texts can be identified as such: from a popular film like Wayne's World, which simply abandons the concept of narrative closure (the film ends with Wayne and Garth offering a variety of "possible" conclusions, including a "Scooby Doo" version that sees the primary villain exposed as a very minor character in a mask) to more academically privileged texts like Barthelme's Snow White and Pynchon's The Crying of Lot 49. Still, as with Taylor's concept of logo centrism, Žižek's perversity tends to suggest a very simplistic "this-or-that" schema: either a text is perverse and, thus, unwittingly complicit with a type of inverted onto-theology or it works to highlight and embrace the inescapable paradox of the lure, or the "Real"—that is, the possible impossibility of the mimetic act. However, such a schema excludes the possibility of texts that, while "perversely" exposing the illusory nature of modernity's logocentric assumptions, demonstrate (like the texts of an early Derrida) a certain awareness of the unsustainability of absolute perversity. Such a schema excludes the possibility that this emergent shift in narrative production is, to a certain degree, a simple shift in emphasis, a development of a narrative tendency that was latently present in postmodernism from the beginning. After all, there is good reason to resist the increasingly prevalent opinion that all postmodern cultural production can be categorized, simply, as irresponsible and naïve nihilism. Unless we are careful, a concept like

Žižek's "perversity" can become dangerously restrictive. The limiting nature of such a term is, perhaps, most apparent if it is rigorously applied to a distinctly postmodern and seemingly "perverse" text—like, say, *The Crying of Lot 49*.

The Crying of Lot 49 quite obviously works to expose the depthless nature of all representational acts. The fact that it works to expose "reality" as nothing more than an infinite layering of contingent surfaces is most obvious when Oedipa Mass, the text's central character, recalls how her desire to be "rescued" from her discursively constructed prison-tower only *seemed* to be satisfied by her once boyfriend, Pierce Inverarity. Oedipa becomes disillusioned when Pierce takes her to Mexico and she sees a painting "by the beautiful Spanish exile Remedios Varo," the description of which seems to echo the famous Borges allegory about cartographers, which Baudrillard employs at the beginning of "The Precession of the Simulacra":

> a number of frail girls with heart-shaped faces, huge eyes, spun gold hair, prisoners in the top room of a circular tower, embroidering a kind of tapestry which spilled out the slit windows and into a void, seeking hopelessly to fill the void, for all the other buildings and creatures, all the waves, ships and forests of the earth were contained in this tapestry, and the tapestry was the world. (21)

Because of what it suggested, "Oedipa, perverse, had stood in front of the painting and cried" (21). We might, given the above discussion, make some tenuous claims about Pynchon's use of the term "perverse," but such claims are, perhaps, unnecessary; the specifics of Oedipa's "realization" clearly speak to the text's overall endorsement of the type of perversity in question: "She looked down at her feet and known, then, because of the painting, that what she stood on had only been woven together a couple thousand miles away in her own tower, was only by accident known as Mexico, and so Pierce had taken her away from nothing, there'd been no escape" (21). This sense of ultimate groundlessness—of reality as a weave, or "textile," of so many intersecting narrative constructions—pervades the entire novel; it is evident in the unstable nature of the stories and rumors surrounding the Tristero (which exists, in the end, as nothing more than an unstable sign, or pictograph), and it is further articulated by the slow "dissipation" of Oedipa's husband, Mucho: " 'He's losing his identity. . . . Day by day, [he] is less himself and more generic. He enters into a staff meeting and the room is suddenly full of people, you know? He's a walking assembly of a man' " (140). Just as the basic events in the novel can be recognized as nothing more than the effects of an innumerable number of other narratives/texts—for example, the plot of *The Courier's Tragedy*, a fictional play that interrupts the first half of the novel, begins to echo throughout, or "predetermine," the remainder of the text—the disintegration of Mucho[13] works to expose history and identity as the contingent interstices of signs without depth, the perpetually unstable effects of " 'Words' " (150).

Still, even a text as ostentatiously "perverse" as *The Crying of Lot 49* seems to understand that the very promise of the "Real" it aims to expose as illusory must be maintained as a possibility, even if we know it to be a false ideological lure. After all, Oedipa (once she has seemingly accepted the impossibility of understanding, or locating, the Tristero and, thus, the final solution to the mystery of Inverarity) optimistically attends the crying of lot 49. In other words, a postmodern text like *The Crying of Lot 49* is perverse, but to a degree; it is perverse insofar as it focuses *primarily* on the impossibility of apprehending the real and *not* the persistent and ironically necessary faith that such apprehension is possible. As with logo centrism, then, perversity is not synonymous with postmodernism. It is an emphasis on, or application of, perversity that marks postmodernism, not perversity itself. To be clear, though: I am not here simply recasting the argument that postmodernism anti-utopianism always retains, as Marianne DeKoven puts it, a "muted, partial, local, [and/or] diffuse" (25) utopianism; such an argument does not differentiate between the spectral and, thus, *unwelcome* utopianism of postmodernism and the subtle, yet strategic, moments when postmodern texts acknowledge the impossibility of any truly perverse, logo centric, and/or anti-utopian aesthetic.[14] And, of course, these "strategic moments" are what I want to highlight. Another approach, though, might help to clarify things.

A critic like Little is quite right to identify a process of "differance" working itself out in Pynchon (or postmodernism generally, for that matter). But we should be careful to align Pynchon's articulation of a type of differance—at least in texts like *The Crying of Lot 49* and *Gravity's Rainbow*[15]—with the differance we see employed in Derrida's early texts like "Differance," *Speech and Phenomena* and *Of Grammatology*. The differance of/in Pynchon's seminal works is far more identifiable as a type of logo centrism, or "perversity" than is the differance at work in Leyner's texts. Pynchon's early work (unlike Leyner's *Tetherballs* or, for that matter, Lynch's *Lost Highway*) is not interested in overtly performing "a pop critique of modernism's vacuous attempts to re-present presence by making figure absent [*and*] a critique of modernist postmodernism's attempt to re-present presence by making figure all there is" (Little 158). Rather, a text like *The Crying of Lot 49* seems to be emphatically focused on expressing, as Žižek would have it, "the pure symbolic order, the signifier's game running its course, unencumbered by the Real of human finitude." Like Derrida's early work on differance, a postmodern text like Pynchon's is far more interested in exposing the fundamental absence of a transcendental signified than it is in reembracing the possibility suggested and/or promised by its impossibility. In his essay on paranoia and semiotics in *The Crying of Lot 49*, John Johnston makes this point succinctly: "In reading the novel . . . we are compelled to consider paranoia less as a mental aberration than as a specific 'regime of signs,' that is, as a basic type of organization of signs in which the semiotic or signifying potential is dominant" (47). To a degree, then, it makes sense to read a text like *The Crying of Lot 49*—which is, I would argue, a signpost of "postmodernism" generally—the same way that someone like Rorty reads the early Derrida, or as Taylor reads Johnson. At the same time, though, we should not ignore the ways in which even the most seemingly perverse, or inversely onto-theological, text can subtly express a distinct awareness of the lures to which it has necessarily succumbed.

As a quintessential postmodern text, *The Crying of Lot 49* does indeed work to eviscerate the sign utterly, challenging the modernist impulse toward meaning; it aims to expose the dangerous lure of logocentrism, the illusion that the sign can be made to signify *once and for all.* But as Johnston notes, "Oedipa *hopes* to learn how to move from 'sign' to 'reality' " (67, my emphasis). While this desire ultimately highlights how "signs themselves possess a seductive power" (Johnston 51), it also speaks to postmodernism's willingness to accept the unavoidable necessity of a certain promise of the end, a certain teleological lure. In short, the postmodern text *can be* defined by an absolute emphasis on absence, or groundlessness, but this emphasis is often tempered, if only subtly, by an awareness that the promise of meaning—like, as Derrida would argue, the messianic or spectral promise—ironically and necessarily animates the very discourse that aims to expose such a promise as an impossible ideological lure. For this reason, the difference between a postmodern aesthetic and a renewalist one can be reduced, as I have been suggesting throughout, to a matter of emphasis. The postmodern text is *too* caught up in a struggle to repudiate logocentric impulses to be overtly concerned with the paradoxical and necessary reassertion of presence that occurs in any articulation of absence. Just as Rorty reads Derrida's early work, we can read the postmodern emphasis on the unfixed nature of the signifier as a type of inverted idealism, or negative theology, a reification of the very claims repudiating any and all reifying impulses. The apparent "failure" of postmodernism can be read, then, as the effect of an increasingly persistent and eventually hegemonic focus on the impossible, the absent, the illusory. This increasingly emphatic insistence on a type of perverse aesthetic ultimately exposed the pointlessness of postmodernism's own *raison d'être*. By failing to address explicitly the impossibility of its own project, postmodernism ironically failed to justify its own efficacy: why continue writing about the futility of writing? Ironically, though, and as I explain in more detail below (via an analysis of Barth's early work), it is this "spectral" para-dox that accounts for *both* the persistence *and* the perceived failure of postmodernism, its motivation to continually communicate/represent the impossibility of communication/representation.

Still, what is important to note at this point is that postmodernism can be understood via its endorsement of *a certain* perverse aesthetic, a perverse aesthetic that cannot be simply discarded, *à la* Taylor and Žižek, as a sign of postmodernism's utter complicity with a type of negative theology. I would argue, in fact, that the work of the major "postmodernists"—for instance, Barthelme, Barth, Pynchon, Coover, Vonnegut, Acker—endorses, what we might begin to think of as an "ethics of perversity." It is this ethical impulse that accounts for the didactic tone that typically "haunts" the postmodern text. Take, for instance, Vonnegut's *Breakfast of Champions*. Like many of Vonnegut's texts, *Breakfast of Champions* is narrated by a fictionalized "Kurt Von-negut" and includes one of Vonnegut's various reoccurring characters: the curmudgeonly science-fiction writer, Kilgore Trout. While Trout's character typically voices a type of nostalgia for the possibility of truth and stable meaning—his frequent summations of his various novels and short stories tend to function as satirical critiques of postmodern society[16]—Vonnegut (as narrator) repeatedly suggests that a writer has a responsibility to express the impossibility of truth, meaning, stable categories, order:

> As I approached my fiftieth birthday, I had become more and more enraged and mystified by the idiot decisions made by my countrymen. And then I had come suddenly to pity them, for I understood how innocent and natural it was for them to behave abominably, and with such abominable results: They were doing their best to live like people invented in stories and books. This was the reason Americans shot each other so often: It was a convenient literary device for ending short stories and books. (215)

For this reason, Vonnegut decides to "shun storytelling" and "bring chaos to order": "If all writers would do that, then perhaps citizens not in literary trades will understand that there is no order in the world around us, that we must adapt ourselves to the requirements of chaos instead" (215).[17] Grounds for a postmodern metafictional imperative, Vonnegut's assumption that the promise of "order" animating "realist" forms of narrative ultimately fosters dangerous impulses is verified by Dwayne Hoover's rampage at the end of the novel. Significantly, it is a novel by Trout that sparks Dwayne's final violent outburst. After speed-reading Trout's *Now It Can Be Told*—a novel written in the form of a letter from the creator of the universe to the only "human" on earth—Dwayne comes to believe that the novel is actually a letter to himself and that, as the novel claims, he is the only human in a world of robots designed to test Dwayne as the prototype for a new race of beings. Convinced that only he can think or feel, that only he has "free will"—that only he is *real*—Dwayne decides to attack people at random. And, when he is finally apprehended by the police, Dwayne fails to notice his "restraints" because he believes that he is now "on the virgin planet promised by the book by Kilgore Trout" (280). This idea of a "virgin planet" is central to Dwayne's rampage. As we are told earlier in Vonnegut's novel, Trout's fictional creator, after apologizing for his "experiments," promises to transfer "The Man" to a "virgin planet." On this virgin planet, which will eventually include all sorts of creatures with free will, "The Man" frequently swims in icy water and screams out random phrases: "The creator never knew what he was going to yell, since The Creator had no control over him. The Man himself got to decide what he was going to do next—and why" (179). In direct contrast to Vonnegut's own novel—a novel in which Dwayne, Trout, and even the author (i.e., Vonnegut) himself are repeatedly identified as nothing more than effects of intersecting narrative acts[18]—Trout's *Now It Can Be Told* is represented as a dangerous form of "storytelling," a form of storytelling that encourages its readers to impose hegemonic order, or a sense of finite meaning, on the arbitrariness that surrounds them. Echoing the logocentric faith in the transcendental signified—a faith that is inextricably linked to humanist conceptions of autonomy and free will—Trout's "virgin planet" encourages a dangerous desire for a finally liberated state of being, a state of being in which, we might say, all "ideological state apparatuses" have been dismantled.[19] In the form of an edenic, or utopian, ideal, this "virgin planet" thus represents the impossible, the spectral promise.

Although it is certainly fair to say, along with a critic like Peter Reed, that Trout's work in *Breakfast of Champions* ultimately "brings chaos" (74), we should be wary of assuming that Trout's text is *not*, in Vonnegut's eyes, a lamentable form of "storytelling." We should, that is, be wary of reading Trout *as* Vonnegut.[20] It is, after all, more accurate to say that Trout's book brings about violence and oppression, not chaos—or, at least, not the chaos Vonnegut seems to have in mind. In the end, Trout's book is represented as dangerous because it fails to *celebrate chaos*, because it voices frustration with the arbitrary and the contingent. The "irresponsible" nature of Trout's text is, perhaps, most obviously highlighted when it is juxtaposed to Vonnegut's book (i.e., *Breakfast of Champions*) as a whole. Like Trout's book, *Breakfast of Champions* addresses the problem of free will and the apparently mechanical processes affecting, or animating, the individual. Quite simply, both books suggest that reality is an artificial construct and that our sense of autonomy is an illusion of "programming." Like Trout's, Vonnegut's "suspicion" is "that human beings are robots, are machines" (3). Vonnegut, however, offers no possibility of escape. By entering the text himself, Vonnegut (as author/creator) overtly rejects the possibility of an originary position *outside the text*. Trapped within the same economy of textuality that imprisons his "creations," Vonnegut is repeatedly faced with his own lack of autonomy. Without any real "authority," Vonnegut must accept the fact that his characters are, for the most part, beyond his control. Even his attempt to "free" Trout—a moment, we should note, that directly parallels Trout's conception of a creator speaking to his creation—seems hollow; Trout (and, indeed, Vonnegut) remain *in text* and Trout's one real desire (to be made young again) remains an ignored and impossible dream. The suggestion is that the type of freedom Vonnegut offers Trout, and that Trout's creator inadvertently promises Dwayne, is impossible.[21] With this in mind, we might read the opening lines of Vonnegut's later work, *Jailbird*, as an overt reaffirmation of "reality" as an inescapable play of signifiers: "Yes—Kilgore Trout is back again. He could not make it on the outside" (9).

What we see in a work of overt metafiction like *Breakfast of Champions* is the extent to which a certain ethics of perversity informs, or animates, the postmodern aesthetic. Vonnegut, if we can apply Hutcheon's phrasing, seems intent on pointing out that "postmodern relativity and provisionality are not causes for despair; they are to be acknowledged as perhaps the very conditions of historical knowledge" (*Politics* 64). But, with such a claim in mind, we are immediately faced again with the problematic situation Rorty identifies in the early work of Derrida; we are faced, that is, with a supposedly post-ideological imperative that, because it *demands* a rigorous critique of "something as big as logocentrism," needs to be understood as "one more logocentric hallucination" ("Is Derrida" 139). A type of ineffaceable remainder, or revenant, the logocentric impulse returns, as Taylor argues, at the very moment it seems to be *finally placed to rest*—that is, identified as immaterial, as impossible, as a dangerous and beguiling illusion. At the same time, though, it is important to stress that Vonnegut *does* offer—or rather, promises—Trout freedom. Of course, this freedom is ultimately identified as impossible, as a promise that will always be yet to come; but the fact that Vonnegut makes the offer speaks to a post-modern willingness to accept the necessity of the promise and, thus, the belief that the promise can be fulfilled. Still, Vonnegut's overtly postmodern desire to critique "something as big as logocentrism" does result in a certain didactic and/or political tone. And, as I have dem-onstrated throughout, this tone that "haunts" the general spectrum of postmodern production can be understood as the effect of a latent and paradoxically impossible ideal: the ideal of finally exposing, if not wholly abandoning, all ideals *as impossible*.

The work of Kathy Acker is a good illustration of this paradox. Via its desire to expose "reality" as the effect of hegemonic ideological apparatuses, Acker's work comes to repeat the very ideological ges-tures it aims to critique and, *finally*, discard as dangerously false. In the work of a writer like Acker, we get the distinct sense of a virtually hegemonic ethical imperative, an imperative that typically results in the *angry* and, at times, violent repudiation of all spectral promises. Perhaps not surprisingly, when this latent idealism—an idealism, of course, that is quite distinct from the subtle "proto-renewalist" accep-tance of the transcendental lure we see in Derrida, Pynchon, Vonnegut, and others—becomes hegemonic, the distinctive humor and irony of postmodernism is often effaced. In Acker's texts we thus see the post-modern ethics of perversity at its most imperative—which is to say that in texts like Acker's postmodernism's spectral contamination becomes most obvious. The specter (or, we might say, the ordeal of indecision) is stripped of its ironic duality; all that seems to remain in Acker's work is one aspect of the specter, one aspect of indecision. By emphati-cally suggesting that we are ethically compelled to reject the spectral promise of identity (of an end, of reality, of a final decision, etc.) as an immaterial lure, Acker's texts paradoxically betray the postmodern desire for a utopian state of absolute, or purely "mythic," indecision, a state in which no decision is necessary, a state in which the correct, or mythic, decision is finally known. In short, Acker's texts—texts that, as Christina Milletti suggests, are defined by "Acker's 'terrorist' aesthetics" (353)—are particularly representative of postmodernism at the point of outright imperiousness: when it is most obviously dependent upon the very spectral promise(s) it is striving to repudiate as impossible, as dangerously false and restrictive.

Take, for example, Acker's *In Memoriam to Identity*. Not only does the title of the text suggest an explicitly "perverse" aesthetic, the stories of the three central characters—Rimbaud, Airplane, and Capitol—repeatedly challenge and problematize the politics of identity, working to expose as illusory the dangerous and hegemonic constructs that determine our "reality." Like her other texts (*Empire of the Senseless*, for instance), *In Memoriam to Identity* persistently—and, we might say, violently[22]—explodes the illusion of what Acker seems to identify consistently as a restrictive and patriarchal symbolic order. A text like *In Memoriam* is thus filled with moral outrages: rape, pedophilia, incest, a mix of all three. The sense we get is that the arbitrary categories we passively accept as "reality" impose dangerous restrictions upon our perception of the world, and thus our desire. Like Vonnegut, Acker suggests that our desire to avoid the uncertainty and instability of "chaos" results in violent efforts to cling to the ideological interpellations that provide us with a sense of self and/or solidity. Consequently, and in a manner that makes Dwayne Hoover's rampage in *Breakfast of Champions* seem perfectly benign, Acker's characters find themselves participating in all manner of violent and obsessive acts, acts that are typically animated by an ideologically determined desire to reaffirm a certain patriarchal order, and thus certain "comforting" categories of identity. Acker, though, opposes this dangerous logo(or, phallogo)centrism with her own type of textual violence. Her overt use of syntactic ambiguity, pastiche, and characters that defy categorization—her characters are often transgendered, bisexual, cybernetic, and so on—forces us to recognize the untenable nature of our logocentric assumptions.

Ultimately, then, Acker's texts seem to endlessly repeat a single lesson, a single "perverse" ethical imperative: only when we have recognized and accepted the logocentric assumptions of modernity as illusory are we truly free and responsible for our own actions. Milletti puts it like this:

> Acker's message is clear: if language is inflected with systems of power, then readers must begin to recognize their culpability within the discourses they embody or reject, and become equally accountable in the endeavor to resist those structures of power that marginalize the Other. Acker's prose is therefore specifically designed to shock readers into an awareness of the normative systems they embody. (360)

Texts like *In Memoriam* attack "the social order that controls normative constructions of identity" (361). Acker thus works to expose the fact that even something as seemingly "real" as "biology is . . . nothing less than a material ploy" (363). The suggestion is that, by realizing and embracing this fact, we can begin to frustrate the hegemonic system of codes imposed by the prevailing social order. Indeed, Airplane and Capitol seem to become more and more liberated as *In Memoriam* progresses; and, not surprisingly, this sense of liberty is intimately tied to a disintegration of gender barriers. Toward the end of the text, in fact, we are told that Capitol could use her "feminine or masculine charms to persuade" (202) and that Harry (one of Capitol's lovers) "could love this man or woman without being upset by her need to be alone" (229). As I suggested above, though, this ostentatiously didactic endorsement of a postmodern ethics of perversity highlights the way in which postmodernism was necessarily animated by the very idealism, or utopianism, it strove to dismantle and reject; instead of the illusion of fixed gender categories, racial barriers, class distinctions, or whatever, postmodernism seemed to be offering us the idealistic and fixed assumption that such illusions had to be and, thus, *could be* rejected *once and for all*. In short, and in a manner that speaks to postmodernism's most rigid rejections of humanist teleology, texts like Acker's necessarily begin to echo a distinctly humanist mantra: this is how, or what, humanity is supposed to be.[23] As Zygmunt Bauman suggests in *Postmodernity and Its Discontents*, postmodernism ultimately and perhaps more and more obviously seemed to be rejecting modernity's quest for "purity" by reinscribing a utopian quest of its own.[24] Such quests, though, Bauman argues, inevitably become obsessed with the possibility of a *final* expulsion of impurity—which we might understand, simply, as a final expulsion of the ironic spectrality of the specter. And, as we see with Acker and Vonnegut, an increasingly didactic and/or political tone speaks to the reality of a distinctly postmodern quest for pervasive anti-foundationalism, a quest that became increasingly—or, better, *more obviously*—dependent upon the very spectral promise (of an end, a final solution, a state of pure indecision, etc.) that it sought to exorcise.

Of course, this didactic/political tone—while most ostentatious in the work of Vonnegut and Acker, as well as a writer like Tom Robbins—is necessarily evident, to one degree or another, throughout the general spectrum of postmodern cultural production. Even the work of Pynchon, which often seems to temper its distinctly "perverse ethics," is susceptible to this didacticism. Jerry Varsava's article on "Thomas Pynchon and Postmodern Liberalism" makes just this claim: "I read Pynchon as an exponent of liberalism, though not a retro-liberalism determined by the social and political exigencies of 1776 or the 1930s, but a 'postmodern' version shaped by both liberal traditions and those cultural circumstances and impetuses peculiar to the late twentieth century" (64). Varsava, in short, views Pynchon's postmodernism as representative of Rorty's concept of postmodern liberalism, a liberalism that insists on plurality and (one assumes, following Rorty) the celebration of the private "liberal ironist." Resistant to both the excesses of libertarianism and the hegemony of consensus, this strain of liberalism (which, as I suggested in the previous chapter, could be read as a defining characteristic of postmodernism generally) endorses a Rortian concept of pragmatism that denies absolutely the possibility of closure, consensus, or some "final vocabulary." Viewed (from the perspective of the postmodern liberal) as the remains of an outmoded Enlightenment project, these "logocentric" concepts must be rejected utterly if we wish to avoid slipping back into the stifling discourse of metaphysics. However, Rortian postmodern pragmatism inevitably enters into public discourse, becoming itself a type of reified nonground for consensus. As we saw with Derrida, then, the postmodern pragmatism that Varsava locates in Pynchon, and that seems to be so obviously at work in Acker, is symptomatic of an effort to flee and/or deny the very thing that animates postmodernism as a discourse: the specter it senses haunting its own critique of the specter (of teleology, of transcendentalism, of onto-theology, of negative theology, of metaphysics, etc.)—or, more specifically, the utopian specter represented by the teleological aporia of the "still incomplete project of modernity."

This paradoxical aporia is, quite simply, the specter of postmodernism—or, we might say at this point, the specter of a perverse ethics, the very ethics that defines the postmodern aesthetic. It is, moreover, the inability, or unwillingness, to identify this aporia *overtly* and embrace it as the necessary element of any radical discourse that defines the apparent "failure" of postmodernism. Assuming, then, that postmodernism is indeed defined by the specific spectral relationship I have detailed above, we might begin to view any narrative strategy that functions as a critique of postmodernism's spectrological "failure"—that, in other words, attempts to transcend overtly the hegemonic reversals of an aesthetic that increasingly insisted upon an ethics of perversity—as symptomatic of an emergent narrative form that can no longer be called, with any real accuracy, "postmodernism."

What Little, Taylor, and Žižek (above) understand as "proper," or late, postmodernism—that is, the solution to the naïve, or perverse, ideological inversions practiced by a past "modernist postmodernism"—can thus be viewed as instances of a narrative impulse that is emerging in *the wake of* postmodernism. Following Žižek's concept of an "art of the ridiculous sublime," we might say that this emergent aesthetic has a tendency to manifest *stylistically* (in certain instances, at least) as postmodernism. David Lynch is, after all, embraced by most critics, and with good reason, as a "postmodern" writer/director. But I would argue that the defining characteristic of these emergent narrative forms is—as we saw in the work of Leyner—their insistence on the possibility of what they paradoxically continue to expose as impossible: meaning, truth, mimesis, telos, communal understanding, and communication. Like Derrida's later work, these texts are *overtly* focused on the ironic nature of the spectral promise, its impossible possibility; they work to expose the necessity of respecting the specter, of embracing the irony of "relation without relation," "meaning without meaning," "religion without religion," and so on. Moving beyond the restrictions of Žižek's Lacanian-inflected criteria, we can begin to reread much of the recent narrative production that continues to be labeled "postmodern" as advocating a type of spectral relationship that is in *anything but postmodern.* Tim O'Brien's *The Things They Carried*—a text that, on the surface, seems to simply redeploy the postmodern and/or metafictional strategies we see played out in the work of writers like Pynchon and Vonnegut—is a perfect example of the way in which recent narrative production attempts to renew the postmodern evasion of hegemonic discourses by abandoning the postmodern, and hegemonic, imperative that the basic goal of all aesthetic production is to expose as illusory the apparent materiality of the specter, or utopian promise.

A novel that is also a collection of short stories, *The Things They Carried* employs a variety of distinctly postmodern strategies. Not only does its very form challenge traditional generic categories, it overtly aims to frustrate our ability to apprehend an "event." In a manner that recalls Vonnegut's work—and parallels Leyner's—O'Brien's text is, for the most part, presented as a type of "autobiography." Both first-person and third-person accounts are offered; in the former, O'Brien is the narrator; in the latter, a character. As a result, the line between the fictionalized narrator and the author himself is much more tenuous then it is in the work of Vonnegut or Leyner. The text refuses to supply overt markers that might lead us to assume that an event described didn't "actually" happen. As far as the typical reader is aware, the O'Brien that narrates is the very same O'Brien whose name appears on the cover of the published text.[25] This overt evasion of categorization is only exasperated by the twenty-two interconnecting stories that make up the text proper. Concerned with the exploits of a certain "Alpha Company" during the Vietnam War, these stories tend to repeat themselves; events that were described in one story are recounted in another, but never with the same result. At times, in fact, the individual stories directly contradict one another. In "The Man I Killed," for instance, we are given a harrowing first-person account of the trauma O'Brien endured after killing a seemingly innocent Viet-Cong soldier. In the later "Good Form," though, O'Brien denies that he participated in the event: "I want to tell you this: twenty years ago I watched a man die on a trail near the village My Khe. I did not kill him" (179). Ultimately, the text as a whole begins to seem circular—or, more accurately, and in terms of the spiral-like process I associated with Derridean indecision, and which we can now view in light of Žižekean repetition discussed above, it insistently returns to the events in question, always trying (in earnest) to *get it right*. Steven Kaplan puts it like this: "the facts about an event are given; they are quickly qualified or called into question; from this uncertainty emerges a new set of facts about the same subject that are again called into question—on and on, without end" (45).

This circular (or spiral) movement is overtly addressed in the story "Speaking of Courage," a story that details the problems one of the Alpha Company (i.e., Norman Bowker) encounters after he returns home. Unable to explain—or rather, *to represent*—the trauma he suffered while at war, Bowker repeatedly circles the lake near his home. This compulsive movement around the lake is, I would argue, a direct representation of O'Brien's own attempts to get *the story right*. O'Brien, in fact, tells us in the following story (i.e., "Notes") that "Speaking of Courage" was written in response to Bowker's own suggestion that O'Brien had failed to tell the *truth* in his earlier novel, *If I Die in a Combat Zone*. Consequently, by the time we read "In the Field," the story (following "Notes") that details the specific event that traumatized Bowker—that is, the sight of a fellow solider drowning in a field of shit—we realize that each of O'Brien's stories can be read as just another pass around the lake. Following a critic like Tina Chen, then, we might argue that Bowker's story explicitly highlights the way in which O'Brien's work "insists upon multiple returns" (81). But what is particularly important to note is that each pass, or "return," seems to be animated by a very sincere desire to arrive at a final representation—or, as in the case of Bowker, a cleansing step into the lake itself. Indeed, as Mark Taylor suggests, "a desire for truth forces O'Brien to go over ground again [and, we should add, *again and again*]" ("O'Brien's War" 223).

This compulsion to *get it right*—a compulsion that results in a distinctly "spiral-like" aesthetic pattern—becomes particularly overt when O'Brien attempts to describe the death of Curt Lemon: "if I could ever get the story right, how the sun seemed to gather around him and pick him up and lift him high into a tree, if I could somehow re-create the fatal whiteness of that light, the quick glare, the obvious effect, then you would believe the last thing Curt Lemon believed, which for him must've been the final truth" (84). Told again and again in "How to Tell a True War Story," the story of Curt Lemon's death comes to be understood, in a rather "postmodern" fashion, as transphenomenal, as impossible to get *just right*. But, unlike the typical postmodern text that would be interested primarily in exposing the promise of the truthful account as dangerous idealism, O'Brien's text insists on the importance of the narrative *return*, on the possibility of the impossible Real. The promise of the truth—the promise, that is, of the *true* war story, the *true* "autobiography"—is given privileged status in O'Brien's text *even though* it is endlessly deferred. Thus O'Brien repeatedly performs, what we might think of as, the Derridean gamble; his text overtly embraces the "the test and ordeal of the undecidable" (*Force of Law* 253). The spiral-like returns in *The Things They Carried* stress the responsibility of making a (narrative) decision, of having faith in the possibility that a correct decision is possible, while simultaneously acknowledging that the absolutely correct decision is always still to come. With each story in *The Things They Carried* O'Brien wagers on the possibility of truth, on the possibility of the transcendental signified. So, while it seems reasonable to assume, as does a critic like Catherine Calloway, that the metafictional strategies in *The Things They Carried* lead "[the reader] to question the ambiguous nature of reality" (251), it is probably more accurate to say that epistemological doubt in O'Brien's work, as in Leyner's, is repeatedly identified as the very thing that animates the promise of certainty.

O'Brien's more recent *In The Lake of the Woods* explores this paradox even further. The narrator clearly suggests that the promise of certainty animating his story is necessarily a condition of inexhaustible doubt: "The thing about Custer is this: no survivors. Hence eternal doubt, which both frustrates and fascinates. It's a standoff. The human desire for certainty collides with our love of enigma" (266). Not surprisingly, the concept of the wager is a recurrent theme throughout *Lake of the Woods*. The main characters, John and Kathy Wade, are, in fact, haunted by "the guilt of a bad wager" (158). For this reason, John Wade is driven by a desire to be free of the decision-making process, to be free of the responsibility associated with the gamble: "The magician in him. Likes to rig up the cards. Luck's irrelevant" (223). However, and in a manner that reads like an implicit critique of postmodernism's insistence on an ethics of perversity, Wade's attempts to eschew his responsibility by transforming reality into mere illusion are repeatedly countered by the narrator's persistent efforts to piece together, or take gambles on, the events that lead to Kathy Wade's mysterious disappearance: "I prowl and smoke cigarettes. I review my notes. The truth is at once simple and baffling: John Wade was a pro. He did his magic, then walked away. Everything else is conjecture. No answers, yet mystery itself carries me on" (266). The possibility of the certainly right decision—that is, in this case, the *finally* accurate narrative representation—is, in other words, repeatedly represented as necessarily contingent upon its impossibility. This paradox is, as Derrida would remind us, the paradox of the specter.

My argument is this: the forms of narrative that have begun to emerge after postmodernism are marked by an overt willingness to respect both sides of the spectral equation. The shift away from postmodernism can thus be understood as an epistemological shift in emphasis, a shift from a postmodern ethics of perversity to a renewalist ethics of indecision. While the postmodern aesthetic can be defined by a need to expose the impossibility of the mimetic text—or, what amounts to the same thing, the messianic promise—the shift away from postmodern metafiction is marked by a pronounced realization that faith in, or a gamble on, the possibility of absolute certainty must necessarily haunt any claim or narrative act, even the claim that such faith is a dangerous ideological illusion. And it is this overtly renewed faith in an impossible "project"—a revenant of the Enlightenment, as it were—that seems to define the narrative forms associated with the current epistemic shift away from postmodernism. However, as we saw via a discussion of Derrida's more recent work, this willingness to respect the specter's spectrality only *seems* to be respect; it is ultimately and necessarily a type of renewed disrespect. That said, I would like to move slowly in terms of identifying this lack of respect in the narrative strategies identified above as renewalist. What is important to note, at this point, is the fact that this renewalist trend extends well beyond the small group of recent texts that remain outwardly (at least) postmodern. Indeed, and not surprisingly, we can locate this same renewalist shift in the "neo-realism" that a variety of critics, since the early 1990s, have associated with the passing of postmodernism.

Metafiction's Failure and the Rise of Neo-Realism

If we were to wager on it—wager, that is, on the exact moment when the "passing" of postmodernism became undeniably imminent—1989 would be, as I suggested in chapter 2, a fairly safe bet. Following a writer like Raymond Federman, we might in fact argue that the first symptoms of some terminal epistemological illness became irrefutable on December 22, 1989—the day Beckett died.[26] However, we might also argue (perhaps more accurately) that a certain undeniable epistemological collapse occurred a month earlier—when the Berlin Wall fell (and, with it, the last viable political alternative). But perhaps we should cast the net wider; the mid- to late-1980s saw a number of events that seemed to herald the impending decline of one aesthetic dominant (i.e., postmodern metafiction) and the emergence of another (i.e., "neo-realism"): the journal *Granta* published an issue dedicated to American "dirty realism";[27] neo-realist writers like Raymond Carver began to rise in status; Beckett died; Tom Wolfe published his "Literary Manifesto for the New Social Novel";[28] and the Berlin Wall fell, suggesting the final triumph of capitalism. Taken together, these events quite clearly signal a new period of mourning. Yet, as I suggested above, the fall of the Berlin Wall resonates with particular significance. Given that postmodernism is typically defined by its opposition to all latent utopian impulses, the fall of the last viable political alternative (i.e., the utopian promise of communism) seemingly speaks to the victory and hegemony of a distinctly postmodern, or late-capitalist, ideology. Not surprisingly, then, it is at the very moment when this victory is imminent, when postmodernism seems to have become the very thing it aimed to destroy, that we begin to see signs of an emergent epistemological configuration. That is, this emergent epoch seems to "mourn" the apparent loss of the very idealistic alternatives that postmodernism strove to efface. And if we recall Derrida's take on mourning this period can be defined by its desire to get over—or, rather, to lay to rest *finally*—that which came before. This particular *work of postmodern mourning* becomes most evident in the early-1990s—when critics began to make claims about the fact that the "high-tide" of postmodernism had finally begun to crash[29] and that a new form of realism had begun to emerge in its wake. Indeed, with the "First Stuttgart Seminar in Cultural Studies"—a conference in 1991 that included writers like Ihab Hassan, John Barth, Raymond Federman, William Gass, and Malcolm Bradbury, and that was aptly titled "The End of Postmodernism: New Directions"—critics began to formally confirm an apparent shift in stylistic privilege. Since then, I would argue, we have been engaged in a process of mourning, a process that sees us trying to break *finally* with postmodernism—or, at the every least, trying to break finally with postmodernism's spectral impulse to exorcise all specters *once and for all.* After all, since the beginning of the 1990s, the suggestion has been that, for one reason or another, postmodernism failed and that its failure, via the emergence of a new form of realism, was inevitable. In short, and in

a manner that highlights my own claims regarding a certain "spectral passing," critics have increasingly stressed the fact that the basic
imperative that animated postmodernism paradoxically necessitated
its demise. And, so, in order to understand how this apparent shift
from metafiction to neo-realism played out, we must first examine the
critical commentary that has developed over the last couple decades—
a commentary, I should add, that isn't always anti-postmodern.

According to Federman, "the search for the means to put an end
to things—an end to language, an end to literature—is what enabled
the postmodern discourse to perpetuate itself" ("Part One" 48).[30] This
aporia, this movement that is animated by a desire to expose the futility, or impossibility, of movement thus becomes the primary cause of
postmodernism's "departure":

> Obviously, [the postmodernist's] work could only be marked
> by doubt and distrust, but especially self-doubt, which, how-
> ever, the stubborn but clever writer, who faced at the same
> time the impossibility and the necessity of writing, quickly
> turned to self-reflexiveness, which for a while at least, helped
> him survive so he could continue to destroy the novel he
> was in the process of writing. ("Part One" 58)

For someone like Federman, as with many of the critics who attended
the Stuttgart Seminar, this is not really a failure so much as it is the
inevitable trajectory of an anti-idealist avant-garde movement. As his
later critical work (particularly in the recent *Symploke* issue dedicated
to the present state of fiction) suggests, Federman sees the current
rejection of the postmodern aporia as lamentable, as an effect of an
increasingly homogonous literary marketplace. For Federman, recent
works of "realism" are less concerned with "reality" than are works of
high-postmodernism: "Most of the books published today no longer
concern themselves with reality, but with the melo-dramatized image
of reality projected by mass media" (164). Federman thus positions the
self-reflexive and fragmented works that aimed to expose the illusion
of reality as (and however paradoxical it may sound) *more realistic* than
recent works of realism. Such an argument, of course, simply speaks
to the way in which a certain teleological specter necessarily animated
the various postmodern attempts to exorcise the specter of a realist, or
"teleological," impulse/imperative. Indeed, postmodernism ultimately
finds itself asserting an anti-realist stance as the *most realistic, as the
most moral.*[31] The sense we get from Federman is that the death of
postmodernism speaks to its success, not its failure; only a truly avant-

garde—and, thus, "moral" and/or "accurate"—movement could write itself to the brink of self-destruction. From this distinctly postmodern perspective, the death of postmodernism is simply an understandable interruption, an inevitable reconfiguration of a radical and ongoing "project": "because it carried in itself its own demise (epistemological and ontological doubt conveyed through disjointed formal structures) Postmodernism had either to die or go elsewhere and become something else, which is what it did, even though it continues to be called by the same name" ("Part One" 52). Federman, as he eventually makes clear, is referring here to the type of fiction discussed above:[32] texts that, at least outwardly, *seem* postmodern yet somehow renew the narrative possibilities that postmodernism denied. These works, and not the "the uninspired Minimalist K-Mart fiction of the last decade" (52),[33] are, for Federman, the result of an interruptive transformation of the postmodern avant-garde spirit. Unfortunately, though, such texts are being out-marketed by the "easy" realism that Federman sees cluttering the shelves at his local bookstore.

Unfortunately, a position like Federman's is simply too nostalgic to be useful. Still, he is right to stress the central aporia that animated the postmodern movement, and his virtually modernist insistence on the privileged status of the postmodern avant-garde—an insistence that echoes Lyotard's often "utopian" claims[34]—highlights the hegemonic position postmodernism eventually came to occupy. Federman's lament for the growing rejection of an avant-garde spirit—for the privileged status of difficult and impenetrable texts—can be read as symptomatic of the awkward position in which postmodernism seemed to find itself. Put differently, Federman's take on the demise of postmodernism suggests the possibility that postmodernism didn't "fail" because it tried to make claims about the futility of attempting to speak the truth; it failed because it *continued to speak*, because it continued to make and privilege *truth claims* about the impossibility of making such claims (while, for the most part, failing to overtly articulate the fact that such claims were necessarily and ironically animated by the latent belief that the truth could finally be expressed). Postmodernism failed *because it didn't die* as it should have. Instead, its increasingly loud movement toward silence and/or the absolute denial of objective truth claims became dogmatic, institutionalized, and programmatic. As a result, and by the late-1980s, we see previously propostmodern theorists criticizing the apparent hegemony of the postmodern project. Ihab Hassan, for instance, begins making gestures toward the need for a new and liberated aesthetic form—what he tentatively calls, following William Gass, "operatic realism" (136). In "Pragmatism, Postmodernism, and

Beyond," Hassan explicitly calls for a return to "belief" and "public criticism" (149), arguing that the hegemony of postmodernism's theoretical claims has damaged our ability to embrace literature and the possibility of social critique.

Significantly, Hassan cites the postmodern imperative to be "inaccessible," or "utterly private," as an example of this absurd—or, we might say, paradoxical—withdrawal from public discourse: "Jonathan Culler tries to make that case by denouncing 'the ideology of lucidity'—how bizarre in a scholar opposed to elitism—and Derrida offers a more considered argument against the ideal of 'universal translatability,' from every language to every other, that the university cherishes" (149). The fact that everything is now homogenously identified as ideology (or politics, or discourse, or whatever)—that, in short, all distinctions have been identified as tenuous illusions—becomes, for Hassan, a sign of decadence and moral vacuity.[35] In a more recent article, "Towards an Aesthetic of Trust," Hassan suggests that "Beyond postmodernism, beyond the evasions of poststructuralist theories and pieties of postcolonial studies, we need to discover new relations between selves and others, margins and centers, fragments and wholes—indeed, new relations between selves and selves, margins and margins, centers and centers—discover what I call a new, pragmatic and planetary civility. (204) This is, for Hassan, a call to reaffirm faith in certain forms of pragmatic, or contingent, truths. It is a call for trust. Of course, as his earlier take on the subject anticipates, Hassan turns to (neo)realism as an aesthetic form that reaffirms the possibility of such trust. Without stretching his argument too far, I would venture that Hassan's call for new "relations" speaks to a much broader "renewalist" call for, what Derrida would understand as, relations without relation, trust without trust, and so on. This call for trust is, after all, as Hassan tentatively suggests, a matter of reaffirming a certain postmodern "spirit," or "spiritual attitude" (210). It is, in other words, a matter of having faith in, or making a decision based on, what we know to be unfounded: the specter that *is* and *is not*: "I need only repeat that fiduciary realism—a postmodern realism, if any—demands faith and empathy and trust precisely because it rests on nothing, the nothingness within all representations, the final authority of the void" (210). Hassan's position thus speaks to much of the more recent criticism on neo-realism, criticism that typically stresses the past hegemony of high-postmodernism and the need for a form of fiction that is no longer confined by a corrosive and socially impractical aesthetic imperative, however paradoxical such an imperative might have been. In brief, and somewhat crudely put, neo-realism, if not renewalism generally, is a direct reaction to the apparent hegemony of postmodernism.

In "Recent Realist Fiction and the Idea of Writing 'After Post-modernism,'" Günter Leypoldt uses a recent Coen Brothers film to highlight this apparent reaction to postmodernism's hegemony—or, perhaps, "exhaustion." In *The Man Who Wasn't There*, the protagonist, Ed Crane (played by Billy Bob Thornton), after being accused of murder, is defended by an attorney named Freddy Riedenschneider (played by Tony Shalhoub). A satirical representation of the typical postmodern hero, Riedenschneider is so convinced that reality is nothing more than an effect of contingent representations he attempts to defend Crane by arguing that what "really happened" can never "really" be known, for the "The more you look, the less you really know." Riedenschneider, though (and this is Leypoldt's point), loses the case, and Crane is "really" sentenced to death. As Leypoldt argues, "Riedenschneider's fixation on uncertainty recalls the playful skepticism of the metafictional tradition, but in contrast to the heroically self-reflexive philosopher narrators of classic postmodernism, he is portrayed as moronic, vain, and ultimately feckless" (20). For Leypoldt, the presence of a character like Riedenschneider in a Hollywood film speaks to the way in which "the metafictional and fabulist devices lost their subversive edge and began to seem less interesting, less 'progressive,' because they had been repeated so often that the self-proclaimed 'literature of replenishment' began to appear no less trite than the 'literature of exhaustion' it had set out to replenish" (26). While I think it is somewhat incorrect to construct postmodernism as a self-proclaimed "literature of replenishment" that sought to move beyond some past "literature of exhaustion"—the terms "exhaustion" and "replenishment," it seems to me (and following Barth), are both applicable to postmodernism—Leypoldt's claim that postmodernism became hegemonically repetitive is indicative of a general critical opinion regarding the rationale for the emergence of a type of neo-realism.[36]

As Robert L. McLaughlin puts it, the emergence of forms of neo-realism can be, and typically is, read as a response to the perceived "dead-end" of postmodernism: "a dead end that has been reached because of postmodernism's detachment from the social world and immersion in a world of non-referential language, its tendency to disappear up its own asshole" ("Post-Postmodern Discontent" 55). As McLaughlin suggests, postmodernism has come to be viewed as an aesthetic failure because it tried to deny what, as I demonstrated in the previous chapter via a discussion of Rorty and Derrida, it could never deny without descending into absolute silence: the relevance of the public, or social sphere. Forms of new realism, like the later work of Derrida, outwardly embrace the impossible and futile project of becoming utterly private, a project (McLaughlin is quick to point out) that the majority of postmodernists never seemed to be completely invested in to begin with:[37] "We can think of this aesthetic sea change, then, as being inspired by a desire to reconnect language to the social sphere or, to put it another way, to re-energize literature's social mission, its ability to intervene in the social world, to have an impact on actual people and the actual social institutions in which they live their lives" ("Post-Postmodern Discontent" 55).

From the perspective of a "neo-realist," then, the failure of postmodernism is twofold. On the one hand, its apparent self-affirmation as an anti-ideological discourse, a discourse that privileged individualism and solipsism over the illusion of communal bonds and the possibility of communication, seems quite naturally to parallel the progress of modernization. Consistent with the trajectory of modern "avant-garde" movements, postmodernism's value as a subversive discourse ends when its dominance appears evident. Not surprisingly, this moment for postmodernism is heralded by many critics of neo-realism by the fall of the Berlin Wall and the end of the Cold War—or, rather, the end of the last viable utopian ideal/impulse. On the other hand, the postmodern withdrawal from public and/or social discourse—that is, the postmodern imperative to be inaccessible, *to expose* as illusory the ideal of shared experience and communal understanding—becomes itself a very public (because academically dominant) claim. An aesthetic that aimed to dismantle binary distinctions, that attempted, more specifically, to destabilize the opposition between high and low culture, becomes itself an aesthetic of the elite. It is, after all, the "elitism" of postmodernism that most critics identify as its most glaring failure. Postmodernism's increasingly emphatic insistence on inaccessibility—on, that is, the utterly private discourse or, rather, the futility of the social or public text—became a dominant ideal, a standard in academia and the artistic community. For critics like Mark Shechner, then, the return of realism speaks to the victory of the popular and, thus, the relevance of the public: "Metafiction was a concept-ridden fiction, whose appreciation depended mainly upon an understanding and acceptance of inflated and dubious concepts for which we have now less patience" (38). From this perspective, "A realist revival might be thought of as the revenge of common sensibility, a demotic upsurge of taste from social orders that lack the leisure, and the will, to cultivate mandarin sensibilities" (39).

This position—a position that is echoed in much of the current criticism on the emergence of neo-realism—tends to ignore the broader affects of postmodernism and thus the fact that its dominance extended far beyond university walls. On a certain level, postmodernism did indeed penetrate the popular front. In fact, it is postmodernism's eventual omni-presence that seems finally to efface its efficacy as a subversive and revolutionary aesthetic program. As McLaughlin notes in a more recent article, postmodernism's increasingly hegemonic celebration of heteroglossia and plurality has been finally co-opted and thus pacified by extremist groups and fundamentalists on the political right: "the Right is using the forms of postmodernism with a clearly nonpostmodern agenda. That is, they make their attacks not by insisting on the truth of their position or rightness of their claims but by gestures toward rhetorical situations, dialogism, and respecting others in their otherness" ("Distracting Discourses" 59–60). Postmodernism's very strategies have become, in short, aligned with the very thing they sought to undermine: fundamentalism (in all its forms). The omni-presence of, if not fundamentalist insistence on, postmodern plurality has, in brief, effaced the possibility of that plurality. Or, as Katherine Hayles and Todd Gannon suggest in a recent article, things have simply become too postmodern to be postmodern any longer. Hayles and Gannon, though, associate the hegemony and, in turn, death of a postmodern "reality" with the 1995 inception of "Netscape" as a user-friendly Web-browser. According to Hayles and Gannon, by the time the world was fully exposed to such browsers and, thus, the everyday experience of virtuality and plurality,

> Fredric Jameson's idea that space, mirroring the inconceivable complexities of the infosphere, had become fractally complex was not so much proved wrong as displaced by the increasingly banal activity of surfing the web; Jean-François Lyotard's assertion that the contemporary period is marked by an "incredulity towards metanarratives" was absorbed into the cultural mainstream, only to come smack against a return to fundamentalism and simplistic global explanations emanating alike from evangelical Christians and Islamic extremists (xxiv); Jean Baudrillard's titillating suggestion that reality had "imploded" into hyperreality ceased to function as a transgressive theoretical conceit, displaced by the everyday-ness of navigating virtual spaces that somehow left no one in doubt reality was as "real" as ever.[38] (99)

The sense we get from both McLaughlin and Hayles and Gannon is that postmodernism ultimately negates its own apparent function as an artistic imperative via its ultimately widespread dispersal as a dominant epistemic configuration. Postmodernism's final success as a pervasive and publicly embraced dominant negates its ability to foster a rejection of all things publicly embraced as the "truth."

The extent to which postmodernism's hegemony pervaded all levels of cultural production is, of course, most evident in corrosively anti-foundationalist television programs like *Seinfeld* and *The Simpsons*. The acutely solipsistic and impenetrable private world(s) portrayed via the unlikable characters in *Seinfeld* and the always ungrounded repudiation of moral authority in *The Simpsons*[39] speaks to the way in which popular cultural absorbed the high-theory of postmodernism by creating what many critics now view as a type of moral vacuum, a vacuum that has been ironically disguised as an ethical, or "morally responsible," world view. As McLaughlin suggests, while discussing the "neo-realist" position of writers like Jonathan Franzen[40] and David Foster Wallace,

> TV has become increasingly about TV and/or TV watching, and, in a reversal of its earlier role as promulgator of American values, TV cynically mocks, deflates, and debunks these values and their spokespeople. . . . The epitome of all this for Wallace is David Letterman, whose talk show is an elaborate parody of talk show conventions in which no guest and no idea escape the smirk and eye-rolling of self-referential irony. ("Post-Postmodern Discontent" 64)

I would argue, though, that television has not ceased endorsing "American Values." Television very much continues to promulgate such values and/or ethical imperatives; the dominant value is simply defined now by an imperative to be utterly skeptical of values as such. If popular television, or even music[41] and film, is not properly ironic and self-aware it is, it would appear, ostracized as irresponsibly sentimental and dangerously idealistic. To a degree, then, the "techniques that were for early postmodernists the means of rebellion have become, through their co-option by television, 'agents of a great despair and stasis'" (McLaughlin, "Post-Postmodern Discontent" 64–5). Consider, for example, a television show like *Seinfeld*.

Seinfeld is, after all, a show that prided itself on being "about nothing." Most episodes, in fact, abandoned the traditional concept of plot altogether. In the first few seasons, most of the episodes depicted a single mundane event—finding a car in a parkade or waiting for a table at a restaurant—while the characters engaged in extended bouts of circular, and often solipsistic, dialogue. "The Contest," for instance, focused exclusively on Jerry, George, Elaine, and Kramer's various attempts to stop masturbating. The fact that all four—George, of course, holds out the longest—ultimately fail can be read as a self-reflexive commentary on the show as a whole: all the characters are defined by an acute inability to escape their private fantasies and limited perspectives. While most of the episodes are driven by exchanges of dialogue, the general suggestion is that all attempts to communicate are ultimately futile; no one is ever *really* capable of understanding the other, of apprehending the "Real." This "co-option" of postmodern technique and ideology becomes most obvious, though, in a later episode: "The Pitch." In this episode, George and Seinfeld are given the opportunity to "pitch" a television show to executives at NBC. George decides that the show should be about Seinfeld's day-to-day life; the show, in other words, should be "about nothing." While George and Seinfeld attempt to solidify the premise of their fictional *Seinfeld* over coffee, we are forced to consider the possibility that they are mimicking exactly the events that lead to the creation of the "real" *Seinfeld*. And, as George and Seinfeld grow increasingly indistinguishable from their "real life" counterparts—that is, Larry David, who is the co-creator of *Seinfeld* and the model for George, and the "real" Jerry Seinfeld—the show itself becomes increasing solipsistic and reflective of a postmodern epoch defined by the prevalence of simulation and vacuous distinctions. Indeed, while they are discussing possible episodes, George pitches an episode that actually aired in the first season of the "real" *Seinfeld*—that is, the episode in which Jerry tries to find his car in a parkade. At this point the line between fiction and reality becomes incredibly tenuous, and the entire show seems to be in danger of folding in on itself, of slipping into infinite regress.

But like most postmodern narratives, *Seinfeld* never dismisses *absolutely* the possibility of some authentic difference between reality and the discursive, or fictional, constructions that define that reality. *Seinfeld* remains distinct from the "real" life of Seinfeld: George is *not* Larry David and Elaine has no "real" counterpart. Moreover, the "fictional" *Seinfeld*, when it finally airs as a pilot on the "real" *Seinfeld*, is unique; it's called *Jerry* not *Seinfeld*; the fictional actors create distinctly original versions of Kramer, Elaine and George; and the set (i.e., Seinfeld's apartment) is distinct from the "real" set.[42] In short, and as I have suggested repeatedly, even the most *perversely* ethical postmodern narratives tend to express a certain necessary belief in the possibility of some finally accurate understanding of reality. However, and as we see with *Seinfeld*, postmodernism can be defined by an almost exclusive emphasis on the impossibility of such a promise. As we have seen, though, this emphasis appears to have finally shifted. In fact, a recent television show like Larry David's *Curb Your Enthusiasm*—which takes a distinctly neo-realist approach to the issues and themes David explored on *Seinfeld*—can be viewed as representative of a larger shift in television programming. Like *The Office,* or *Arrested Development, Curb Your Enthusiasm* (which refuses to supply a laugh track, has certain actors "playing" themselves, and employs documentary-style footage) seems to embrace a type of "dirty realism" that works to *shift the postmodern focus* and thus overtly renew the possibility of apprehending some version of the "Real." Before discussing this renewalist shift further, though, I want to return to the arguments of McLaughlin and Shechner.

The point I want to make is this: critics like Shechner are, to a certain degree, incorrect when they simply blame the failure of postmodernism on the academic impulse to privilege it as an aesthetic ideal. It makes more sense to view postmodernism as an aesthetic imperative that failed to remain or, for that matter, *to become* wholly withdrawn from public discourse. This is not to say that postmodernism *should have been,* or *should have remained,* an elite and esoteric aesthetic. What I am suggesting is that the "passing" of postmodernism can be best understood as the effect of a necessary inability to avoid social and/or public discourse—an inability, that is, to avoid making truth claims, to avoid being repositioned as an aesthetic imperative, to avoid succumbing to the teleological impulse it strove to repudiate.

This brings us back, of course, to Taylor's conception of postmodern logo centrism: the idea that postmodernism, via an increasingly dogmatic emphasis on negation, or relativism, finds itself making overtly positive and/or public claims. The "failure" of postmodern metafiction is, in this sense, a failure to avoid becoming or, at the very least, *seeming* entangled in the totalizing impulse, or dialectic, it claimed to repudiate. As Philip Tew suggests, while discussing Roy Bhaskar's[43] argument that postmodernism was mistaken "to elide the referent," all "aesthetic responses, most particularly negation, depend upon an ontologically persistent 'reality principle,' or a realist dialectic" (48). For Tew, the attempt to evade this paradox is symptomatic of what, not surprisingly, Žižek repeatedly identifies as the fundamental and "perverse" error of most postmodern texts. For this reason, Tew argues, via a Žižekean filter, that "postmodernists" like Hutcheon and Derrida are naively mistaken in their outright rejection of a Hegelian concept of totalization. What such postmodernists fail to embrace, then—fail to embrace, that is, because they are too busy stressing its impossibility—is a

> totalization that never totalizes all and where one perceives
> 'the unattainable, ever elusive excess of the "infrastructure"

which can never be fully mirrored within the text [. . .] a redoubled reflection, the reflective re-marking of the very surplus of reflection,' offering a notion of an absolute that mediates and acknowledges its own impossibility, of which Hegel makes use dialectically as Žižek demonstrates. (40)

The postmodern aesthetic "fails," because, as Žižek might say, it fails to embrace the impossible Real that its perpetuation as a discourse necessarily (re)affirms. Or rather, as Tew puts it, while quoting Bhaskar, "it fails 'especially in its denial of [. . .] the capacity for rational assessment of philosophical and other positions, [whereby] it undermined its own capacity to sustain itself, for the post-modernist discourse must be real, if it is to have any effect at all [. . .]' " (49). In response to this failure, Tew offers the possibility of a "meta-realist" critique, or a type of "critical realism" that, in a manner that echoes Žižek's concept of an "art of the ridiculous sublime," "offers a recuperation of an appeal to a reality principle that involves an extension of an ongoing complexity of understanding of being and objectivity, incorporating an acknowledgement of provisionality (even though this concept presented a challenge that seduced many into attempts to dispel its very elusiveness by prioritizing it as a determining constant)" (36). In this way, Tew anticipates my own position: the apparent failure of postmodernism is the inevitable effect of the very specter that animated it in the first place, the specter of a "still incomplete project of modernity," the specter that promised *the end* of just such a project.

What we begin to see is that this current "realist revival" is not simply "the revenge" of a public that is, as Shechner seems to suggests, too simple or too lazy or too exhausted to bother with the difficult nature of postmodern narratives; rather, it is symptomatic of an epistemic response to postmodernism's inability to do what it claimed to be doing all along. Neo-realism, like Tew's critical mode of "meta-realism," is, in other words, a response to the futile project of exorcising all spectral, or utopian, remainders. The end of postmodernism does not, as critics like Shechner would have us believe, parallel the end of a socialist alternative *because* both communism and postmodernism were privileged in the ivory tower of academia. Rather, postmodernism's decline seems to coincide with the dissolution of the Soviet Union *because* that dissolution marks the very moment when postmodernism, like the process of modernization, became hegemonic and thus utopian[44] in its repudiation of all utopian, publicly shared and/or universalizing impulses (such as socialism). And it is in this inevitable moment of hegemony—the moment in which an epistemic focus becomes a virtually inescapable imperative—that a certain victory of the specter takes place. Simply put, postmodernism begins to "pass" at the moment when, in its attempt to repudiate past hegemonic discourses, it becomes both dominant and restrictive—that is, when it becomes impossible to ignore its own spectral contamination. In the case of postmodernism, a latent and paradoxical impulse—teleological, utopian, humanist, or whatever—becomes undeniable and a new epistemological reconfiguration begins to emerge. This latent impulse is most evident, we might say at this point, in the simple fact that a postmodern "ethics of perversity" should have lead to solipsistic silence; yet, rather than going silent, rather than performing a final act of narrative suicide, postmodernism *necessarily* continued to become louder and more public, insisting all the while that being loud and being public was an effect of false and dangerous ideological imperatives.

Like the still stylistically "postmodern" texts discussed above, then, neo-realism speaks to the way in which this current epistemological reconfiguration can be defined by its relationship to the spectral inheritance that animated postmodernism. This emergent period of renewalism abandons the postmodern *need* to expose, above all else, the impossibility of the specter and, instead, works to embrace both the possibility *and* the impossibility of the specter. Renewalism is, I am arguing, defined by an epistemological willingness—or, we might begin to say at this point, *an imperative*—to, as a later Derrida would have it, "respect the specter." In works that outwardly continue to employ the stylistic devices associated with postmodernism—works by, among others, Mark Leyner, David Lynch, Toni Morrison, Maxine Hong Kingston, Mark Z. Danielewski, Don DeLillo, David Foster Wallace, Tim O'Brien, and (perhaps) Louise Erdrich and Quentin Tarantino[45]—this "respect" is played out via a focus on the necessity of the spectral promise and a renewed faith in its impossible possibility. More overt works of neo-realism demonstrate this same spectral relationship—albeit in a more obvious manner—while also demonstrating a concerted effort to abandon the metafictional imperative that defined postmodernism. For this reason, neo-realism seems to be indicative of a more general epistemological relinquishment of aesthetic imperatives *as such*.

Using Wallace's *Infinite Jest* as an example, McLaughlin argues that recent works of neo-realism focus "less on self-conscious wordplay and the violation of narrative conventions and more on representing the world we all more or less share" ("Post-Postmodern Discontent" 65-7). This is not, however (and as the majority of "neo-realist" critics tend to agree), a simple return to modernism or an outright rejection of postmodern claims: "this new fiction nevertheless has to show that it's a world that we know through language and layers of representation" (11). In his introduction to *Neo-Realism in Contemporary American Fiction*, Kristiaan Versluys puts it like this: "The task [of neo-realism] is to question everything, including the by now rather hackneyed habit of subjecting every assertion or perception to massive onslaught of doubt and endless deferrals of meaning" (8). This isn't a simple return to mimesis; realism is now employed—or, rather, *accepted*—as just another "language game" (8). The renewalist acceptance of the specter's ironic spectrality is, perhaps, most apparent in the fact that neo-realism seems willing to do what postmodernism was not (yet) willing, or able, to do: embrace both realism and metafiction as equally contingent "language games." The defining feature of neo-realism (especially when it is categorized along with recent works that seem, at least stylistically, to be postmodern) is thus its apparent evasion of the paradoxical idealism implied in the postmodern claim that a responsible narrative *must* overtly acknowledge the absolute contingency of all narrative acts. To a certain extent, then, and if we recall Taylor and/or Žižek, neo-realism positions itself as a form of *finally successful* POSTmodernism. By exposing the metafictional imperative of postmodernism as a type of "back-door" idealism, or truth claim, the turn to a postmodern-inflected realism aims to "sidestep" the traps of "pervasion" and/or "logo centrism"; it does this, as Versluys suggests, via an acceptance of realism *as a contingent narrative act*. Rather than insisting on the impossibility of mimesis, of the spectral promise fulfilled, of a telos—rather than enforcing an impossibly corrosive stylistic imperative—neo-realism seems to move beyond the problematic truth claim that all truth claims are dangerous illusions and embraces the need for such claims while simultaneously demonstrating an awareness of their illusory status. Embracing what we might call, following Klaus Stierstorfer, "contingent referentiality" (10), this emergent neo-realism thus aims to reaffirm the necessity of gambling on some type of universal claim, or common ground. By viewing metafiction—or, rather, the need to expose every narrative act as one more contingent *petit récit*—neo-realism or, more broadly, renewalist narrative relaxes the formal restrictions of postmodernism and returns to realist forms that more openly negotiate the mimetic impulse that postmodern metafiction could never truly abandon. This *return* to realism is, then, ultimately symptomatic of a broad epistemological renewal of faith—that is, faith in the promise (of mimesis, of communication, etc.) and the impossible possibility that it will be fulfilled.

As Winfried Fluck suggests, realism seemed to return when "people remembered, or rather finally dared to admit that they had continued to be interested in stories based on the illusion of the referent" (67). What is important to note here is that realism does not simply reemerge along with a renewed insistence on the possibility of the referent; it reemerges, instead and more significantly, along with a desire for narrative strategies that fulfill a latent desire for the referent *as illusion.* Consequently, as Fluck goes on to argue, "the new realism is not just a naïve conservative backlash to postmodern daring and innovation, but a new type of writing with its own potential for contributing to our contemporary cultural situation" (67). However, unlike postmodern metafiction, neo-realism allows for *the possibility* that the referent can be accessed, that a representational act can be accurate. At the same time, though, this new realism is aware of itself as "no more (and no less) than a system of rhetorical strategies . . . It does not simply reflect or mirror reality, but offers a version of it" (67). Focusing on the work of Raymond Carver, Fluck goes on to argue that this current manifestation of realism does not, as it did in its previous "liberal" manifestations, claim to reveal some authentic or universal experience. As Fluck suggests,

> one of the major sources of authorization for the [past] realist text has been a power of experience to provide knowledge. In claiming to depict reality as it *really is,* realism not only refers to the criterion of a shared experience, but, by doing so, also promises to provide a more truthful and relevant version of that experience than other forms of literature. (71)

Exemplified in the work of a writer like Hemingway or, perhaps, Fitzgerald, "This search for authentic experience is part of a modernist project to penetrate to a deeper level of human existence that lies beneath the shallow surface of Victorian conventions" (71). For Fluck, this type of realism is symptomatic of a modernist quest for "deep knowledge," a quest that can be identified as the animating feature of a number of "modernist" discourses.

Recalling Jameson, Fluck asserts that discourses as diverse as "Marxism, psychoanalysis, existentialism and finally structuralism all offered versions of this discourse of 'deep knowledge' " (71). However, according to Fluck, recent works of neo-realism, as exemplified in the stories of Carver, mange to eschew this modernist desire for "deep knowledge":

> In contrast to the skillful insinuations of Hemingway, Carver's stories no longer offer such promises of "deep." In Carver's

work, crises and catastrophes are not heroic moments valued
for their potential to reveal an existential truth but accidental
occurrences in a dehierarchized sequence of daily events.
Consequently, the characters that experience them are not
transformed or deeply affected by them, but continue to
live on as before. (72)

Looking specifically at Carver's "Why Don't You Dance?," Fluck highlights the way in which a work of neo-realism seems to promise *and*
defer the possibility of transcendent truths and/or moments of epiphany. A story that climaxes with a bizarre dance during a mundane yard
sale, "Why Don't You Dance?" is, according to Fluck, a form of realism
that puts into question the easy equation of "defamiliarization and an
anti-mimetic mode of writing" (72). By failing to provide "a climax or
epiphany that could provide the rest of the events with 'actual' meaning," Carver's stories refuse to provide "teleology, sustained argument,
or moral structure" (73). Instead, a work like "Why Don't You Dance?"
simply offers "a chain of events in which one scene acquires an inexplicable, almost surreal transcendence for the briefest of moments—a
moment that seems to carry, in contrast, for example, to Hemingway,
no representative power beyond itself" (73). The modernist moment
of epiphany is thus both promised and deferred as "a moment of
decontextualized experience" (73). Moving on to a discussion of two
paintings that he identifies as neo-realist precursors—Edward Hopper's
Nighthawks and Richard Estes' *Central Savings*—Fluck expands this argument, stressing the fact that a realist mode can be used to recharge
the possibility of meaning, truth, or whatever, while endlessly deferring that possibility. Again, Fluck's position here confirms the assertion (above) that the narrative strategies after postmodernism can be
defined by their willingness/ability to maintain the necessarily ironic
nature of, what a late-Derrida would privilege as a state of, "indecision,"
a state in which the decision process (or, in this specific context, the
act of narrative representation) is animated by *both* the impossibility
of the certainly right decision, or representation, *and* the promise of
pure indecision (or "no decision" in the sense that there is only one
right decision, or true representational act).

Let me clarify this. Because a work of high-postmodern metafiction is overtly focused on emphasizing the impossibility of mimesis, it is
seemingly confined to two readings: either it forces us to acknowledge
the pointlessness of any narrative representation (in which case its
persistence as an art form becomes redundant) or it presents itself as
the *finally right representation* because it accurately represents "reality" as
an ideological illusion (in which case we are left wondering why one

metafictional text is not enough, why one metafictional text isn't simply the final word on all narrative acts as such). In either case, we are left without a reason to move. We are left in a state of paralysis. We are left, that is, in a state of "mythic," or pure, indecision—in the sense that there is no longer a decision, or narrative act, to make/perform.[46] What a work of neo-realism—or, rather, any of the works that we might identify with this emergent period of renewalism—stresses is thus the very thing that *continued* to animate postmodernism: the necessarily possible *and* impossible nature of the certainly right decision, or narrative act. At the very moment postmodern works of metafiction seem to present themselves as *finally decided* on the impossibility of any finally right decision, they continue to be animated by the very fact (however paradoxical it may sound) that such a decision is impossible. Neo-realism, in short, attempts to "get over" this paradoxical problem by embracing it—by embracing, that is, the necessity of the spectrological lure: "What a realist surface manages to quite effectively do is to constantly refuel the viewer's interest and curiosity because of a promise of representation that is ... never fulfilled" (Fluck 77). Rather than simply rejecting the spectral promise as illusory idealism—and thus, like postmodernism, becoming hegemonically opposed to the very promise that necessarily animates any anti-ideological movement—neo-realism endorses an ethics of indecision; it overtly embraces the need to believe in the spectral promise of the certainly right decision while simultaneously embracing, *à la* postmodernism, its infinite deferral.

A nice example of this "neo-realist promise" can be found in the opening chapter of Russell Banks' *Continental Drift*. Entitled "Invocation," Banks' opening chapter seems to outwardly challenge the postmodern rejection of mimesis and the possibility of historical objectivity:

> It's not memory you need for telling this story ... It's not memory you need, it's clear eyed pity and hot, old-time anger and a Northern man's love of the sun, it's a white man's entwined obsession with race and sex and a proper middle-class American's shame for a nation's history ... nothing here depends on memory for the telling. (1–2)

In a manner that recalls Carver's minimalist "dirty realism"—that is, his realistic accounts of middle America, or American "white trash"—Banks promises the possibility of "representative experience" yet consistently populates his text with characters and situations that overtly escape complete apprehension. While moments of climax hold out the promise of positive change and shared understanding, they are consistently eviscerated of meaning. At one point, the main character, Bob Dubois (a middle-aged man who frequently cheats on his wife), is dramatically held up by gunpoint while working at a liquor mart. The scene ends with Bob shooting one of his assailants twice and finding the other, with "shitpants" (104), cowering in a storeroom. While this event seems to *change* Bob, the change we see, as well as the event itself, is quickly diffused by a persistent and unchanging narrative flow; the significance of the event—if, we begin to wonder, it had any at all—is slowly lost on the reader (as it is, we could argue, on Bob). As with Carver, then, "We are . . . constantly moving between a promise of representative experience, its subversion and its subsequent restitution—a movement that is received time and again by [the neo-realist] strategy of recharging the realistic surface of the text with a meaning that cannot be firmly grasped" (Fluck 78).

In brief, neo-realism seemingly escapes the dogmatism of post-modernism by explicitly embracing *and* deferring the possibility of the referent, of mimesis. By embracing the fact that both realist and metafictional strategies are necessarily animated by a belief, even if latent, that there "can be, in principle, only one correct version of reality" (Fluck 69), neo-realism works to escape the postmodern tendency to make a grand narrative out of an "incredulity" to grand narratives. Neo-realism seems to "respect the specter"—it seems, that is, to respect the necessity of an animating, yet impossible, ideal—so as to avoid being dangerously compelled to *either* insist upon the possibility that the spectral ideal can become real and in the flesh *or* to emphatically and repeatedly expose such an ideal as impossible. Viewed alongside the more formalistic texts touched on above, neo-realism can thus be understood as symptomatic of an emergent episte-mological reconfiguration that can be defined, as I suggested above, by a desire to abandon—or rather, to get over, to lay to rest—all aesthetic imperatives. What is most significant about this apparent return to realism—a realism, we need to stress, that is informed by postmodern formalism—is that it signals the end of metafiction as a privileged aesthetic style while simultaneously identifying *both* itself *and* metafiction as equally contingent and equally relevant "language games." More simply, neo-realism or, more broadly, *the literature of renewalism* can be defined as an attempt to *relax the rules*. By overtly acknowledging that all aesthetic imperatives are necessarily animated by, what I have been calling, a certain spectrological aporia, the literature of renewalism works to avoid becoming, like its modern and postmodern predecessors, another hegemonic ideal—which is to say that it works to avoid effacing the necessarily ironic spectrality of the specter. However, as I have suggested throughout, this impulse to "respect the specter" inevitably becomes a new way of "dis-respecting the specter"; it becomes, in other words, another imperative, another *mythic decision* that is itself, and in ways it necessarily cannot control, the effect of a certain spectral compulsion, a certain *absolute* belief in a utopian ideal. Before I can fully reapproach this claim from the perspective of emergent modes of narrative, though, it is perhaps necessary to look more closely at this apparent shift from a postmodern to a renewalist aesthetic. Indeed, with the above discussion in mind, and in a rather spiral-like fashion, I would like to clarify the distinctions, cursively identified above, that separate postmodern narrative strategies from the strategies of an emergent renewalist "episteme."

The Project of Renewalism

In Charlie Kaufman and Spike Jonze's film, *Adaptation*—their follow-up to the particularly solipsistic *Being John Malkovich*—Kaufman writes himself into his adaptation of Susan Orlean's book, *The Orchid Thief*. Played by Nicolas Cage, Kaufman *accidentally* becomes the main character of the film, a film that is supposed to be about Susan Orlean (played by Meryl Streep). In a manner that makes Vonnegut's presence in *Breakfast of Champions* look perfectly normal, Kaufman's fictionalized self comes to dominate the film, effacing, at least partially, the source material that is the film's *raison d'être*. Concerned more with the process of adaptation than with the adaptation itself, the film begins, as the end result of what we see Kaufman attempting to produce throughout, in a state of apparent paralysis; feeling a sense of what we might call postmodern responsibility, Kaufman feels compelled to be corrosively self-reflexive. For the fictional Kaufman, an adaptation *must* ostentatiously acknowledge its process of production, as well as the contingent subject-position of the artist that is engaged in that production. A screenplay mustn't simply reaffirm the romantic illusions of stable meaning, final answers, authorial control, and so on. So, instead of the traditional Hollywood romance, or thriller, or whatever, Kaufman produces, well . . . nothing. Indeed, apart from credits, the film opens with a completely black screen. We then hear Nicolas Cage, as Kaufman, in a voice-over: "Do I have an original thought in my head? My bald head?" The answer is, apparently, no. Rather than what Kaufman would consider to be "an original thought"—or, in other words, the start of the movie—we are given more of the self-critical voice-over: Kaufman tells us that he has a "fat ass," that he "needs to fall in love," that he needs to "learn Russian or something," that he needs to "be real." Eventually, the credits include a line stating that the film is, indeed, "Based on the book, *The Orchid Thief,* by Susan Orlean"; by this point the information seems incidental.

When the film proper finally begins, it doesn't begin with Susan Orlean or John Laroche, the orchid thief who is the subject of Orlean's investigation. The initial sequence occurs on the set of *Being John Malkovich.* The actors and crew—including the "real" John Malkovich—are milling about, preparing for the next shot. Filmed in documentary style, this initial sequence is presented as authentic "making-of" footage. In the background, though, Nicolas Cage *as Kaufman* self-consciously tries to get involved. Ignored by actors and crew alike, Kaufman eventually leaves. This confusion of reality (the Malkovich set) and fiction (Cage as Kaufman) sets up the basic conceit of the film: the only "real" thing Kaufman can write is himself, yet the self he writes is inevitably forced, fictionalized, discursively determined. All Kaufman can do—as a *responsible* postmodern artist—is draw attention to the fact that everything he produces is inevitably caught up in this inescapable paradox.

After the scene on the set of Malkovich, we see Kaufman getting the job of adapting Orlean's book. He informs the studio representative—a beautiful young woman—that he doesn't want to write anything that is artificially "plot driven." He's not going to write an "Orchid Heist" movie, or a movie about poppies and drug runners. He's not going to "cram in sex." There won't be any car chases or "characters, you know, learning profound life lessons. Life isn't like that." However, Kaufman inevitably fails to realize a way out of the romantic archetypes that he repudiates. So he stalls. He gives us Susan Orlean's story, randomly cut in with his own, up to the point when the film studio buys the rights to *The Orchid Thief* and gives him the job of adapting it. At the same time, he creates another character: his own twin brother, Donald, who is writing a screenplay of his own. The screenplay, Donald tells Charlie, is a Hollywood thriller in which a female detective is hunting a male serial killer who feeds his victims to themselves in small bits. The "big payoff" is that the detective is really the killer. So, in the end, "when he forces the woman who's really him to eat herself he's also eating himself to death." Charlie, of course, thinks that Donald is a "sell-out." He repeatedly tells Donald, who has been attending a seminar by Robert McKee, that he needs to be more original, that there are "no rules," that screenwriting seminars are "bullshit," that "Anybody who says they have the answer is going to attract desperate people." Apart

from the rule that there are no rules, the basic *postmodern rule*, according to Kaufman, is that the true artist is always on a "journey into the
unknown." Taking the Lyotardian "incredulity toward metanarratives"
and the imperative to "make it new" to its extreme, Kaufman's position
becomes virtually suicidal, or cannibalistic. His screenplay—that is, the
film we're watching—becomes transfixed on his own inability to write a
screenplay. For much of the film he sits in front of his computer, trying
to write. When he's not trying to write, he's masturbating.[47] Eventually,
he decides that the only thing he can do is write about himself. This
"realization" is articulated in another voiceover: "I have no understanding of anything outside of my own panic and self-loathing and pathetic
little existence. It's like the only thing I'm actually qualified to write
about is myself and my own self. . . ." This "epiphany" (of sorts) is followed by a look of excitement on Kaufman's face and an abrupt cut.
In the next shot we see Kaufman at home, speaking into a recorder:
"We open on Charlie Kaufman, fat, old, bald, repulsive, sitting in a
Hollywood restaurant across from Valerie Thomas, a lovely statuesque
film executive. Kaufman, trying to get a writing assignment. . . ." After
another cut, Kaufman is in bed. He's still recording himself, but now
he's reading from notes: "Fat, bald, Kaufman pitches furiously in his
bedroom. He speaks into his handheld tape recorder and he says:
'Charlie Kaufman, fat, bald, repulsive, old, sits at a Hollywood restaurant with Valerie Thomas. . . .' "

In danger of slipping into infinite regress, the film seems to run
into a—or rather, *the*—postmodern dead end. Kaufman, once again,
begins to despair, and when Donald tells him that he got the idea
for his "trick" ending from a tattoo he saw of a snake biting its own
tale—a symbol Kaufman recognizes as the Ourobouros—he realizes
that his own work has become pointlessly and dangerously cannibalistic: "I'm insane. I'm Ourobouros. . . . It's self indulgent. It's narcissis-
tic. It's solipsistic. It's pathetic." At a loss, Kaufman goes to New York
and attends McKee's seminar. At the same time, the segments about
Orlean become subtly more dramatic; Orlean becomes obsessed with
both Laroche and the possibility of seeing a "Ghost," an elusive and
legendary orchid. At the seminar, McKee tells Kaufman that voice-
overs are ridiculous and that any attempt to make a film in which
"nothing much happens" will be both boring and unrealistic. Love,
murder, sacrifice, pain: these things are occurring everyday. If you're
making a movie, McKee tells Kaufman, "you got to put in the drama."
If Kaufman's film is to be a success, if it is to be relevant at all, it
needs "an ending." It needs to assume, or embrace, a certain teleological impulse; it needs to animate itself with the promise of an end,

a final answer, the truth. Excited, Kaufman has Donald, who begins to function much more obviously as Kaufman's double, come to New York and help with the script. As Donald and Charlie begin to investigate Orlean in the present day, the segments that involve Orlean at the time of writing the *Orchid Thief* begin to take on a different tone. We discover that Orlean despises her passionless marriage and job; she wants to be passionate in the way that Laroche (who continually becomes obsessed with hobbies and then abandons them altogether) is passionate. Moreover, Laroche tells Orlean that he has been trying to find the "Ghost Orchid" because it produces a drug that "seems to help people be fascinated"—which is to say that it allows people to believe in a type of telos, a type of animating goal (even if such a telos/goal is impossible). In the narrative present, Charlie and Donald discover that Orlean has become addicted to the Ghost drug, and that, while writing her book, she began an illicit affair with Laroche, who is now mass-producing the drug in Miami. In brief, then: after a drug cartel subplot, a foot chase through a swamp, a car chase in which Donald is killed, Charlie's epiphany that "you are what you love, not what loves you," and some gratuitous, and crammed in, sex, the film ends with Kaufman telling us, in another voice-over, that he's ready to finish his adaptation: "It ends with Kaufman driving home after his lunch with [his ex-girlfriend] thinking he knows how to finish the script. Shit, that's a voiceover. McKee would not approve. Well, who cares what McKee says? It feels right. So: Kaufman drives off from his encounter with Amelia filled for the first time with hope."

On the most superficial level, the shift in narrative strategy that the film—or, rather, Kaufman undergoes—is a compact representation of the current shift I have attempted to articulate above. It is a shift away from the basic imperative that animated, and eventually came to dominate, the postmodern aesthetic: corrosive and ultimately paralyzing self-reflexivity. Indeed, the first part of the film—the acutely metafictional part—functions as a conscious articulation of the postmodern "failure" I described above. Kaufman's initial need to be self-reflexive, to be responsible, to demonstrate that there is no final "answer," no possible telos, or end, inevitably forces him to turn on himself. If he is to escape the archetypes and predetermined discourses that his work inevitably perpetuates, he must withdraw *à la* Rorty from all public, or coherent, discourses; he must become utterly and inaccessibly private. At the same time, though (and quite paradoxically), he must enter into public discourse if he is to make his point—which is, ultimately, that all points are contingent and pointless. We see this problem play out most obviously in those moments when Charlie corrects Donald.

There are no rules, there is no answer, but "don't say 'pitch,' " "don't say 'industry,' " art has to be original, new, and so on. Quite simply, the first portion of the film—its paralysis, its inability to "progress"—can be read as a critique of a postmodern "ethics of perversity" and, thus, the ostentatious metafiction that postmodernism has always privileged. What Kaufman seems to suggest is that the postmodern aesthetic necessarily leads to silence, paralysis, utterly private self-reflexivity, masturbation in the dark.

John Barth, the postmodern writer *par excellence*, makes a similar point in "The Literature of Exhaustion." Using Beckett as an example, Barth notes that silence is the ultimate ideal of any artist who aims to escape the discursive confines in which he or she necessarily works: "For Beckett . . . to cease to create altogether would be fairly meaningful: his crowning work; his 'last word.' What a convenient corner to paint yourself into" (68). The sense we get, from both Kaufman and Barth, is that this move toward absolute withdrawal is a type of failure.[48] By recalling Lyotard's terms, as well as the above discussion, we can rephrase the problem like this: not only does the imperative to deny all grand narratives become, itself, a type of grand, or hegemonic, narrative, the postmodern recourse to the *petit récit*, or personally contingent narrative, ultimately leads to the denial of all possible communication, or shared understanding. Again, though, this is not to say that postmodernism was wholly blind to this problem.[49] After all, Barth himself seems to be acutely interested in the paradoxical implications of postmodern solipsism.[50] Still, what we see in the work of a writer like Barth is an investment in provisionality that does not yet seem willing to outwardly embrace the possibility of a truth, or ideal, it knows to be impossible. Consequently, in much high postmodernism we see an emphatic movement toward silence and/or paralysis.

However, the fact that postmodernism—like the beginning of *Adaptation*—never *really* ceased to move, never *really* dissolved into so many fragments of private incoherence, speaks to its often repressed desire, its faith in the very promise of the telos it worked to expose as impossible. The postmodern desire to claim that history is over, that nothing original can be said, that the Real is an illusion, becomes the very reason to continue writing. As Barth suggests, "an artist may paradoxically turn the felt ultimacies of our time into material means for his work—*paradoxically*, because by doing so he transcends what had appeared to be his refutation" (71). Along with someone like Baudrillard, then, the postmodern writer is spectrally compelled to write about the pointlessness of writing, or the impossibility of communication or meaning. Silence is always evaded because the promise of an end (a ghost) is nether possible nor impossible. And, as I demonstrated in the previous two chapters, a promise, like a specter, is never here and now, but it is never entirely absent either; if it were absent or if it were here now and, thus, an actuality, it would cease to animate. This spectral paradox of transcending the very refutation that animates the transcendence of that refutation—a paradox we see Kaufman struggling with and finally embracing as an inescapable part of any narrative act—is played out most obviously in Barth's first novel, *The Floating Opera*. A text that we might readily identify as the first work of American postmodernism, *The Floating Opera* is an overtly metafictional piece that articulates its own *raison d'être*, for the text as well as the main character/narrator, by denying the possibility of ever locating a purpose, or meaning, for the text (or character).

Narrated by the lawyer Todd Andrews, *The Floating Opera* begins by questioning its own narrative relevance. Throughout, though, the promise of an end—that is, in this case, the promise of a satisfactory conclusion to, and explanation for, Andrews' story—is repeatedly identified as a type of illusory lure. As Andrews continually insists, this end (which we are always, as Derrida would say, "awaiting") is never going to arrive. Andrews' makes this point most clearly when he decides to explain the novel's title: "*The Floating Opera*. Why *The Floating Opera*? I could explain until Judgment Day, and still not explain completely" (13). Significantly, the apparent impossibility of a conclusive answer does not prevent Andrews from offering some sort of explanation. In fact, Andrews goes on to supply us with his reflections on the name of a showboat—*Adam's Original and Unparalleled Floating Opera*—that "used to travel around the Virginia and Maryland tidewater areas" (13). A setting for the final portion of the book, *Adam's Original and Unparalleled Floating Opera* gives Andrews the idea of a large boat on which a play is running continuously. This imaginary boat, Andrews tells us, would "drift up and down the river on the tide" and audiences would sit along the bank to watch: "They could catch whatever part of the plot happened to unfold as the boat floated past, and then they'd have to wait until the tide ran back again to catch another snatch of it, if they still happened to be sitting there. To fill in the gaps they would have to use their imaginations" (13). Like any work of historiographic metafiction, *The Floating Opera* included, Andrews' "floating opera" functions as a way of highlighting the illusory nature of narrative coherence: "Most times the [audience] wouldn't understand what was going on at all, or they'd think they knew, when actually they didn't" (13). The promise of full disclosure compels the audience of this "floating opera," just as it does Andrews as narrator of *The Floating*

Opera, to reassemble the fragments, to *re*-member the event. Nevertheless, and as Andrews repeatedly notes, the event always remains absent.
By continually highlighting this inevitable and necessary absence, *The
Floating Opera* (as text) *perversely* highlights, as Maurice Couturier puts
it, the "impossibility of all true communication between author and
reader" (7). Not surprisingly, then, Andrews, like Kaufman, is driven
by a need to justify his work. And it is because of this need to justify
his reason for writing that Andrews arrives at his "final solution," his
final *postmodern* answer: "I awoke, splashed cold water on my face, and
realized that I had the real, the final, the unassailable answer; the last
possible word; the stance to end all stances. . . . Didn't I tell you I'd
pull no punches? That my answers were yours? *Suicide!* . . . *Suicide* was
my answer; my answer was *suicide*." (23). What is interesting here is
that Andrews is telling us, some sixteen years after his epiphany, that
the *final* true answer is suicide—or rather, we might accurately infer,
artistic silence. While the entire text is, in fact, an account of the day
Andrews planned, and tried, to commit suicide, it is also, as Andrews
repeatedly tells us, a story of the day he changed his mind. The text
itself, as the impossible attempt to articulate the impossibility of articulating anything, delays the moment of silence that the text anticipates
on, or at, its horizon. More simply, the text's desire to expose the
impossibility of its own narrative telos remains spectrally animated by
the possibility of just such a telos.[51]

At the end of the text, and right before Andrews commits his
final act—or, rather, before he performs what Barth would consider to
be Beckett's final artistic solution—he finds that he is paralyzed, that
he is unable to do anything, suicide included.[52] This paralysis is, significantly, articulated as a narrative problem: "why explain at all? Why
move at all? . . . there was no reason to do anything, and I will say that
the realization of this worked upon me involuntarily. This is important: it was not that I decided not to speak, but that, aware in every
part of me of the unjustifiable nature of action . . . I simply could not
open my mouth" (264). At this moment, the text seems to be in real
danger of losing all faith, however latent, in the promise, or specter,
of its own narrative end; via the model of the narrator's physical body,
this moment exposes the danger of a seemingly inevitable postmodern
textual collapse, the absolute cessation of narrative movement. Put differently, this moment seems to be dangerously close to fulfilling the
promise of a truly POSTmodern text. It points to the silence—without
itself being "silent"—that would be the effect of any successful rejection
of spectral compulsion, of the impossible promise, of what the later
Derrida would call the messianic. Ultimately, Barth and Andrews—or

perhaps, Barth *as Andrews*—realizes this. Instead of *going through with it*, though, Andrews (like any good postmodern narrator) continues to explain why there is simply no reason why he *shouldn't have gone through with it*. Shocked out of paralysis by the danger in which he has inadvertently placed his illegitimate daughter, Andrews once again finds a reason to mobilize himself. With this return of "desire," however illusory he understands it to be, Andrews decides—quite arbitrarily, he insists—to change his mind. He then spends the next sixteen years preparing to do what he knows is impossible: communicate, to himself and to his readers, his reasons for deciding that suicide was the final and only answer *because there are no answers*.[53]

In *the end*, the promise of a final answer, or telos, ironically becomes the animating "goal" of *The Floating Opera* as a discourse, or narrative act. Like the postmodern texts examined above, *The Floating Opera* highlights the way in which postmodernism, and thus postmodern metafiction, is spectrally compelled to expose the specter as impossible, as an ideological illusion, as the cause of all past discursive hegemonies. As a type of response to this paradox, then, the current narrative "turn" overtly embraces this animating specter—this specter that postmodernism attempted to exorcise *once and for all* and that, consequently and paradoxically, animated its major narrative strategy. Simply put: because it was intended to exorcise the very thing that animated its exorcisms, the stylistic mode typically associated with the still residual episteme of postmodernism ultimately and necessarily "failed," becoming the very thing it sought to undermine: an aesthetic, if not an ethical, imperative. This, of course, brings us back to *Adaptation*.

While the initial portion of *Adaptation* seems to expose and, indeed, mock this particularly postmodern problem, the latter portion seemingly functions as a type of solution. Like any narrative mode we might associate with a renewalist episteme, works of "neo" or "dirty" realism included, the final portion of *Adaptation* speaks to the way in which, as Robert Rebein puts it, "contemporary realist writers have *absorbed* postmodernism's most lasting contributions and gone on to forge a new realism that is more or less traditional in its handling of character, reportorial in its depiction of milieu and time, but is at the same time self-conscious about language and the limits of mimesis" (20). The latter portion of *Adaptation* speaks to the way in which this emergent epoch *after* postmodernism seems to reject postmodernism's stringent focus on anti-foundationalism. What "renewalist" works like *Adaptation* overtly announce and accept is the fact that the desire to deny the possibility of any stable truth, or grand narrative—that is, the desire to abandon as a dangerous illusion "the still incomplete project of modernity"—is ultimately animated by some type of (blind) faith, or teleological impulse. Without descending into absolute silence, which itself becomes a type of "ideal" end, postmodern narrative strategies must, to a certain extent, remain blind to their own teleological, or positivist, contamination if they are to identify themselves as truly POSTmodern. Kaufman's acceptance of this "truth" allows him to abandon the implicit and *perverse* ethics of postmodernism and relax his allegiance to its ultimately unsustainable strategies. So, in the end (of *Adaptation,* or of postmodernism generally), we get forms of narrative that revive the possibility of communal understanding, humanism and/or consensus. They renew, in short, the possibility of a "still incomplete project of modernity," which is to say that they no longer attempt to do without what Jameson would call a latent utopian impulse (and what Žižek understands as the impossible Real) that animated postmodernism in the first place; renewalism, in short, outwardly embraces the necessary and inevitable "return of the repressed." It is, I would argue, hardly coincidental that the concept of a Ghost Orchid—that is, an elusive, if not mythical, flower that stimulates compassion and compels action—becomes a major theme in the last half of *Adaptation.* While it might be going too far to suggest an intentional link between the Ghost Orchid and Derrida's theory of the specter, the presence and discussion of the orchid does highlight the distinctly renewalist assumption that we *must* believe in a certain impossible telos, a certain impossible "Real." It is this ability to "hope"—or, perhaps, to gamble—that is finally articulated as the solution to Kaufman's distinctly postmodern dilemma. Quite simply, then, renewalist forms of narrative are defined by an overt willingness to respect the specter, to endorse, in other words, a certain ethics of indecision.

And, significantly, these renewalist forms of narrative are not restricted to any one specific style. While many critics have associated the end of postmodernism with the growing dominance of neo(or, dirty)-realism, the examples above seem to suggest that, whether or not we call them "neo-realist," the emergent forms of narrative are marked by an overall rejection of past aesthetic imperatives. For the most part, these narratives do indeed seem more "realistic"—especially as evidenced in the work of overtly "dirty" realists like Carver and Banks—but I am arguing that such narratives are better defined by the relationship they reestablish with a certain spectral inheritance, a spectral inheritance *passed on* by postmodernism. Rather than just new "realisms," then, what we see—in the work of writers and/or directors like Leyner, Morrison, Banks, Richard Powers, David Foster Wallace, Lorrie Moore, Danielewski, Lynch, Sophia Coppola, Wes Anderson,

Paul Thomas Anderson, Noah Baumbach, Jared Hess, Maxine Hong Kingston, Nicholson Baker, and Dave Eggers—are narrative forms that renew the realist faith in mimesis while simultaneously deferring and frustrating that faith via the irony and stylistics of a now past, or *passed*, postmodernism. For the sake of clarity, let me employ another example: the early work of Nicholson Baker. After all, if Barth's *The Floating Opera* is one of the first overtly postmodern novels, *The Mezzanine* (i.e., Baker's first novel) is one of the first clearly identifiable works of renewalism.[54] Just as Kaufman, in the end, saves his film by abandoning, or relaxing, his postmodern convictions, Baker works to reestablish the possibility of mimesis and universal understanding while remaining wary of the dangers that postmodernism struggled to expose and move beyond. To a degree, then, a novel like *The Mezzanine* continues to be postmodern; but, then again, and as we have seen, postmodernism (for its own part) seemed to anticipate the renewalist sensibilities Baker overtly embraces.

A novel that consists of nothing more than one man's memories concerning the day he bought shoelaces on his lunch break, *The Mezzanine* (via a series of footnotes) repeatedly draws attention to its own textuality and thus the fragmentary and unstable nature of any narrative reconstruction of the past. Moreover, the narrator's (i.e., Howie's) focus on everyday minutia—how he learned to enjoy sweeping, the problem with floating straws, the strange effect of farting in a bathroom stall while your boss washes his hands and talks business with a colleague—functions as a conscious acknowledgment of the absolutely private nature of existence. At the same time, though, Baker's text remains outwardly "realistic"; it is always coherent, straightforward, and accessible.[55] In fact, the absolutely private thoughts of the narrator become a way of drawing the reader into the text, a way of reaffirming community; the narrator's idiosyncrasies speak to our own idiosyncrasies. While there is little point in the narrator's conclusion that, when paying for groceries, "the differential in checkout speeds between a fast, smart ringer-upper and a slow, dumb one [is] three transactions to one" (117), it is likely that such a conclusion is not unlike other conclusions to which the reader has, somewhat pointlessly, arrived. Like the work of Leyner, this particular brand of narrative is neither a simple rejection of postmodern strategies nor a "back-lash" return to Lukásian realism. In other words, critics like Philip Simmons are, to a certain extent, correct when they associate *The Mezzanine* with a "postmodern historical imagination" (603). The text is, after all, "so extremely solipsistic, so limited to the domestic, the personal, and the resolutely mundane, that any larger historical frame . . . is gestured at only through the irony of its absence" (603). Still, as even Simmons admits, Baker's text (like, as I suggested above, Leyner's) "performs the most fundamental comic function of validating our perceptions in unexpected ways" (611). In the end, the postmodern fragmentation—that is, Baker's willingness to privilege innumerable "microhistories" (Simmons 605) over a single grand narrative—is employed in a manner that seems designed to ironically frustrate the postmodern rejection of communal understanding and/or essentially "human" experience; "we gain," as Simmons himself suggests, "a pleasurable shock of recognition" (611).

Instead of suggesting that Baker works to endorse a "postmodern historical imagination," then, we might argue, along with a critic like Arthur Saltzman, "that *The Mezzanine* does not feature the vanquishment of historical nostalgia, as Simmons contends, so much as it alters its course; it does not eliminate depth per se but posits 'deep surfaces' " (27). In a manner that recalls Fluck's discussion of Carver—in particular, his suggestion that neo-realism is defined by a willingness to privilege "surface knowledge"—Saltzman's take on Baker highlights the way in which a text like *The Mezzanine* can be read as overtly reaffirming the possibility of communication, or communal understanding, while simultaneously deferring the realization of that possibility. What we get, and what makes *The Mezzanine* utterly distinct from a text like *The Floating Opera*, is the promise of a type of communication without communication, an articulation of community without community. *The Mezzanine* readdresses the postmodern denial of shared understanding—of representational accuracy, of mimesis—by identifying its impossibility as the very grounds of its possibility. Like Blanchot's "community without community"—or, what the later Derrida associates in *The Politics of Friendship* with the term "lovence," a term that seems to suggest the possibility of connection via disconnection, touching without contact— the communal promise offered by *The Mezzanine* is continually made possible by the impossibility that it will be fulfilled (or, put differently, *finally effaced as promise*). The ruminations of Howie in *The Mezzanine* offer us, as Saltzman puts it, "contact and privacy simultaneously" (69). I don't want to suggest, though, that a text like *The Mezzanine* ultimately reaffirms a traditional notion of privacy, and thus a notion of the subject as "essentially" anterior to the social, or symbolic. Instead, by pointing to the possibility of a type of community without community, a text like *The Mezzanine* seems to present the subject's "privacy" as an effect of its singularity, but a singularity that, as a theorist like Jean-Luc Nancy[56] would suggest, is singular only insofar as it is simultaneously and paradoxically "with" others. This "singularity" is not "individuality; it is, each time, the punctuality of a 'with' that establishes a certain origin of meaning and connects it to an infinity of other possible origins [or 'singularities']" (*Singular Plural* 85). It is in this sense that I agree with Saltzman that the text offers the possibility of "contact and privacy simultaneously." The text, in other words, "renews," as does a work like Leyner's, the possibility of connection *as* disconnection. If we return again to the work of Nancy, we might in fact say that *The Mezzanine* works to suggest that the "common measure . . . is not some unique standard applied to everyone and everything," but rather "the commensurability of incommensurable singularities." (75). And, I would argue, this paradoxical renewal of the possibility of connection and/or communication (and, thus, of a finally correct and successful representational act, or decision) is even more obviously endorsed in Baker's later, slightly pornographic, novel *Vox*.

Another seemingly minimalist piece, *Vox* also focuses on the mundane and the personal. However, *Vox*, which is nothing but recorded dialogue between a man (Jim) and a woman (Abby) on a "phone sex" line, is much more overt than *The Mezzanine* in terms of suggesting the utterly private nature of human existence. Jim and Abby spend most of their time telling each other about their sexual habits, habits that tend to be extremely fetishistic and personal. At the same time, though, and as does *The Mezzanine*, *Vox* reembraces a type of sentimental faith in social experience and communal sharing. However, this "faith" is not naïve in the way that prepostmodern realism is understood as being. Like *The Mezzanine*, or Leyner's *Tetherballs*, *Vox* remains postmodern in terms of its articulation of a type of inescapable solipsism, or "singularity." The conversation, after all, takes place on a phone. There is no "real contact." Still, as Mikko Keskinen notes, "In phone sex, bodies are disconnected, but minds are connected by disembodied voices. . . . The point in phone sex seems to be to embrace and indulge in the distance rather than to grieve or curse it" (102). Jim and Abby's quest for the "real thing" is thus fueled by its impossibility; their desire is, in fact, repeatedly identified as an effect of the impossibility of its fulfillment. What produces their desire is the absence of the Real; its promise, its *possibility*, is the effect of its impossibility. Jim, as we eventually learn, phoned the "hot line" because he wanted to move beyond the artificial: "I felt at that moment that I wanted to talk to a real woman, no more images of any kind, no fast forward, no pause, no magazine pictures. And there was the ad" (33). What Jim gets, though, is a phone conversation and another night of masturbation. On a certain level, in fact, the entire conversation can be read as Jim's private fantasy: "Although nominally divided into two voices, two speakers, the novel gives the impression of one narrative voice characterized by wit,

wordplay, and stylistic virtuosity" (Keskinen 111). Once again, then, we
are given an overt promise of communication, of a mimetic utterance,
that is simultaneously deferred as impossible. Like Fred speaking to
himself through his own intercom at the end of *Lost Highway*, Jim's
conversation in *Vox* can be read as an articulation of an always and
necessarily deferred movement toward the articulation of some "impossible Real": "The long-distance call from Abby's place to Jim's is, in this
sense, a local one, or even an intercom call: Jim attempts to speak to
himself through a thin inside wall—the borderline separating narrative
levels—of the house of fiction" (Keskinen 112).

What I want to stress here is the fact that this "renewalist" reaffirmation is marked by a certain redeployment of postmodernist strategies, a certain *relaxing of the rules* that seems to have resulted in both the
growing relevance of a type of neo-realism and the persistence of narrative strategies that remain outwardly postmodern—or, in other words,
metafictional. As the end of *Adaptation* suggests—that is, the return to
the metafictional framework with which the film began and Kaufman's
realization that he shouldn't adhere blindly to McKee's rules any more
than he should adhere to the postmodern rule that all rules must be
rejected—this period after postmodernism is defined by a renewed willingness to abandon all imperatives, including postmodernism's. Texts
like Baker's thus seem to point to the postmodern "failure" around
which I have been circling since the beginning. As an example of emergent renewalist narratives, Baker's work suggests that postmodernism
"failed" *because* it refused, or was unable, to acknowledge *clearly* that
it ultimately and necessarily reaffirmed the very positivist ideology it
claimed to be refuting.

As I have suggested throughout, emergent narrative forms, in
a manner that parallels late-phase deconstruction, seem to take into
account *outwardly* a certain postmodern failure, or limitation. What
these narrative forms suggest—and what a film like *Adaptation* seems to
expose, or play out—is that the corrosively self-reflexive works of postmodernism were necessarily haunted by the very specter they attempted
to exorcise: the specter of a telos, the specter of positivism, the specter
of humanism. In brief, the very specter we see at work in postmodernism is the very same specter the later Derrida locates in Marxism
and, in turn, deconstruction: a past revenant, or ghost, of "emancipatory and *messianic* affirmation, a certain experience of the promise."
And it seems clear that this current narrative "turn" is marked by an
acceptance of the very spectrality of this particular specter, a ghost that
ultimately and necessarily haunted postmodernism's desire to exorcise all past ideological revenants. As an apparent reappraisal of the

postmodern relationship to the spectral remainder that animated the aesthetic strategy of metafiction, this current movement away from the recent hegemony of postmodern narrative strategies is, in short, the latest attempt to "deal with" the specter of postmodernism—which is, quite simply, the specter of "a still incomplete project of modernity," the essential specter haunting both Marxism *and* deconstruction.

A Conclusion . . . *Perhaps*

One final example. In Toni Morrison's *Beloved*, the concept of the specter—of the ghost, of the repressed—is pivotal. For this reason, *Beloved* can help us to clarify two distinct yet intimately related concepts. On one hand, the text exemplifies a distinctly renewalist aesthetic; its narrative strategies overtly endorse and embrace the ironic spectrality of the mimetic promise. On the other hand, *Beloved*, like *Hamlet*, offers us a very specific model of the specter, a model that speaks to the very narrative in which it is articulated. And it seems more than a mere accident that the spectral negotiation that determines the plot of *Beloved* comes to highlight the distinctly renewalist negotiation that defines the text's overall aesthetic.

Like all of the renewalist texts discussed above, *Beloved* redeploys a series of overtly postmodern stylistic devices. Most obviously, *Beloved* (like Morrison's later novel, *Jazz*) approaches its central animating event—that is, Sethe's protective, yet brutal, slaughter of her child, Beloved—again and again via a spiral-like series of narrative returns. Indeed, the event is recounted several times and from a series of different perspectives. As in O'Brien's texts, this repetition comes to suggest the impossibility of the certainly accurate narrative act, the certainly right narrative decision. However, and as we see in a text like O'Brien's *The Things They Carried*, the event's essential inexplicability (or, rather, the specter's essential spectrality) becomes the very thing that animates the narrative act. Ryan P. McDermott puts it like this:

> The "unspeakable scene(/seen)" of *Beloved* is not only an unwittingly productive critical construction—it is symptomatic of the novel's own desire to break and yet preserve the fungibility of its pervasive silence through the production and reproduction of the image outside of the symbolic order of language. As such, the "unspeakable scene" works a structural device that both appeals to and frustrates our attempts to translate this silence into narrative. (77)

The promise of complete narrative apprehension is made possible by the fact that the event—or rather, the impossible "Real"—continually resists narrative apprehension. We see this paradox—that is, the paradox that the impossibility of the certainly right narrative act allows for the possibility of such an act—in Sethe's own circular attempts to tell her story: "Sethe knew that the circle she was making around the room, him, the subject, would remain one. That she could never close in, pin it down for anybody who had to ask" (163). Like O'Brien's narrators, though, Sethe empathically yields to the belief, however contradictory it may be, that her story and, thus, the reality of her trauma can be made manifest; she yields to the belief that, eventually, she will no longer be haunted by the past. Put differently, and in a manner that speaks to the ethical imperative that defines renewalism, Sethe determinedly and ironically opposes the paralysis of narrative indecision (i.e., the effect of knowing that no finally correct decision is possible) with the certainty of indecision (i.e., the belief that there is, indeed, an absolutely correct decision). This ethics of indecision is doubly stressed via the actual event that Sethe, among others, repeatedly tries to apprehend/understand. The text's emphatic willingness to undergo "the ordeal of indecision" is, in short, mirrored by the impossible decision with which Sethe was faced: to kill her children or to let them be taken as slaves. As deplorable as her ultimate decision might appear *prima facie*, the fact that she makes a decision *at all* can be read as a clear endorsement of the ethical imperative animating the entire text: the ethical imperative that any decision or narrative act *must* endure both aspects of indecision, that any decision *must*, respect both the possibility and the impossibility of the spectral promise.

Of course, this "ethics of indecision"—or rather, this apparent endorsement of the renewalist imperative to respect the specter—is also mirrored by the text's theme of revenants, of ghosts. The narrative, after all, begins with the assertion that Sethe's house is haunted; Sethe and Denver (Sethe's other daughter) live in a house "palsied by the baby's fury at having its throat cut" (5). From the very beginning Sethe and Denver are invested in the possibility of some type of exorcism and/or conjuration. In the initial pages of the text, in fact, we are told that "Sethe and Denver decided to end the persecution by calling forth the ghost that tried them so" (4). What is important to note here is that the desire to call forth (i.e., "to conjure") the spirit is intimately tied to a desire to explain things *once and for all*, to make the baby (Beloved) understand *at last*. "If she'd only come," Sethe asserts, "I could make it clear to her" (4). To begin with, then, Sethe is animated by the promise that the specter can be made manifest and, thus, that the traumatic event can be finally and accurately related.

But, in the beginning at least, this promise is continually deferred and Sethe and Denver continue to be haunted. However, when Paul D, an ex-slave with whom Sethe was once held captive, returns and performs a type of exorcism on the house, Sethe and Denver seem to get their wish. The promise is, in short, fulfilled; and, for a time, everything seems better. The sense we get is that Paul D's presence allows Sethe to repress her trauma, to believe that it's finally over, to believe that it has been reckoned with *at last*. Paul D frees Sethe from her responsibility—from, especially, the responsibility of her decisions both past and present. Not surprisingly, though, and in a manner that speaks to the spectrological argument I have been employing throughout, Paul D's exorcism is followed almost immediately by the manifest appearance of Beloved. The suggestion is that the utter rejection of the ghost's presence is tantamount to an utter rejection of its absence; in either case, the ironic spectrality of the specter is effaced. An exorcism is, after all, always also a form of conjuration. Still, combined with Paul D's presence, Beloved's manifestation as an adult woman seemingly liberates Sethe *once and for all*. However, we are slowly brought to the realization that Beloved's manifestation and, thus, *the absence of the ghost* is a dangerously seductive reality, a reality that slowly and quite necessarily tears the makeshift family apart.

Eventually, both Denver and Sethe begin to sense the dangerous effects of Paul D's exorcism/conjuration; they both seem to realize that the ghost continually promised and opened up certain possibilities *because* those possibilities remained deferred. While Denver admits that her and Sethe's attempts to "reason with the baby ghost . . . got nowhere" and that, in the end, "It took a man, Paul D, to shout it off and take its place for himself," she also comes to realize that "she preferred the venomous baby" (104). Likewise, Sethe begins to lament the loss of the ghost, while simultaneously falling prey to the comfort that Paul D and Beloved seem to offer:

> Alone with her daughter in a haunted house she managed every damn thing. Why now, with Paul D instead of the ghost, was she breaking up? getting scared? needing Baby? The worst was over, wasn't it? She had already got through, hadn't she? With the ghost in 124 she could bear, do, solve anything. Now a hint of what had happened to Halle and she cut out like a rabbit looking for its mother. (97)

Significantly, this troubling train of thought is interrupted by the pleasure of a massage that Sethe is, at the time, receiving from Beloved: "Beloved's fingers were heavenly. Under them and breathing easy, the anguish rolled down. The peace Sethe had come there to find crept into her" (97). Still, and regardless of the apparent comfort that Beloved and Paul D seem to offer, the dangerous absence of the ghost and/as the presence of Beloved becomes increasingly evident; we are even led to believe that Beloved may be intent on harming Sethe. What I want to highlight, though, is the fact that, with Beloved *finally present*, Sethe slowly loses the reason to explain herself, to tell her story, to make (in short) decisions about the representative acts that define her past. Beloved, after all, knows what happened. She was there. She is, we might say, the manifestation of the event itself.

As McDermott suggests, "Beloved's reincarnation can . . . be read as a materialization of the visual trace that eludes appropriation into the sphere of narration—the latter being the condition which makes the visual trace not fully recoverable and consequently outside the bounds of historiographic discourse" (79). This materialization becomes a comforting, if problematic, *presence* for Sethe: "Sethe's own investment in the newly returned Beloved—more pointedly, in Beloved's bodily presence—becomes a way of compensating for the failure of language to account for this lost object" (McDermott 79). I would like to take this suggestion a bit further, though. By finally "compensating for the [necessary] failure" of the narrative act, Beloved's presence—or rather, *the presence of the event itself*—annihilates the possibility of all future narrative acts. Beloved's presence doesn't, as we might expect, exacerbate the weight of Sethe's responsibility—that is, her future responsibility to make narrative decisions about her past; instead, Beloved's presence (like, to a certain extent, Paul D's) strips Sethe of all (narrative) responsibility. Consequently, Beloved's presence strips Sethe of her authority and her control:

> Then the mood changed and the arguments began. Slowly at first. A complaint from Beloved, an apology from Sethe. . . . Wasn't it too cold to stay outside? Beloved gave a look that said, So what? Was it past bedtime, the light no good for sewing? Beloved didn't move; said, "Do it," and Sethe complied. She took the best of everything—first . . . and the more she took, the more Sethe began to talk, to explain, . . . Beloved wasn't interested. . . . Sethe pleaded for forgiveness, counting, listing again and again her reasons . . . (241–42)

Paul D's exorcism and/or conjuration of the specter—for, as we have already seen, the two are ultimately synonymous—leaves Sethe in a state of mythic indecision; she no longer has a reason to get her story right, to tell it *in truth*. The story has become, for all intents and purposes, manifest, and its presence leaves no room for other possible accounts. All Sethe can do is apologize (to Beloved) or forget (with Paul D). Either situation, though, can be read as an effect of the ghost's absence. Without the ghost, without the possibility *and* the impossibility of finally apprehending the moment of Beloved's death, without the possibility *and* the impossibility of forgiveness, Sethe loses both the ability and the need to make decisions about her own story. More simply, Morrison's distinctly renewalist text suggests, via its own narrative strategies and its employment of a specific model of the specter, that without the ghost, without the ironic spectrality of the specter, there is no ordeal of indecision and, thus, no possible decision, no possible responsibility (narrative or otherwise).

This renewalist endorsement of spectrality, or narrative indecision, becomes particularly explicit when, in the concluding portions of the novel, the women in the Sethe's community finally come together to perform what *seems to be* a second and final exorcism. At this point, though, Beloved is no longer the ghost that haunted 124. She has become real: *in the flesh*. For this reason, we should avoid referring to this communal act as an exorcism. If anything, it is the exact opposite of an exorcism. The community seemingly comes together to insist upon Beloved's spectrality, her status as ghost. The women reject her material presence *so as* to reaffirm her possibility *and* her impossibility as a ghost of the past. And while we are told that, afterward, the community "forgot her like a bad dream" (274), it would be a mistake to assume that she is finally expelled. After the community confronts her *presence*, Beloved, as Roger Luckhurst astutely notes, "*remains*" (249). Or better: *her remains* persist. The community reopens the possibility of remembering the dismembered past by performing a ritualized act of forgetting, by *dematerializing* Beloved, by insisting upon her essential spectrality. Once this ritual act is performed, Derridean indecision once again becomes possible. Paul D is told that, "Maybe," Beloved "disappeared," *maybe* she "exploded," *maybe* she is "hiding in the tress waiting for another chance" (264). Once again, no one knows with certainty what happened; and, in the absence of certainty, the process and possibility of making "sense out of the stories" (267) is renewed. By coming together to insist upon her impossibility, the community makes possible the act of making narrative decisions about Beloved (and all the past traumas with which she is associated).

The conclusion of *Beloved* stresses the impossible possibility of exorcising the past *finally*, of remembering *or* forgetting. Because "It was not a story to pass on" the community works to forget Beloved. But, because "This is not a story to pass on," Beloved's spectral "footprints" necessarily continue to "come and go, come and go" (275). The novel thus concludes with an almost audible call to "respect the specter." Even the slippage in this line that repeats *without repeating*—"It was not a story to pass on" *and* "This is not a story to pass on"—is utterly spectral in nature. It demands a reading that can never be settled, or decided upon. One meaning ("to forget") is wholly present only when the other ("to remember") is wholly absent. The condition of absolute meaning is here the condition of its impossibility. As a result, *Beloved* works to "pass on" *and* "pass on" the very specter of a telos that animated postmodernism. On the one hand, Morrison's text accepts, or "passes on," postmodernism's rejection of the modernist compulsion to conjure this specter into being *once and for all*; on the other, *Beloved* clearly moves beyond, or "passes on," the postmodern imperative to utterly deny the possibility of the specter's materiality, its potential as a promise of an ideal future still "to come." *Beloved*, in short, outwardly works to suggest that the impossibility of social justice, authentic experience, and/or true and final decisions need not prevent us from sincerely struggling for such things. What we see, then, as I said above, is that only in the absence of absolutely just decisions (and/or narrative acts) are any decisions (and/or narrative acts) possible.

Put differently and, *perhaps*, in conclusion, *Beloved*'s distinctly renewalist imperative to respect and endure the "ordeal of indecision" is, if we follow Derrida, an ethical call to embrace the spectral contingency of the "perhaps." In *Politics of Friendship*, and while elaborating on the ethical implications of the specter (implications that he began to address overtly in *Specters of Marx*) Derrida spends an entire chapter reading, enumerating, and interpreting Nietzsche's use of the word "perhaps." The question Derrida wants to answer is this: what does this "perhaps" suggest about the possibility and the impossibility of friendship, of an ethical and finally true understanding of the other. Derrida, of course (and while reading Nietzsche's own discussions of friendship alongside the famous Aristotle quote, "0 friends, there are no friends"), comes to suggest that the frequency of the term "perhaps" in Nietzsche's work can be read as symptomatic of a type of promise. This promise is, as are most things for Derrida, twofold. On the one hand, this promise promises the veracity of what has been said while simultaneously rejecting the certainty that a promise typically seems to afford: "there will come, *perhaps*; there will occur, perhaps, the event of that which arrives (*und vielleicht kommt*), and this will be the hour of joy, an hour of birth but also of resurrection" (28). This promise promises, like the ghost that originally haunts Sethe, that the event will become manifest. It promises the absence/manifestation of the ghost, *perhaps*. In terms of Morrison's text, this promise could be said to promise the true narrative representation of the event, *perhaps*. The perhaps thus defers the possibility of the promise while simultaneously opening up, yielding to, hoping for, the possibility that the deferral is only temporary, that "there will occur, perhaps, the event of that which arrives"—that there will occur, that there *can* occur, a finally right decision, a finally right narrative and/or interpretive act. On the other hand, this promise promises the perhaps itself; it promises the possibility that we can, finally, accept the "dangerous" irony of the perhaps: "What is going to come, *perhaps*, is not only this or that; it is at last the thought of the *perhaps*, the *perhaps* itself. The *arrivant* will arrive *perhaps*, for one must never be sure when it comes to *arrivance*; but the *arrivant* could also be the *perhaps* itself, the unheard-of, totally new experience of the *perhaps*. Unheard-of, totally new, that very experience which no metaphysician might yet have dared to think" (*Politics* 29)

For Derrida, the future to come is the future of the perhaps. It is the future of the specter, of that which is *and* is not, that which we know we can never know yet somehow believe we will know . . . *perhaps*. *Perhaps*, then, we might argue, the future is already here and now? Doesn't Derrida, after all, position himself as the philosopher to come? Indeed, Derrida argues for a future of the "perhaps" *as* a philosopher of the perhaps: "the thought of the 'perhaps' *perhaps* engages the only possible thought of the event" (29, my emphasis). Furthermore—and assuming that the above analysis is, to a degree, accurate—are not these narratives *after* postmodernism, are not these narratives of renewalism, narratives of the perhaps? Are these not narratives that seemingly embrace the spectrality of the specter, narratives that embrace the necessary possibility of the impossible? Yet, if this is true—if, that is, the future of the perhaps is now—does it not suggest, quite paradoxically of course, that the *perhaps* is, itself, an impossibility? Does not this apparent claim (and imperative) to achieve the perhaps—to respect, that is, the specter—efface the ironic danger of the perhaps, the ironic danger of the specter's spectrality? Aren't we once again in the domain of certainty; are we not, once again and quite necessarily, forcing the ghost to become manifest/absent? We might argue, in fact, that it is not a simple accident that, in his endorsement of this future of the perhaps, Derrida occasionally drops the "perhaps": "there is no more just category for the future than that of the 'perhaps' " (29). What happened, here, to the perhaps? Why is this promise of the perhaps no longer, itself, a condition of the perhaps, a condition of epistemological doubt? Let me rephrase the question: what is implied by the fact that, when it comes to a renewalist ethics of indecision, a decision is no longer necessary? After all, the suggestion (as we just saw in a text like *Beloved* and as we are seeing, again, via a look at Derrida's later work) seems to be that, when it comes to the ordeal of indecision, we have no decision. The ordeal of indecision *must* be endured:

> The possibilization of the impossible possible must remain at one and the same time as undecidable—and therefore as decisive—as the future itself. What would a future be if the decision were able to be programmed, and if risk [*l'aléa*], the uncertainty, the unstable certainty, the inassurance of the "perhaps," were it not suspended on it at the opening of what comes, flush with the event, within it and with an open heart? (29)

In a claim like this, has not the specter, like Beloved, once again and, perhaps, quite necessarily obstructed us with its apparent manifestation/absence?

What I am trying to suggest by way of a tentative conclusion—a conclusion, *perhaps*, of the "perhaps"—is this: by positioning itself as a narrative/theoretical strategy that no longer feels compelled to reject, as dangerously impossible, the spectral promise that drives all narrative acts, by defining itself as a narrative strategy that no longer insists on any single type of narrative strategy, this emergent discourse of renewalism slips quite necessarily, *perhaps*, into the same spectral trap that lead postmodernism to its apparent demise. The very specter that is seemingly "dealt with" in this shift away from a postmodern stylistic imperative *necessarily* returns at the very moment it is thought to be, finally, placed to rest. Most obviously, this specter continues to haunt the claim that what we are witnessing at the end of postmodernism is "an improvement" that manages to successfully "lay to rest" the spectrally determined imperatives of postmodernism, that manages to bring our mourning to an end. Yet this specter of positivism must always "pass on." Certainly, postmodernism has "given up the ghost." And, *certainly*, it would seem that this ghost has *passed on* to a much more welcoming home, a home of the gamble, a home of the perhaps; but the new imperative to respect the specter, to embrace the dangerous irony of the perhaps—an imperative we see in this emergent fiction, as well as in the later work of theorists like Derrida—suggests that the specter is once again being denied, or *passed on*, that it is once again compelling us in ways we cannot control. In brief, what I think we need to note (especially now, at the swell of this new epistemological tide) is that this spectral relationship does not cease to be a problem—that is, a source of teleologies and/or absolutes—simply because we claim to recognize it, to accept it. It is, I am arguing, *necessarily impossible to respect the specter*. This seems to be implicit in the teleological imperative that we *must* respect the specter, that we *must* endure the ordeal of indecision. For to say this is to locate another *final answer* and thus to deny the impossibility of such a solution—the impossibility that the specter represents in the first place. So, what we begin to see in this strange moment of passing, in this strange and ongoing period of mourning, is the fact that the specter works to produce work, if it works at all, because it compels us to destroy it, to efface its spectrality, to disrespect it *as specter*, to always and forever *pass on it*.

Notes

Chapter One: The Phantom Project Returning

1. I should note that the release of the second edition of *Poetics* coincides (to a certain extent) with Hutcheon's publication of "Postmodern Afterthoughts," an earlier, more condensed, version of the epilogue.

2. A fact, of course, that Hutcheon herself admits: "For decades now, diagnosticians have been pronouncing on its health, if not its demise" (*Politics* 165).

3. For example: Neil Brooks and Josh Toth's *The Mourning After: Attending the Wake of Postmodernism*; José López and Garry Potter's *After Postmodernism: An Introduction to Critical Realism*; Robert Rebein's *Hicks, Tribes and Dirty Realists: American Fiction After Postmodernism*; and Klaus Stierstorfer's *Beyond Postmodernism: Reassessments in Literature, Theory, and Culture*. For the most part, these texts (along with the ones mentioned above) are discussed in detail in chapter 3.

4. Another useful example would be the fairly recent collection of essays, *God, the Gift and Postmodernism*, edited by John D. Caputo. Considered in some detail in the following chapter, this collection aims to examine the way in which recent theoretical shifts (those of Derrida included) have reopened the possibility of discussing religion and god as the ground for ethical reasoning.

5. To be clear: while I find these terms (i.e., "emergent," "dominant," "residual") useful in articulating the dynamics of shifting epistemological configurations, I do not mean them in their strictest sense. That is, I do not use them in same way Williams, as a Marxist critic, does. Rather, I use them in a manner that is more in line with the way they are employed in Jameson's *Postmodernism* or, better, Marianne DeKoven's recent book, *Utopia Limited: The Sixties and the Emergence of Postmodernism*. Like DeKoven, I use these terms to "describe the shift or pivot to the postmodern" (18)—as well as, in my case, *away from* the postmodern—but I use them, as DeKoven does, "without the implications of progress from capitalism to socialism (or of any teleology) that inhere in Williams' Marxist development of [them]" (18).

6. That Olson wholly dissociates the postmodern from the vast period separating Homer and the end of modernism is, perhaps, worth noting. If such a broad period can be associated (however loosely) with the gradual formation and eventual dominance of an enlightenment sensibility, then the fact that Olson's postmodern is overtly opposed to such a period suggests that it is far less removed from our current understanding of the term than we might initially expect. Olson's apparent anticipation of our current sense of the term—an anticipation noted by both Jerome Mazzaro and Hans Bertens—is perhaps further exemplified in an earlier document, a letter to Robert Creeley (dated 9 August 1951). In this letter, Olson seems to suggest that the "post-modern" is the effect of a type of finally completed process of modernization, a type of pervasive globalization: "the post-modern world was projected by two earlier facts—(a) the voyages of the 15th and 16th Century making all the earth a known quantity (thus, geographical quantity absolute); and (b) 19th Century, the machine, leading to (1) the tripling of population and (2) the same maximal as the geographic in communication systems and the reproductive ones" (75).

7. Olson's "post-modern," although never clearly defined, appeared to be a description of a successful fusion of poetic innovation and revolutionary politics "linked to a prophetic history" (12), a form of artistic production akin to that of the prewar avant-garde. It is conceived of as a shift away from the rational humanism that *haunted* the modern movement, yet it remains, to a certain degree (as its similarity to a modernist/heroic avant-garde suggests), *complicit with* modernism, "with the original *Stimmung* of modernism, in an electric sense of the present as fraught with a momentous future" (Anderson 12).

8. In an attempt to be accurate, I should note that this quotation ends "... beginning around 1875." Köhler is in fact arguing—and this is what Bertens is skeptical of—that Olson and Toynbee's construction of postmodernism represents an epistemic shift beginning sometime in the late-nineteenth century. Of course, Bertens is right to suggest that the net has been cast too wide if the beginning of postmodernism is associated with an epistemic break that occurred in the late-nineteenth century. As we've already seen, though, Olson seems to construct the postmodern as a break from an identifiable (even from today's perspective) "modern aesthetic." And, as I suggested above, Toynbee's discussion of a period that attempted to define itself as posthistoric and which was subsequently succeeded by an emergent multinational period of Western civilization might be more important than the accuracy of his terminological applications. Moreover, the fact that both Olson and Toynbee conceive of an epochal rupture in the early 1950s is of considerable more importance than Toynbee's choice of 1875 as the date of *his* post-Modern break.

9. The double genitive is intentional, as it is in the title of Derrida's *Specters of Marx*. This particular specter, as I will attempt to demonstrate, *belongs to* the postmodern period as a unique manifestation; however, it is also ironically, or paradoxically, a repetition, having come (or arrived) from the outside, from *before*, as a *revenant*. This will become clearer as we progress.

10. See also Bertens' discussion of Olson in the more recent *The Idea of Postmodernism: A History*. Here, Bertens considers Olson's possible connec-

tion to Heidegger (and even his anticipation of Derrida): "To free oneself from the straightjacket of rationalistic liberal humanism, Olson proposes what would seem to be a Heideggerian poetic practice that breaks with the western rationalist tradition and its compulsive and arrogant urge to make reality subservient to itself" (21). Nevertheless, Bertens insists that Olson's seemingly Heideggerian theories are much less radical than those of Derrida, even if critics like William Spanos would disagree. In short, according to Bertens, Olson maintains a very traditional poetic sensibility, repeatedly intimating that "the real speaks for itself, and is allowed to do so by the poet who merely functions as a mediator" (21). As I suggest below (as well as in the following chapters), though, this peculiarly "post-modern" return of the real, or "repressed," can be read as a necessary effect of a certain persistent specter. Even the most overtly postmodern rejection of the mimetic impulse is inevitably presented as a *finally* accurate representation of reality. Still, it seems reasonable to say, along with Bertens, that (while close) Olson's "post-modern" is not *quite* "postmodern."

11. Mazzaro's discussion of Olson occurs primarily in the preface to *Postmodern American Poetry*. He argues here (and this is, in part, the portion that Bertens quotes) that, for Olson and Jarrell, "Without the technical language of the structuralists, the formulation of the essential differences between 'modernism' and 'postmodernism' becomes: in conceiving of language as a fall from unity, modernism seeks to restore the original state often by proposing silence or the destruction of language; postmodernism accepts the division and uses of language and self-destruction—much as Descartes interpreted thinking—as the basis of identity" (Mazzaro viii). Of course, this take on Olson is not unique to Mazzaro; as Bertens also notes, Donald Allen and George Butternick, in their introduction to *The Postmoderns: The New American Poetry Revised*, make a similar argument, suggesting that "Olson's postmodernism rebelled against a formalist Modernism" (Bertens 12).

12. Indeed, the above (or some slight variation of it) remains as the dominant take on the distinction between modernism and postmodernism. Take the basic argument of Joseph Conte's *Design and Debris* (2002) as an example: "The postmodern artist expresses an affinity for—rather than an aversion to [as does the modernist artist]—forms of disorder" (8). Still, it is important to point out that Conte's postmillennial desire to stress, or locate, a source of order, or unity (or even a type of ethics), in the postmodern penchant for chaos is representative of a way of thinking that is identifiable with this current epistemological moment *after* postmodernism.

13. As Bertens explains it, Howe lamented the fact that "The postmodern writer must do without heroes and without heroic conflicts; he can only fictionalize the 'malaise' of the 'increasingly shapeless' world he lives in and of his 'increasingly fluid' experience" (13).

14. Howe seems to rely quite heavily on a very traditional, or "liberalist," notion of the subject. Consequently, his "reading" of mass society is heavily inflected by what we might think of as "existential angst." In fact, as Thomas Schaub argues, Howe's sense of a "mass society" seems to be characteristic of a type of postwar liberalism that attempted to distance itself from a prewar liberalism that appeared to be dangerously susceptible to totalitarian

tendencies, tendencies that were (by the end of the war) directly linked to communism. This "neo-liberalism," Schaub suggests, positioned itself in opposition to the apparent positivism and unchecked humanism of a prewar liberalism that "subscribed to 'facile' ideas of progress and 'history' " (7). However, because it struggled to distance itself from communism (and thus totalitarianism), this "revisionist liberalism" increasingly subscribed to distinctly conservative views. In particular, and as we see with Howe, the new liberal becomes increasingly opposed to the masses, or mass culture. Rather than becoming a revolutionary and liberating proletariat, mass society seemed to submit quite happily to totalitarian regimes. The new liberal sees a need to "preserve high culture from the degradations of mass culture" (17). Not surprisingly, then, Howe celebrates individual writers who critique the apparent dissolution of the subject via the dangerous effects of rapid modernization. Arguably, as Schaub seems to suggest, this postwar liberalism can be said to permeate, in one way or another, the majority of postmodern discourse. We might in fact say, if only tentatively, that the revisionist liberalism we see in Howe persists in the high postmodernism of writers like Pynchon and Barth (if not, also, theorists like Rorty and Derrida). Schaub's extended discussion of Barth's *The End of the Road*, a text that I touch upon briefly in chapter 3, seems to suggest just this possibility. See, specifically, chapter 8 in *American Fiction in the Cold War*.

15. Howe names writers like Bernard Malamud, J.D. Salinger, Saul Bellow, and Ralph Ellison. For the most part, critics today would identify such writers as late-modernists—or as writers who, in one way or another, continue a type of modernist tradition. But we must remember that, for Howe, the postmodern, or postwar, experience is to be resisted. Consequently, it is not surprising that Howe's postmodernists are defined by their penchant for nostalgia: "They do not usually write about postwar experience per se: they do not confront it as much as they try to ambush it" (432). In short, Howe's postmodernists are not the postmodernists of today—that is, Barth, Burroughs, Vonnegut, and so on; they are not, that is, defined by their endorsement of a finally POSTmodern (or POST-human, or POST-ideological, or whatever) society.

16. It is perhaps worth noting that Howe's view of the postmodern is not entirely negative. Not only does he celebrate various works of postwar fiction, he suggests that, while the absence of clearly defined social relations results in various aesthetic difficulties, it also creates "new possibilities" (426).

17. Arguably, the claims concerning the death of postmodernism are not as outwardly "apocalyptic" as were the claims regarding the end of modernism; however, as I demonstrate in chapter 3, the arguments surrounding the passing of postmodernism are, like those that surrounded the passing of modernism, inflected by a certain sense that things have finally been, once and for all, *figured out*, or solved. In other words, and as we see (if only briefly) in Hutcheon's epilogue to *The Politics of Postmodernism*, the end of postmodernism is marked by a certain sense of finality, of completion.

18. Of course, we might read Fielder as saying something quite different than this. On one level, a critic like Fiedler seems to be celebrating the fact that the end of modernism—and, thus, the end of modernism's posthistoric

claims—marks a certain return of history; if modernism has been succeeded than the modernist claim that history is over is no longer viable. However, it is important to note that Fiedler, like most of the early advocates of a postmodern period, explicitly identifies postmodernism as an apocalyptic break, as a hitherto unknown period free of the limiting and hegemonic ideologies of a now defunct modernism. So, even if Fiedler sees the postmodern turn as a return to history, such a view remains tied to the assumption that history is finally at an end. Put differently, if somewhat crudely, the assumption that we have *at last* corrected certain false understandings of history is implicitly haunted by the belief that progress is now at an end. Obviously, and as we will see, this same paradox is (necessarily, I might add) at work in the claims regarding the end of postmodernism.

19. That is, Toynbee's discussion of what we would today call modernism highlights the way in which the recent claim regarding the end of postmodernism echoes the claims surrounding the end of modernism. Toynbee's "post-Modern"—as an epoch that claimed to be posthistoric—was ultimately and ironically succeeded by postmodernism proper. The fact that another epoch seems to have arrived at the end of history (or *after the end of modernity*) is thus less surprising than it might seem.

20. For instance, in *Literature Against Itself*, Graff "argues that postmodernism should be seen not as a break with romantic and modernist assumptions but rather as a logical culmination of the premises of these earlier movements, premises not always clearly defined in discussions of these issues" (32).

21. Of course, either argument can be used to explain the apparent fact that postmodernism has become as obsolete—or, rather, as implicated in a still incomplete and historically contingent project—as the epoch that it apparently succeeded. In order to account for the fact that a POST-postmodern, or something *more than* postmodernism, is possible, it would appear that we must view the postmodern *either* as not truly POSTmodern *or* as an unsuccessful version of *a truly* POSTmodern epoch. However, as I suggest below, a simplistic dichotomy such as this is ultimately too limiting.

22. See chapter 2 for a more in-depth discussion of the often contested relationship between poststructuralism and postmodernism.

23. We might think of Derrida's 1966 paper, as well: "Structure Sign and Play in the Discourse of the Humanities." As with "Ends of Man," a certain rupture is announced—the end of a previous mode of representation: "Perhaps something has occurred in the history of the concept of structure that could be called an 'event,' if this loaded word did not entail a meaning which it is precisely the function of structural—or structuralist—thought to reduce or to suspect. But let me use the term 'event' anyway, employing it with caution and as if in quotation marks. In this sense, this event will have the exterior form of a *rupture* and a *redoubling*. . . . Nevertheless, up until the event which I wish to mark out and define, structure—or rather the structurality of structure—although it has always been involved, has always been neutralized or reduced, and this by a process of giving it a center or referring it to a point of presence, a fixed origin" (*Writing and Difference* 278). This rupture, this end

of an ideology of the center, then, echoes the Foucaultian understanding of the latest (that is, the latest in the mid-1960s) epistemic break. Still, unlike Foucault, Derrida—even as early as "Structure, Sign and Play"—hints at a sense of "redoubling" or "repetition" that confounds an entirely simplistic sense of a final and complete rupture, or end. Of course, what Derrida calls here "redoubling" is the hinge upon which my central thesis depends.

24. As I have already suggested, it is, perhaps, this way of rethinking a postmodern anti-historical theory that makes my own thesis a product of an episteme after postmodernism; of course, at this point, the veracity of such a statement remains to be seen.

25. Although discussed in more detail below, this paradox may require some further clarification. For Derrida, the "specter is the future, it is always to come, it presents itself only as that which could come *or come back*" (39, my emphasis). Put simply, the specter is a metaphor of the promise. And, of course, in *Specters*, the specific promise under discussion is the promise of Marxism itself—or, more broadly, the promise of any radical democracy "to come." It is important to note, though, that what makes the effect of the specter so problematic (and yet so productive) is that its arrival *as promise* is always a type of return, a coming back. A ghost, after all, is a "revenant." It is a return of what is already past/passed. But, in returning, the ghost, as in what has "passed," is never the same, just as the ghost of Hamlet is not the King himself. Thus, "what seems to be out front, the future, comes back in advancement from the past, from the back" (10). And it is in this way that Derrida's understanding of the specter is intimately tied to his understanding of mourning and the messianic. The specter promises the future (i.e., the messianic return), a time when the work of mourning (what is past) is over, a time when the specter (of what is past) is finally put to rest. The promise, then, *as specter*, is always a promise from/of the past, but (at the same time and however paradoxically) it always returns *anew*, beckoning us toward the future. A ghost is always, in short, a matter of "Repetition *and* first time" (10).

26. In other words, this specter of the messianic is the promise of emancipation, meaning, justice, and so on. It is the possibility of a "to come" that, according to Derrida, drives (or is the very ground of possibility for) *all* radical discourses. The specter that all radical discourses—and, let's say tentatively at this point, *all* epistemological *re*configurations—can never, *must* never, permanently exorcise, is thus, as Werner Hamacher puts it, "The messianic eschatology underlying every fundamentally critical thought, every longing, and every one of the simplest statements" (167–68).

27. What I am calling an aporia, Derrida would probably call the secret that defines an inheritance, the impossibility of its apprehension or final "conjuring": "If the readability of a legacy were given, natural, transparent, univocal, if it did not call for and at the same time defy interpretation, we would never have anything to inherit from it" (*Specters* 16). The very spectrality of the inheritance, its incomprehensible uniqueness, is the very condition of its function as a legacy. And while it is impossible to conjure fully—and, "to conjure," here, suggests both to call into being and "to exorcise" (*Specters*

48)—it is the legacy's power to compel us to attempt conjuration that is its most important characteristic.

28. The first line of the *Communist Manifesto*: "A spectre is haunting Europe—the spectre of Communism" (473).

29. See pages 40–48 in *Specters of Marx* for a more complete discussion of the double meaning of "to conjure."

30. For Derrida, this is a very dangerous impulse. It is on this point that Derridean ethics become most explicit. Derrida is insistent that certain specters of Marxism need to be abandoned, while the one I have been discussing must be inherited. Marxism's refusal to temper its own teleological assumptions is, for Derrida, a result of a spectral compulsion that needs to be avoided in the future: "Marx continues to want to ground his critique or his exorcism of the spectral simulacrum in an ontology. It is a—critical but pre-deconstructive—ontology of presence as actual reality and as objectivity. This ontology means to deploy the possibility of dissipating the phantom, let us venture to say again of conjuring it away as representative consciousness of the subject, of bringing this representation back to the world of the labour, production, and exchange, so as to reduce it to its conditions" (170).

31. For this reason, as Derrida puts it, "Haunting belongs to the structure of every hegemony" (37).

32. "Discursive" because we can understand Marxism, like deconstruction, as a discourse—that is, as a discursive effect of a given episteme, or epistemological configuration. And, of course, while Marxism appears to be a discourse of a modern episteme, deconstruction aligns nicely with postmodernism.

33. Such an argument, in fact, wouldn't be far removed, if it is removed at all, from Foucault's claim that the modern episteme is defined by the birth of the subject.

34. See Hassan's *The Postmodern Turn*, 91.

35. As Jameson argues in *Postmodernism: Or, The Cultural Logic of Late Capitalism*, "What is meant in the specifically architectural context, is that where the now more classical high-modernist space of a Corbusier or a Wright sought to differentiate itself radically from the fallen city fabric in which it appeared—its forms thus dependant on an act of radical disjunction from its spatial context (the great *pilotis* dramatizing separation from the ground and safeguarding the novum of the new space)—postmodernist buildings, on the contrary, celebrate their insertion into the heterogeneous fabric of the commercial strip and the motel and fast-food landscape of the postsuperhighway American City" (63). Jameson's prime example of postmodern architecture is, of course, John Portman's Bonaventure hotel. Jameson focuses on Portman's building because of the way in which its exterior walls of reflecting glass mirror the rather low-class area in which it is located; in this way, it blends into its surroundings and does not stand out as a type of heroic monument. For Jameson, postmodern buildings "no longer attempt, as did the masterworks and monuments of high modernism, to insert a different, a distinct, and elevated, a new Utopian language into the tawdry and commercial sign system of the surrounding city, but rather they seek to speak that very language, using its lexicon and syntax" (39).

If Jameson's argument—which is, in reality, based on an enormous glass building that looms above a slum-like area—seems somewhat unconvincing, other
useful discussions include the entire fourth chapter of Jameson's *Postmodernism*
as well as Charles Jencks, *The Language of Post-Modern Architecture* and Robert
Venturi et al.'s *Learning From Las Vegas.*

36. The fact that, ultimately, postmodernism seemed to fail in this endeav-
or—that it seemed to find itself occupying the newly defined position of elite
cultural production—is, to a certain degree, the focus of chapter 3. We might
say, at this point, though, that this apparent failure can be read as an inevitable
effect of postmodernism's spectral compulsion.

37. See Foucault's reply to the various detractors of *The Order of Things*
in "What Is an Author?"

38. The shift that I'm attempting to highlight—from a modernist tendency to ontologize the specter to a postmodernist tendency to abandon
the possibility of ontology altogether—is, to a degree, noted by Bertens. For
Bertens, "ontological uncertainty is absolutely central" (46) to postmodernism.
The suggestion seems to be that the distinction between modernism and postmodernism is marked by the presence or absence of an ontologizing impulse:
"Whereas the Modernists sought to defend themselves against their own awareness of cosmic chaos, of the impossible fragility of any 'center' they might
perceive, the Postmodernists have accepted chaos and live in fact in a certain
intimacy with it. This Postmodernist recognition of the final demise of all
Authority, of all higher discourse, of all centers, leads to an acceptance of chaos
and sometimes even to a mystical attunement with a chaotic universe" (28).
From a spectrological perspective, Bertens' take on the modernist attempt to
defend against an apparently chaotic universe seems to anticipate my claim
that modernism is defined by "an *ontological* treatment of the spectrality of
the ghost." Moreover, the suggestion that postmodernism embraced a type of
"mysticism" can be reread as a description of the postmodern refusal to *believe*
in the possible materiality of the specter.

39. In either case, then, we must struggle necessarily to, as Derrida puts it,
"distinguish between the analysis that denounces magic and the counter-magic
that it still risks being" (*Specters* 47). More simply, in either case (modernism
or postmodernism), we can locate a certain faith in magic, or the ability to
"conjure" *once and for all*, that inevitably frustrates, while simultaneously animating, any attempt to exorcise all traces of past magics or ideological illusions. In
both epistemological reconfigurations—modernism *and* postmodernism—one
side of the spectral equation is denied. In modernism, the specter's immateriality is denied; in postmodernism, its materiality. This impulse to reject the
spectrality of the specter is, as I have already suggested, the most essential
effect of the specter. And, as I demonstrate in chapter 3, the specter persists
after postmodernism—or, rather, its ironic spectrality is once again and necessarily rejected. Indeed, in the case of this *re*configuration after postmodernism
(which is, perhaps, best represented by the late-Derridean theory of specters
that I have employed as a guiding framework) we are confronted with another attempt to solve the problem of the specter—this time by accepting the

specter's spectrality *once and for all*. This is, as we will see, the inevitable telos of late-deconstruction, or deconstruction *after postmodernism*.

40. In *Language as Symbolic Action*, for example, Burke claims that "even something so 'objectively there' as behavior must be observed through one or another kind of *terministic screen*, that directs the attention in keeping with its nature" (*Symbolic* 49). The suggestion is that, because it is not possible to account for everything at once (or, for that matter, *once and for all*), we are forced to employ and embrace certain necessarily limiting discursive perspectives, or "terministic screens," so as to organize and/or understand "reality." What is of particular interest, though, is Burke's claim that, "any such screen necessarily directs the attention to one field rather than another" (*Symbolic* 50). For this reason, Burke comes to describe these necessary "screens" as mystifications, mystifications that can become dominant (or "ultimate") in their absolute exclusion, or rejection, of all other possible "screens," or discourses.

41. The concept of "Mystification" is discussed at length in Burke's *A Rhetoric of Motives*. Burke points to both Hegelianism and Marxism as examples of "mystifications." For Burke, Marxism works to demystify Hegelianism: "instead of some generally human motive, such as 'the essence of mankind,' Marx stresses the specifically *class* nature of ideologies. And the imputing of universal or generic motives is then analyzed as a concealment of specific motives (hence, 'mystification')" (110). However, Burke's point is that any dominate discourse, or terministic screen, becomes (after a process of apparent demystification) a new form of mystification. Indeed, Burke goes on to compare Marxism to the mystifying rhetoric of providence employed by Cromwell: "there is a very close parallel between both Cromwellian and Marxist appeal to 'necessity'; for any ultimate terms of motivation must, by their very nature as 'high abstractions,' omit important ingredients of motivation. The general statement of historical motives in terms of dialectical materialism is as 'mystifying' as any such statement in terms of 'Providence'—for in both, all reference to minute administrative situations is omitted. In either language, the bureaucratic, administrative details are 'spiritualized.' As regards the pragmatic operations of production and government, the treatment of conditions in terms of 'necessity' is as 'mystifying' when the necessity is identified with the inevitable laws of history as when it is identified with the will of Providence manifesting itself through such laws" (114).

42. Habermas attributes the weakening of this spirit to the neoconservative attempt to misconstrue the effects of societal modernization—the progress of capitalism, industrialization and individualism—with the subversive effects of cultural modernity. According to neoconservatives like Daniel Bell, or so Habermas suggests, the temperament of cultural modernity "unleashes hedonistic motives irreconcilable with the discipline of professional life in society" ("Incomplete" 5)—that is, the protestant work ethic. The neoconservatives blame cultural modernity for what, according to Habermas, is really (for the most part) an effect of societal modernization: "The neoconservative does not uncover the economic and social causes for the altered attitudes towards work, consumption, achievement and leisure" ("Incomplete" 6). But these attitudes,

Habermas argues, "are rooted in deep seated reactions against the process of *societal* modernization" ("Incomplete" 6). Habermas, though, does not want cultural modernity to be viewed as a simple effect of societal modernization. Instead, he wants to reassert its own autonomous program, a program that is antithetical to societal modernization but also troubled by its own aporias. These aporias, generated by cultural modernity's attempt to successfully recast the aims of the Enlightenment, are the very reason, or pretence, for the various—in Habermas' opinion, conservative—positions that "either call for a postmodernity, or recommend a return to some form of premodernity or which throw modernity radically overboard" (7).

43. Habermas seems to suggest that all "poststructuralists" are "young conservatives" who "claim as their own the revelations of a decentered subjectivity, emancipated from the imperatives of work and usefulness" (13). From Habermas' perspective, this "line" of theorists—a line that, in France, "leads from Bataille via Foucault to Derrida" (14)—works to "justify an irreconcilable anti-modernism" (13). Habermas, of course, doesn't outwardly identify these theorists as "poststructuralists"; however, besides Bataille, who may very well be viewed as a precursor to poststructuralism proper, Habermas' list of young conservatives can be safely read as a list of poststructuralists.

44. See Habermas' "Modern and Postmodern Architecture," in which he attempts to account for the reaction against modernist architecture, arguing that it was at least partly due to the fact that such architecture overestimated the possibility of actualizing the promise of a utopia that animated it in the first place. Quite simply, Habermas argues, "it had readily allowed itself to be overburdened" (325). The idea being that any stringently actualized ideal will ultimately fail to account for the multiplicity and diversity of possible social configurations. According to Anderson, this argument is a recurrence of "the schema traced by the Frankfurt address, derived from the same paralysed dualism set by Habermas' theory of communication action: inviolable systems and inoperative life-worlds" (43).

45. It is, perhaps, important to note that *The Postmodern Condition* was published (in French) in 1979, one year before Habermas' Frankfurt Address, but several years after (and apparently as a type of response to) Habermas' *Legitimation Crisis*. Although most tend to read the Frankfurt Address as a response to *The Postmodern Condition*, Anderson argues convincingly that "it was probably written in ignorance of the latter" (37).

46. See Jameson's Foreword to *The Postmodern Condition*, specifically viii.

47. While attempting to counter Lyotard's later claim (in *Postmodern Fables*) that only narratives of emancipation can be considered grand narratives, Anderson argues that "Nothing in Lyotard's original account of metanarratives confined them to the idea of emancipation—which was only one of the two modern discourses of legitimation he sought to trace" (34). A close reading of *The Postmodern Condition*, though, seems to validate Lyotard's claim (as one might expect, it being Lyotard's work and all). Indeed, Lyotard clearly suggests that a theme of emancipation is an integral characteristic of a metanarrative—whether that narrative is the story of physical human eman-

cipation, as it is in Marxism, or the history of some type of absolute spirit, as it is in German idealism.

48. Of course, to a certain extent, Lyotard comes to recognize, and overtly embrace, this problem. As he suggests in "Rewriting Modernity," postmodernism, which includes his own discussions of the term, can be defined as an ongoing attempt to rewrite, or *write beyond*, modernity: "If we understand 'rewriting' modernity in this way, like seeking out, designating and naming the hidden facts that one imagines to be the source of the ills that ail one, i.e. as a simple process of remembering, one cannot fail to perpetuate the crime, and perpetuate it anew instead of putting an end to it. Far from really rewriting it, supposing that to be possible, all one is doing is writing again, and making real, modernity itself. The point being that writing it is always rewriting it" (28). The postmodern is thus the promise that animates the rewriting of modernity; it is the spectral promise that such a rewriting will be *finally* successful. However, to believe that such a promise will be, or has been, fulfilled—to believe that the postmodern will, or has, arrived *once and for all*—is to slip (back) into the hegemonic confines of another grand narrative. In a manner that seems to anticipate a theorist like Žižek, then—or, put differently, in a manner that anticipates a mode of thinking *after* postmodernism—Lyotard turns to the psychoanalytic process as a way of accounting for the always deferred but necessarily incessant desire to finally apprehend a certain (we might say, spectral) lure: "Postmodernity is not a new age, but a rewriting of some of the features claimed by modernity, and first of all modernity's claim to ground its legitimacy on the project of liberating humanity as a whole through science and technology. But as I have said, that rewriting has been at work for a long time now, in modernity itself" (34). Or rather, as Lyotard suggests in "Note on the Meaning of 'Post-,' " it is a dangerous mistake to assume that the " 'post-" of postmodernism . . . indicates something like a conversion: a new direction from a previous one" (76). Such thinking, Lyotard argues, "is in fact a way of forgetting or repressing the past, that is, repeating it and not surpassing it" (76). Ultimately, though (and as I suggest above), Lyotard seems to find himself perpetuating the very "crimes" he wishes to avoid. Indeed, he seems unable to avoid "repeating the myth" that we can "surpass," or break with, the past; to do so, Lyotard seems to repeatedly suggest, we need merely to stop believing that we can.

49. While discussing Lyotard's more recent *Postmodern Fables*, Anderson makes a similar argument. According to Anderson, Lyotard's postmodern fable ultimately fails in its attempt to evade becoming another metanarrative. In fact, Anderson argues, Lyotard's fable becomes as much a story of emancipation as "the legitimating narrative whose obituary Lyotard had set out to write" (35).

50. As Lyotard puts it, "A self does not amount to much, but no self is an island; each exists in a fabric of relations that is now more complex and mobile than ever before. Young or old, man or woman, rich or poor, a person is always located at 'nodal points' of specific communication circuits, however tiny these may be. Or better: one is always located at a post through which various kinds of messages pass" (*Postmodern* 15).

51. Huyssen, in *After the Great Divide*, makes an argument similar to the one proposed. See, specifically, 134–44.

52. For example, in *Postmodernism*, Jameson's discussion of the postmodern schizoid has several interesting "omissions." Initially—that is, in "Postmodernism and Consumer Society"—Jameson argues that the postmodern schizoid "is *condemned* to live an eternal present . . . , a by no means pleasant experience" (137, my emphasis). By the time he publishes *Postmodernism*, though, this same passage has been altered significantly. As a portion of the first chapter of *Postmodernism*, his discussion of schizophrenia takes on a notably positive tone—words like "condemned" are removed altogether and there is no longer a sense that postmodern schizophrenia is, necessarily, an unpleasant experience. In fact, Jameson's virtually celebratory tone in *Postmodernism* has garnered the condemnation of leftist critics like David Harvey. "In reading Jameson's account of schizophrenia[,]" Harvey suggests, "it is hard not to impute euphoric qualities to the hallucinogenic rush of intoxicating experience behind the surface appearance of anxiety and neurosis. But . . . Jameson's selective quotations from the autobiography of a schizophrenic girl eliminate the terror that attaches to her unreality states, making it all seem like a well-controlled LSD trip rather than a succession of states of guilt, lethargy, and hopelessness coupled with anguish and sometimes tremendous dislocation" (351–52). Ultimately, though, Harvey misses the point. By attacking the view that the postmodern symptom of schizophrenia is a possibly positive state of being, Harvey seems to forget that Jameson's concept of schizophrenia is removed (via Lacan and Deleuze) from the much more negative experience of clinical schizophrenia.

53. For instance, as Jameson argues, "Utopia is a spatial matter that might be thought to know a potential change in fortunes in so spatialized a culture as the postmodern; but if this last is as dehistorized and dehistorizing as I sometimes claim here, the synaptic chain that might lead the Utopian impulse to expression becomes harder to localize. Utopian representations knew an extraordinary revival in the 1960s" (xvi).

54. This question is dealt with more completely in the third chapter. While tracing the specter of postmodernism (as it passed from a narrative stylistic intent on ostentatiously denying the possibility of mimesis to an emergent stylistic that re-embraces the possibility, or *the always deferred promise*, of mimesis) I argue that the postmodern movement toward paralysis and solipsistic silence was continually and necessarily deferred by a spectral (or utopian) impulse to repeatedly articulate such movement *as progress*.

55. After all, Jameson's *Postmodernism* arguably marks the beginning of the end of postmodernism as an epistemological dominant, its final consolidation into a confirmed canon and a defined set of cultural assumptions. Or, put differently, Jameson's text can be said to mark the moment when postmodernism's dominance becomes hegemonic and untenable. As I point out in the following chapters, the very socioeconomic symptoms now associated with high postmodernism (the cold war, the Reagan administration, etc.) are over by 1989. It's fair to say, then, that by 1991 (when Jameson's text is published)

the cultural production that was seemingly married to certain socioeconomic manifestations had also reached a point of saturation and (thus) decline and/ or dissolution. In short, Jameson's text seems to arrive just as a new, or "emergent," epistemological configuration is able to appear on the horizon.

Chapter Two: Spectral Circumventions (of the Specter)

1. See, for instance, Rajan's recent book, *Deconstruction and the Remainders of Phenomenology*, in which she "uncovers" latent elements of phenomenology in the deconstructive project, a project that she associates with a broad range of "poststructural" (or even, "structural") texts (i.e., texts that both predate and run contemporaneously with Derrida's more overt articulation of "deconstruction"). Rajan's book considers "the 'fragments' of phenomenology that produce deconstruction and continue to disconcert both deconstruction and its permutation into poststructuralism" (23). In a manner that seems to anticipate my own claim that poststructuralism (and, or *as*, deconstruction) can be read as a postmodern discourse that is haunted by a still incomplete project of modernity, a certain utopian desire, Rajan suggests that the project of deconstruction betrays symptoms of a phenomenological discourse that is still "unfinished." Similarly, Gasché (whom I discuss in more detail below), seeks to reestablish a "relation, however critical, between Derrida's work and structuralism and phenomenology" (4).

2. As I noted in the previous chapter, Habermas resists postmodernism because it "gives in" to the hegemony of societal modernization; it interrupts, by abandoning or denying, the "still incomplete project of modernity" that sustained the possibility of critique and political intervention. From this perspective, postmodernism should be rejected because it goes too far in its denial of modernist assumptions—that is, the remnants of an Enlightenment project (or, what Norris would call, post-Kantian idealism). Harvey puts it like this: "postmodernism, with its emphasis upon the ephemerality of *jouissance*, its insistence upon the impenetrability of the other, its concentration on the text rather than the work, its penchant for deconstruction bordering on nihilism, its preference for aesthetics over ethics, takes matters too far. It takes them beyond the point where any coherent politics are left, while that wing of it that seeks a shameless accommodation with the market puts it firmly in the tracks of an entrepreneurial culture that is the hallmark of reactionary neoconservatism" (116). What is worth noting here is that critics like Habermas, Norris, and Harvey would like us to condemn postmodernism for the very same reason that Huyssen would have us reject poststructuralism: it is complicit with the hegemonic processes of societal modernization. The very possibility of these two contrary positions suggests that postmodernism, like poststructuralism, needs to be defined by its absolute rejection of, *as well as* its complete complicity with, the project of modernity. As I suggested in the previous chapter, the Enlightenment assumptions that permit, or animate, the possibility of critique are necessarily locatable in the very discourse(s) that claim to reject

them. At the very moment that he identifies the source of poststructuralism's teleological tendencies to be a latent complicity with modernism and, in turn, celebrates postmodernism for its *progressive* ability to abandon that complicity, Huyssen inadvertently and unknowingly relocates that same complicity within postmodernism. In short, and as I point out below, the fact that Huyssen can make the argument he does puts into question the grounds for a leftist rejection of postmodernism while it simultaneously reaffirms the apparent connection between postmodernism and poststructuralism.

3. In a manner that anticipates Kristeva's more psychoanalytically inflected discussion of the genotext, Barthes' *Text* is understood as the expression of "a serial movement of disconnections, overlappings, variations" (*Image* 158). The *Text*, as "tissue of quotations" (*Image* 146), announces the subject's reality as the unstable focal point of a multiplicity of intersecting discursive traces. For Barthes, like Kristeva (in her own way), the "*more* plural the text" (*S/Z* 10), the *more* its meaning becomes contingent upon its reading, the *more its writing is its reading*. Once again, then, textual criteria is reestablished; ostentatious plurality and the evasion of prior categories of classification—including categories of good and bad, avant-garde and classic—becomes the determining factor of a *Text*: "What constitutes the Text is . . . its subversive force in respect of the old classifications. How do you classify a writer like Georges Bataille? Novelist, poet, essayist, economist, philosopher, mystic? The answer is so difficult that literary manuals generally prefer to forget about Bataille who, in fact, wrote texts, perhaps continuously one single text" (*Image* 157).

4. Jameson makes a similar point while discussing Paul de Man: "It is certain that DeMan's [sic] form of deconstruction can be seen as a last-minute rescue operation and a salvaging of the aesthetic—even a defense and valorization of literary study and a privileging of specifically literary language—at the moment in which it seemed to disappear without a trace. This he first secured through a strategic redefinition of the concept of a *text*, which is now restricted to apply only to those writings that 'deconstruct themselves,' to speak loosely" (*Postmodernism* 251). As with Barthes and Kristeva, de Man needs to be read within a larger "poststructural/postmodern" context. Indeed, as Jameson's look at de Man suggests, and as I attempt to demonstrate below via a discussion of "early" deconstruction, poststructuralism should be read "against a larger context in which it offers the spectacle of an incompletely liquidated modernism" (255). As with (and however paradoxical it may sound) postmodernism, "the positions and arguments [of poststructuralism] are 'postmodern' . . . even if the conclusions are not" (255). Consequently, no matter how much someone like Christopher Norris would like to label some (Baudrillard, de Man, Rorty, etc.) nihilistically postmodern—while praising others (Derrida, Habermas, etc.) for their perpetuation of certain Enlightenment, or modern, ideals—the fact is that certain remainders of the critical project of modernity necessarily motivate and thus connect all radical discourses *since* modernism.

5. A good number of "poststructuralists" do not limit themselves to discussions of modernist cultural production: Barthes (in *Mythologies*) talks about everything from "The World of Wrestling" to "The Face of Garbo"; Foucault is

quite fond of de Sade (among others); and Derrida has a strange tendency to discuss Plato, Rousseau, and Kant. According to Huyssen's logic, we would have to call Derrida an Enlightenment philosopher when reading *Of Grammatology* (or *Truth in Painting*) and a Classical philosopher when reading "Plato's Pharmacy." After all, Derrida seems to be as critical with Rousseau in *Grammatology* as he is with Lévi Strauss (the "modernist"). Of course, this is not to suggest that modernist ideals do not have a tendency to return in poststructuralist discourse, that there isn't at times a certain "unmasked" desire for elitist categories of aesthetic distinction in contemporary theory; these "returns" are, in fact, the very thing I want to stress.

6. As I demonstrate below, a critic like Christopher Norris would wholeheartedly agree that, unlike Derrida or Habermas, Baudrillard is unfortunately a postmodernist. For Norris, Baudrillard's denial of all post-Kantian *revenants*—that is, his "drive to extend the aesthetics (i.e. the realm of imaginary representations) to the point of collapsing every last form of ontological distinction or critical truth-claim" ("What's Wrong" 23)—speaks to his postmodern, or neopragmatic, attitude, an attitude that Norris repeatedly blames Richard Rorty (as well as Stanley Fish and, to a lesser degree, Lyotard) for disseminating.

7. While most tend to read his work as a "celebration," if not a fullfledged promotion, of the nihilism of postmodern "hyperreality" and "simulation," I would argue that Baudrillard—like all poststructuralists, or (as I'd like to begin considering them) postmodern "deconstructionists"—is motivated to critique (which is to say, "to write" *at all*) by a certain nostalgia for the past and, more importantly, a certain hope for a future "to come." Of course, it is not within the scope of my project to consider the spectral impulses animating every postmodern discourse, but I'd like to suggest that Baudrillard's various attempts, as in the seminal "Precession of Simulacra," to distinguish a postmodern period of hyperreality from a period in which "the real" was still a possibility speaks to his, somewhat Habermasian, sense of historical deterioration. And while one could argue that Baudrillard's work becomes more and more "aesthetic"—or, as someone like Rorty would suggest, more and more "privately ironic"—even works as late as *The Illusion of the End* betray a certain *condemnation* of the present. For instance, while discussing the way in which current "historical" events have become predetermined by the inescapable economy of postmodern "mediation," Baudrillard asserts that, "In these conditions, such events, which are nonetheless important, have the strange aftertaste of something that has already happened before, something unfolding retrospectively—an aftertaste that does not bode well for a meaningful future" (19). The question we need to ask is why Baudrillard, the most postmodern of all postmodernists, would bother questioning the possibility of a "meaningful" future. As Baudrillard has admitted, and contrary to popular opinion, to point out the hyperreality of postmodern culture, "the dilution of history as event . . . , isn't to believe in nothing any more, . . . but to register this curving back of history and to try and thwart its lethal effects" (*Paroxysm* 8). On a certain level, then, Baudrillard should be read—along with, as we will see, Derrida and even Rorty—as a participant in what he identifies in *Illusion* as the

"Stealth Agency": "The aim of the agency was precisely to set up against this simulation a radical desimulation or, in other words, *to lift the veil on the fact of events not taking place*. And thus to make itself secret and enigmatic in their image, to get through to a certain void, a certain non-meaning, by contrast with the media, which are frantic to plug all the gaps" (15).

8. Indeed, as I suggest below, and in line with someone like Rajan, we might very well argue that poststructuralism can be understood more generally as a type of postmodern, and/or linguistically inflected "permutation" of, deconstruction.

9. Of course, we might wonder here to whom Huyssen is referring. Not only is it unclear what "postmodernists" are engaged in this radical reconsideration of the subject, Huyssen seems to have a very partial list of "poststructuralists" in mind. Although he does admit that Kristeva has done some work in terms of questioning modes of subjectivity, he seems to be unaware, or in denial, of Foucault's various attempts to theorize modes of subject-formation. By focusing solely on "What Is an Author?," Huyssen fails to address, for example, Foucault's more sustained and subtle discussions of disciplining and subject-formation in *Discipline and Punish* (which are, moreover, direct developments of Althusser's theories of interpellation). As well, for one reason or another, Huyssen does not consider Lacan's work in texts like "The Mirror Stage" as a useful rethinking, and "re-inscription," of questions of subjectivity. In fact, Huyssen completely fails to recognize the fact that poststructuralism rarely, if ever, refutes the importance of subject position. Certainly, poststructuralists reject the possibility of a cohesive or self-identical subject; but only the most naïve of readers would fail to notice that poststructuralists are very much concerned with who is speaking and when. For example, Derrida (albeit, post-1984) makes various appeals to his "French-Algerian" subject-position.

10. Of course, such a definition of "poststructuralism" (and thus deconstruction) suggests that deconstruction somehow predates both postmodernism and poststructuralism. While it is beyond the scope of this project, such a suggestion should not be simply dismissed. As we see in the work of Rajan, deconstruction is not limited to Derrida, postmodernism, or poststructuralism. The questions I would ask (while deferring them for another time) are: how do different discursive/epistemic permutations affect the manner in which deconstruction *works* (if "works" is even the correct word)? How closely aligned is a (basically) "transhistorical" deconstructive project to what we have been calling a "project of modernity"—or, even (for that matter), the logic of the specter? To a degree, I suppose (and if only indirectly), these questions are worked out in the following pages.

11. Of course, this not to say that Rorty's pragmatism is the defining characteristic of postmodernism; the pragmatism Rorty endorses needs to be read, rather, as symptomatic of postmodernism *generally*. As we saw in the previous chapter, postmodernism, at its peak, was defined as a complete repudiation of bourgeois liberalism and/or humanism. That is, postmodernism is identifiable, if it is identifiable *at all*, as a rejection of naïve—which is to say, from a postmodern perspective, unironic—views of the subject. Consequently, a person would

be, to a certain extent, correct to argue that Rorty's celebration of the "post-modern bourgeois liberal" frustrates any attempt to align Rorty's pragmatism with postmodernism *as a cultural dominant.* Still, we need to remember that Rorty's "postmodern bourgeois liberal" is *not* the same thing as a prepostmod-ern liberal humanist. Rorty's liberal is celebrated because "she" has a distinctly ironic understanding of the subject. On a certain level, then, Rorty's terms (i.e., "bourgeois" and "liberal") are misleading; we might, in fact, say that Rorty employs them simply *to be difficult,* to seem brazen and unsympathetic to radi-cal or utopian rejections of current sociopolitical structures. Ultimately, then (and this is the point I am trying to make above), Rorty's take on pragmatism and the "postmodern bourgeois liberal" is representative of a broad range of postmodern discourse. At the same time, though, and as I already suggested, there is some accuracy to the claim that Rorty's "liberal" is, if only latently, very much tied to a past tradition of humanism and political moderateness. However, and as I explain more fully via a discussion of postmodern writers (like Pynchon) in chapter 3, latent "liberalism" such as this can be read as an effect of the very specter I have been examining throughout.

12. As we will see, there is a certain amount of "irony" here. Rorty doesn't like the idea of mixing the private with the public, yet he views "liberal ironists" (i.e., those who refuse to make public claims) as "exemplars." In other words, he seems to point implicitly toward the "didactic" function of "ironism": liberal ironists teach us (the public) that the best thing we can do (for the public) is understand that private vocabularies, or modes of understanding, cannot be applied to the public.

13. As Rorty puts it, "ironists theorists like Hegel, Nietzsche, Derrida, and Foucault seem . . . invaluable in our attempt to form a private self-image, but pretty much useless when it comes to politics" (83).

14. For Rorty, the *ideal* "liberal ironist" is always a "she."

15. In other words, "There is no reason the ironist cannot be liberal, but she cannot be a 'progressive' and 'dynamic' liberal in the sense in which metaphysicians sometimes claim to be" (*CIS* 91).

16. By way of clarifying my use of the term "propositional"—and, thus, its specific function in Rorty's discussions of Derrida—it might be useful to quote from one of Rorty's footnotes in *Contingency, Irony and Solidarity.* While address-ing the work of John D. Caputo, Rorty claims that "[Caputo] is wrong in saying that my view, or Derrida's, ensures that we 'get no further than propositional discourse.' All that I (or, as far as I can see, Derrida) want to exclude is the attempt to be nonpropositional (poetic, world-disclosing) and at the same time claim that one is getting down to something primordial—what Caputo calls 'the silence from which all language springs' " (CIS 123, n4).

17. See, for example, chapter 3, "Limited Think: How Not to Read Derrida," in Norris' *What's Wrong with Postmodernism?* In this chapter, Norris actively resists John Ellis' claim, in *Against Deconstruction,* that deconstruction simply reinscribes itself within the metaphysical, and binary, discourse it claims to critique.

18. See Irene Harvey's *Derrida and the Economy of Différance.*

19. In *What's Wrong with Postmodernism?*, Norris is concerned specifically with the negative claims, concerning Derrida and deconstruction, that Habermas makes in *The Philosophical Discourse of Modernity*.

20. Of course, what I am attempting to do (and as should be clear from my discussion of Lyotard in the previous chapter) is very similar. However, I think Norris is wrong to separate deconstruction from postmodernism/poststructuralism. The "crucial respects" in which deconstruction fails to be (completely) "counter-enlightenment" are similar, if not the very same, "crucial respects" in which postmodernism has never been totally "counter-enlightenment."

21. Take, for instance, Rorty's assertion that "all that supposedly deep stuff about the primordiality of the trace in Derrida's earlier work looks like a young philosophy professor, still a bit unsure of himself, making quasi-professional noises" ("Response" 41).

22. On various occasions, in fact, Derrida makes reference to the necessity of what might be understood as a "transcendental lure." For instance, in *Positions*, and while discussing his claim that language is "expression," Derrida notes that "The representation of language as 'expression' is not an accidental prejudice, but rather a kind of structural lure, what Kant would have called a transcendental illusion" (33). Put more simply, the possibility of representing language *as such* is an illusion, a *necessary* illusion. As Derrida explains in another context, the experience of signification, in which the signifier "seems to erase itself or to become transparent, in order to allow the concept to present itself as what it is, referring to nothing other than its presence[,] . . . is a lure, but a lure whose necessity has organized an entire structure, or an entire epoch" (22). The lure can be understood as the promise of presence; it is what compels us to move, to deconstruct. However, the very thing that entices us about the lure (i.e., the possibility of the transcendental signified, of full presence) is the very thing that threatens to close off the possibility of actualizing the lure. The lure is (determined by) the logic of differance, the logic of supplementarity. We might in fact argue that, as lure, the supplement's "economy exposes and protects us at the same time according to the play of forces and the differences of forces. Thus, the supplement is dangerous in that it threatens us with death. . . . Pleasure itself, without symbol or suppletory, that which would accord us (to) pure presence itself, if such a thing were possible, could only be another name for death" (*Grammatology* 155). The lure promises, and represents the threat of, the wholly other, the aneconomical, god. Not surprisingly, then, the possibility of differance (as, we might say, a *thematic* device) is dependent upon the possibility of the lure: "To recognize writing in speech, that is to say differance and the absence of speech, is to begin to think the lure. There is no ethics without presence of the other but also, and consequently, without absence, dissimulation, detour, difference, writing" (*Grammatology* 139–40).

23. While it is true that, in the early and mid-1980s, Derrida's work became increasingly performative, or "literary," by the time he publishes texts like *Force of Law* and *Specters of Marx* he has, I would argue, returned to the more argumentative/analytical style that defined his earlier work.

24. Gasché makes a similar observation. By "evoking" Derrida's own discussion of the "invention" in "Psyche: Inventions of the Other," Gasché highlights the fundamental flaw in Rorty's "readings" of a later Derrida. What Rorty misses is that "an invention cannot simply be private—it is the arrival of something new only on condition that it is publicly recognized as such" (*Inventions* 9). As Gasché repeatedly suggests, any *expression* of absolute singularity is necessarily contaminated by a very public movement toward totalization. Moreover, the very desire to be singular, to break absolutely with what came before is, according to Gasché, *the very desire* that defines the philosophical tradition. Consequently, any "claim that Derrida's texts would announce the end of philosophy, irreversibly break with the history of philosophical ideas, and undermine all possibility of localizing his thought within, or with regard to the course of, the history of philosophy . . . does nothing but reactivate one of the most crucial self-determinations of philosophy since its inception" (*Inventions* 60).

25. See note 15 in chapter 6 of *Contingency, Irony and Solidarity*, "From Ironist Theory to Private Allusions: Derrida."

26. Rorty makes this particular connection most overtly in his *Philosophical Papers: Vol. 2*: "How can Derrida's 'trace,' 'différance,' and the rest of what Gasché calls 'infrastructures' be *more* than the vacuous nonexplanations characteristic of a negative theology?" In a footnote, and while addressing Norris, Rorty goes on to clarify his position: "Norris is quite right in saying that, on my view, early Derrida is 'falling back into a kind of negative theology that merely replaces one set of absolutes (truth, meaning, clear and distinct ideas) with another (trace, *différance*, and other such deconstructive terms).' But the main justification for distinguishing between an earlier and a later Derrida is that he *stops* doing this" (113).

27. In a manner that seems to mirror (almost exactly) Derrida's own discussions of the necessary impossibility of presence, or self-identical being, Sartre most clearly refuses the possibility of the *ens causa sui*—that is, the possibility of the "for-itself" (or consciousness) ever becoming a being 'in-itself-for-itself'—in the conclusion of *Being and Nothingness*: "Everything happens therefore as if the in-itself and the for-itself were presented in a state of disintegration in relation to an ideal synthesis. Not that the integration has ever *taken place* but on the contrary precisely because it is always indicated and always impossible" (792).

28. For more on the often denied connection between Derrida, Sartre and/or negative theology, see also: Steve Martinot's *Forms in the Abyss: A Philosophical Bridge Between Sartre and Derrida;* Baugh's *French Hegel: From Surrealism to Postmodernism* and " 'Hello, Goodbye' Derrida and Sartre's Legacy"; Howells' *Derrida: Deconstruction from Phenomenology to Ethics*, "Sartre and Derrida: Qui Perd Gagne" and "Sartre and Negative Theology"; Caputo's "Apostles of the Impossible"; Rajan's *Remainders of Phenomenology*; Arthur Bradley's "Thinking the Outside: Foucault, Derrida and Negative Theology"; and my own "A *Différance* of Nothing: Sartre, Derrida and the Problem of Negative Theology" (which is ultimately an extension of the above discussion).

29. I am here basically repositioning Derrida's discussion of what he sees as the totalitarian tendency inherent in Marxism, and the way in which the capitalist reaction to the "ghost" that Marxism represented encouraged Marxism to view its "ghost," or Utopian dream, as a material reality: "But since Marxist ontology was also struggling against the ghost in general, in the name of living presence as material actuality, the whole 'Marxist' process of the totalitarian society was also responding to the same panic. We must, it seems to me, take such a hypothesis seriously. . . . It is as if Marx and Marxism had run away, fled from themselves, and had scared themselves. In the course of the same chase, the same infernal pursuit" (105).

30. For Caputo, the arguments of Rorty and Norris fail because they are *too* polemical. While Rorty is too forceful in his attempts to identify Derrida, along with someone like Genet, as an entirely private ironist, Norris "does not take enough precautions to keep Derrida out of the Hegel [and Kant] column. His transcendental Derrida is too strong, too erect, too stiff" ("Quasi-Transcendental" 161).

31. For instance, in "Apostles of the Impossible," Caputo asserts that, for Derrida, "God is neither simply present or absent, neither simply given or not, for the name of God is the name of what is to come. God escapes the play of being and non-being, to be or not to be . . . because God is the specter of what is to come, the stuff of things to hope for" (199).

32. This distinction—between the future "to come" and the "future present"—is highlighted, as Jean-Michel Rabaté notes, in Derrida's *Archive Fever*. In this text, Derrida states that he would prefer affirming the "to come" "with the 'to come' of *avenir* rather than *futur* so as to point toward the coming of an event rather than toward some future present" (as qtd. in Rabaté 179).

33. This paper was delivered at a 1989 conference entitled "Deconstruction and the Possibility of Justice." It was later published (as *Force of Law*) along with a second paper, "First Name of Benjamin," which was read at a colloquium in 1990 held under the title "Nazism and The Final Solution." What is important to note is that both papers were read (and presumably written) around the time of the Soviet Union's dissolution and the fall of the Berlin Wall. As they mark the beginning of Derrida's interest in the arena of ethics, justice, spectrality, and the messianic—an interest that, arguably, becomes most overt in *Specters of Marx* and *Politics of Friendship*—I would argue that these papers represent the first stages of a period of mourning, a period of mourning that marks, more broadly, the dissolution of the postmodern episteme. That is, beginning with these two papers, Derrida's work begins to speak to a period of cultural, or epistemic, mourning, a period of mourning for a certain specter of Marxism: the specter of the messianic, of the promise, of the utopian, of the Enlightenment. In other words, and as I suggested in the previous chapter, the fall of the last overtly utopian discourse effects the dissolution (also) of a postmodern, or hegemonically "counter-Enlightenment" epoch; because postmodernism's spectrally motivated hunt of utopian discourses begins to seem totalitarian and dangerously utopian, a new reconfiguration of "the project" becomes preferable; the specter that was seemingly chased away by

postmodernism thus returns in this period of mourning to animate an epoch that can be defined by its imperative to "respect the specter" so as to deal with the specter *once and for all.* Obviously, then, I use "mourning" here to describe a specific relationship to the specter. The term suggests a lament for that which has passed (or is past), as well as a desire to (re)gain, or to do, something in the future (even if it is, *only,* to get *over* who, or what, is now past). Focusing on Blanchot's use of the phrase "since Marx," in "The Three Voices of Marx," Derrida indirectly expounds on this idea of mourning, which we might understand as a type of paradoxical relationship with the ghost(s) that haunt us: "a 'since Marx' continues to designate the place of assignation from which we are *pledged.* But if there is pledge or assignation, injunction or promise, if there has been this appeal beginning with a word that resounds before us, the 'since' marks a place and a time that doubtless proceeds us, but so as to be as much *in front of us* as *before us.* Since the future, then, since the past as absolute future, since the non-knowledge and the non-advent of an advent, of what remains to be: to do and to decide (which is first of all, no doubt, the sense of the 'to be or not to be' of Hamlet—and of any inheritor who, let us say, comes to swear before a ghost)" (*Specters* 17).

34. Of course, the same can be said of deconstruction. Deconstruction is caught up in the structure of the promise, is haunted by the promise, because what mobilizes it is the promise *of deconstruction*—that is, every work of deconstruction is drawn, however subtly, by the promise that it will deconstruct *finally,* and at last.

35. Hence, Derrida's repetition throughout *Specters* of phrases like "the past as absolute future" (*Specters* 17)—or even, more famously, the line from *Hamlet*: "The time is out of joint."

36. Similarly, in *Specters,* Derrida argues that "the effectivity or actuality of the democratic promise, like that of the communist promise, will always keep within it, and it must do so, this absolutely undeterminable messianic hope at its heart, this eschatological relation to the to-come of an event and of a singularity, of an alterity that cannot be anticipated" (65). Simply, the possibility that the future "to-come" will finally arrive and be *present,* or contemporaneous with "itself as the living present," mobilizes democracy, or communism, or justice, or deconstruction, or whatever.

37. This is again another way of saying "a messianic without messianism." As Peter Fenves points out, for Derrida, "to be without a determinate messiah may not only be possible, it may be the condition for the possibility of messianic expectation, a dry and deserted condition, the desert itself" (268).

38. Indeed, "one of the reasons [Derrida keeps] a distance from all these horizons—from the Kantian regulative idea or from the messianic advent, for example, at least in their conventional interpretation—is that they are, precisely, *horizons*" (*Force of Law* 255).

39. The idea of "touching on" a particular concept (or even a particular theorist—like Derrida) is, of course, particularly germane to the above discussion. After all, to touch upon something truly or fully—as in to apprehend it *at last,* to get it right *absolutely*—is to be decisive, without doubt. For Derrida,

such a state is only ever an illusion, even if its impossible possibility drives us forward in some endless and futile spiral of activity. What I am suggesting here, though, is that it is impossible to act if we believe (as Derrida seems to teach) that our activities can never be truly justified. We cannot sustain a state of belief *without belief*. We believe absolutely (on some level) or we cannot move, we cannot act, we cannot deconstruct. I "touch upon" this issue of touching (as it relates to Derrida and the problem of indecision) much more fully in "A Certain Perhaps: Touching on the Decisiveness of Derrida's Indecision."

40. Derrida states this explicitly in *Specters*: "without this experience of the impossible, one might as well give up on both justice and the event" (65).

41. We might say, in fact, that what Derrida's "religion without religion" demonstrates is that, contrary to Caputo's claims, an *active* discourse cannot be "*without* the dogmas of the positive religious faiths" (*Prayers and Tears* xxi, my emphasis). At the same time, though, I do not think that it is reasonable to simply, if not crudely, accuse deconstruction of slipping into a type of negative theology. Derrida's laborious and endless attempts (like, we might add, Sartre's) to evade the pitfalls of negative theology are, perhaps, reason enough to rescue deconstruction from such accusations. As I intimate below, it would appear that it is the constant struggle (however unsuccessful it might be) to evade becoming a negative theology that distinguishes deconstruction from any negative theology.

42. This need to frustrate a reader's tendency toward absolute decisiveness is stressed in Derrida's discussion of the Nietzschean philosopher "to come"— the philosopher of the "perhaps." See *Politics of Friendship*, in particular the second chapter: "Loving in Friendship: Perhaps—the Noun and the Adverb." I discuss this reading of the Nietzschean "Perhaps" in chapter 3.

43. This epistemic view is, perhaps, articulated most ostentatiously in the current revival (via Caputo, Kearney, Clayton Crockett, Jean Luc Marion, etc.) of theological discussions. Take, for instance, Clayton Crockett's claim that "both modernity and postmodernity are religious histories (not histories of religion), organized around an essentially religious secret—a religion without religion, or a secret without a secret" (499).

Chapter Three: Writing of the Ghost (Again)

1. To avoid confusion, I will refer to the thirteen-year-old narrator as "Mark," while continuing to identify the "real life" (or rather, the "adult") author as "Leyner"; it should be pointed out, though, that it is impossible to know (with any certainty) whether the preface is written by "Mark" or "Leyner"; given the fact that the "author" of the preface refers retrospectively to the "mid-eighties" (11), I have assumed that the preface is the work of the "adult" Mark Leyner. However, as anyone who has read the text knows, narrative markers—such as references to the "mid-eighties"—are often misleading (if not simply and unabashedly inconsistent with the text as a whole).

2. Leyner's style throughout this text (as well as others) is strikingly reminiscent of the traditional stand-up comedian; he continually seems to be offering

up, or suggesting, the possibility of various recognizable (because archetypal) behaviors, motivations, and/or situations, situations with which we can *all* relate. However, the principal humor in Leyner's texts is produced via Leyner's ability to completely and simultaneously undermine these universals by repeatedly associating them with behaviors, motivations, and/or situations that are anything but recognizable, or universal. I discuss the full import of this below.

3. See the final section of chapter 2.

4. We might think here of any number of male or female stand-up comedians, from Jeff Foxworthy to Wanda Sykes and Chris Rock. Typically, a comedian's humor, on stage or on the half-hour television "sit-com" based on their comedy, preys on an audience's desire to reaffirm certain group, or communal, characteristics. The comedian will often relate mundane stories—stories that typically begin with the line "Have you ever . . . ?" Designed to garner the "it's funny because it's true" response, these stories inevitably reaffirm certain ideological categorizations: the differences between men and women, the reasons why one racial group is better or worse in bed than another, and so on. In most cases, the humor is specifically designed to produce a sense of recognition in the audience, a sense of recognition that ultimately works to further solidify the identity categories to which the audience members subscribe.

5. Indeed, "Mark" once again seems to be raising (even as his comedic, or ironic tone, simultaneously undermines) the possibility of some type of transcendental act of communication, a moment of pure insight.

6. We will see a similar argument played out in the discussions (discussed below) concerning the emergence of a type of neo-realism. As various critics have noted, the postmodern aversion to the realistic impulse can be recast as another effect of the realist impulse. That is, postmodern metafiction seems (perhaps inadvertently) to present itself as the most realistic representation of reality *because it represents reality as unrepresentable.* As Taylor insists, "the aim of postmodern aesthetic education remains reconciliation with the 'Real' " (189).

7. I discuss Burke's concepts of terministic screens and mystification at some length in the chapter 1. See, specifically, the third section: "Exorcisms without End."

8. Although I make more of this below, I think it is important to highlight the fact that Little wishes to associate differance with a literature that somehow avoids the traps of negative theology. Ironically (and in terms of Little and Taylor's arguments, quite significantly), differance is, according to critics like Rorty, the most obvious example of Derrida's initial inability to avoid the onto-theological legacy he wishes to circumvent. See the second section of chapter 2.

9. Although we see this satirical look at postmodernism throughout Leyner's work, it is (perhaps) best exemplified in a question asked by one of the many anonymous characters/narrators in *My Cousin, My Gastroenterologist*: "who are the new intellectuals who are the new aesthetes now that the old new intellectuals and the old new aesthetes have been decimated by the self-decimating ramifications of their old new ideas?" (37).

10. After all, if we simply conflate modernism and postmodernism because we can locate the same spectral impulse animating their respective aesthetics

we run the risk of losing the ability to make *any* historical distinctions. As I
have suggested throughout, a certain specter is, in one way or another, always
compelling movement; if this is indeed the case, then all periods (since at
least the Enlightenment) have been, and will continue to be, if we follow
Taylor, "modernist." The fact is, though, even if a certain spectral compulsion
necessarily persists, the way in which that compulsion is played out can be a
useful way of determining epochal transitions. And, indeed, the way in which
the period after modernism deals with its spectral inheritance seems to be, as
many critics tend to agree, distinctly *post*modern.

11. Taylor, of course, recognizes this failure as the effect of a certain
continuation of modernism. Ultimately, then, and as we saw with critics like
Huyssen and Hutcheon in chapter 1, Taylor betrays the logocentric or "utopian" impulse animating his own claim that this emergent period is, at last,
a truly *final* break with modernism. In other words, Taylor's sense of a truly
POSTmodern epoch speaks to the way in which the imperative to respect the
specter becomes, quite necessarily, another way of disrespecting the specter, of
refusing to accept *both* the possibility *and* the impossibility of a *final solution*.

12. These representational objects/events, or "projections," can be understood as instances of, what Žižek understands as, the "Lacanian sublime." And,
as Marek Wieczorek notes in his introduction to *The Art of the Ridiculous Sublime*,
"Žižek shows how the obstacle in the life of the protagonist [in a Lynch film]
is precisely of the order of a fantasmatic projection onto an impossible object
of desire" (ix). Even more so than in *Lost Highway*, this sense of an inevitably
circumscribed traumatic "Real" is evident in Lynch's more recent film, *Mulholland Dr.* For a major portion of the film, Betty Elms (played by Naomi Watts)
encounters a series of inexplicable events, characters, and objects. Eventually,
we are led to the realization that these events and objects are disruptions in
a fantasy/dream world, a world in which Betty is able to become a successful
Hollywood actress and a "Nancy-Drew-like" sleuth. Unable to sustain these disruptions—at one point Betty is faced with what the audience understands to be
her own dead and decomposing body—Betty's "fantasy" turns into a "reality" in
which she is no longer Betty Elms but Diane Selwyn, a down-and-out waitress
who never managed to "make it" in Hollywood. At this point, the inexplicable
aspects of Betty's "fantasy" world become logically integrated into the "reality" of Diane's. However, even though Diane's reality seemingly reestablishes
a coherent symbolic order, the traumas we see manifest as inexplicable disruptions in the "Betty fantasy" take on a much more sinister (because less
fantastic) form; unable to cope with her current reality, Diane shoots herself,
becoming the decomposing body to which Betty, in the initial portion of the
film, found herself drawn and then repulsed. Once again, then, we are given
the circular, or repetitive structure of the psychoanalytic process; only, in this
case, the impossible object of desire is represented much more obviously as
absolute closure, or death.

13. The dissolution of Mucho is, of course, echoed in Pynchon's later
novel, *Gravity's Rainbow*. In both texts, though, the dissolution of a central
character seems to be a way of highlighting identity as construct, as nothing
other than the effect of contingent discursive forces. It is not, in other words,

a contingent negotiation of some unrepresentable Lacanian Real or Kriste-vean chora. Without a certain faith in the possibility of signification—without, that is, the ability to believe in the discursive constructs of history and/or time—Pynchon's Slothrop in *Gravity's Rainbow* becomes, quite simply, nothing. Nothing *but* the illusion of time holds him together—or, rather, makes him *present*: " 'Temporal bandwidth' is the width of your present, your *now*. It is the familiar 'Δt' considered as a dependent variable. The more you dwell in the past and in the future, the thicker your bandwidth, the more solid your persona. But the narrower your sense of the Now, the more tenuous you are. It may get to where you're having trouble remembering what you were doing five minutes ago, or even—as Slothrop now—what you're doing *here*, at the base of this colossal curved embankment . . ." (509).

14. In *Utopia Limited*, and while demonstrating the way in which the post-modern "shift" was actually a complex and extended "pivot" during the 1960s away from distinctly modernist/utopian ideologies, DeKoven works to "reg-ister the persistence in postmodernism of modes of sixties utopian desire" (24). While I certainly agree that we can locate a persistent "utopian desire in tension with post-utopian assumptions characteristic of the most important postmodern fiction" (274), I want to be careful to distinguish this "tension" as distinctly spectral and, thus, as the effect of a certain inevitable and unsought-for *return*. In postmodernism, I am suggesting, this return is the result of an increasingly hegemonic, or ostentatious, application of a "perverse" mode of critique. What I am trying to point out above, though, is that postmodern cultural production often evaded such tension by consciously embracing, if too subtly, the utopian, or logocentric, lures that an argument like DeKoven's seems to suggest are *always* resisted outright (though inevitably and necessarily present) in postmodernism.

15. We might argue, in fact, that, like the later Derrida, the later Pynchon entertains the very shift in emphasis that I have been associating with "renewal-ism" generally. While a text like *Mason and Dixon* seems to be a direct continu-ation of Pynchon's earlier work—it employs real historical events, meandering and unfixed syntax, arbitrary musical interludes, absurd and impossible char-acters (such as singing dogs and talking clocks), and so on—it is ultimately far more invested in articulating a need for faith, or some of type of belief, in the possibility of representational accuracy. Not only are the main characters, Mason and Dixon, initially driven by the promise of locating the accurate value of the solar parallax, the obvious presence of a narrator—whose own story (of telling the story of Mason and Dixon to a group of children) frequently inter-rupts the story proper—reminds us of the text's unavoidable and animating desire to achieve a type of mimetic truth. Indeed, in a passage that is oddly reminiscent of the passage I cited above from Leyner's *Tetherballs*, the narra-tor describes the possibility of ascertaining the solar parallax as the possibility of seeing the earth accurately from the sun: "thro' the magick of Celestial Trigonometry,—to which you could certainly be applying yourselves,—such measurements may yet be taken,—as if the Telescope, in some mysterious Wise, were transporting us safely thro' all the dangers of the awesome Gulf of Sky, out to the object we wish to examine" (96). According to the narrator, then,

this hypothetical telescope is a "Vector of Desire" (96), a vector that, like his own story of Mason and Dixon, promises the absolute and impossible apprehension of a particular object or event.

16. For example, while traveling with a truck driver, Trout notices a moving van with pyramids painted on its side. The name of the company to which the van belongs is, Trout realizes, "Pyramid." Bewildered, Trout asks his traveling companion why " 'anybody in the business of high speed transportation [would] name his business and trucks after buildings that haven't moved an eighth of an inch since Christ was born?' " Trout's companion, we are told, responds with a certain amount of contempt: " 'He just liked the sound of it' " (112). Shocked by this affirmation of the ultimately hollow and unstable nature of signs, Trout conceives of a new story: "It's about a planet where language kept turning into pure music, because the creatures there were so enchanted by sounds. Words became musical notes. Sentences became melodies. They were useless as conveyers of information, because nobody knew or cared what meanings of words were anymore" (113). As Vonnegut would put it, "Like so many Trout stories, [this one] was about a tragic failure to communicate" (58).

17. In a manner that sums up the basic critical response to Vonnegut, Lorre Rackstraw succinctly highlights the fact that Vonnegut's work can be defined by its desire to expose the dangerous illusions fostered by narrative order: "it is worth noting that Vonnegut was one of the first American writers to make explicit through his self-reflexive fiction the irony that he was using language to explore the curious and powerful and sometimes dangerous nature of language itself—how it functions as 'signs' or symbols that can influence our perceptions and what we take to be real, and thus can actually shape our system of values and ethics" (53).

18. Given the image of an "asshole" that runs throughout the text—that is, the image of a number of randomly intersecting lines—we might say that, for Vonnegut, all people (like, Vonnegut might add, all phenomena) are "assholes," arbitrary locus points of an innumerable number of intersecting discursive strands.

19. As Josh Simpson argues in a recent article on, what he calls, the "Troutean Trilogy" (i.e., *God Bless You, Mr. Rosewater, Slaughterhouse Five,* and *Breakfast of Champions*), "At the center of [Vonnegut's] canon resides the notion that science fiction [as exemplified in the nostalgic texts of Trout] is capable of filling humanity with false realities and empty promises for Utopian societies that do not and, perhaps most important, cannot exist" (262). Simpson also quotes, for use as an epigraph, a line from Frank McLaughlin's 1973 interview with Vonnegut that, I think, is worth requoting here: "I resent a lot of science fiction. This promising of great secrets just beyond our grasp—I don't think they exist" (Vonnegut as qtd. in Simpson 261).

20. At the same time, though, Trout often seems to represent Vonnegut's own latent nostalgia and humanistic sentimentality, feelings that Vonnegut feels he must repress or efface. Reed, in fact, makes a similar point. While pointing out that *Slaughterhouse Five,* like much of Vonnegut's work, "is a novel in which a serious, direct statement of ethics . . . would seem didactic and false," Reed

argues that "Trout's simple, humorous, hyperbolic stories deliver the message effectively without changing the author's narrative stance in the novel" (73). Through Trout, then, Vonnegut often appears capable of having his cake and eating it too. Still, as we see in a text like *Breakfast of Champions*, Trout is often and, perhaps, necessarily punished for his nostalgic satires. On a certain level, then, we might read the abuses Trout suffers at his author's hands as Vonnegut's way of performing a type of postmodern self-flagellation. Trout, in other words, speaks to Vonnegut's latent desire to escape "the chaos" he knows he must embrace.

21. As Rackstraw points out, it is possible to read Trout's final cries for youth as symptomatic of the dangerous desires of a past patriarchal—or, in Derrida's terms, a logo/phallogocentric—order: "In the distance [Vonnegut] hears Trout call out, in his father's voice, '*make me young, make me young, make me young!*' It is the voice of 'logical' patriarchal civilization with its ecstatic torment and mortal need—if not for transcendence, at least for the power to find renewal and direction in the void" (62).

22. The main characters in *Empire of the Senseless* (i.e., Thivai and Abhor) are, after all, terrorists. There seems to be a suggestion in Acker's work that we need to be violently shocked out of our ideological stupor, our passive acceptance of the artificial categories that determine our reality. Indeed, we could make the obvious argument that the excessive violence and spectacle in Acker's texts force us to recognize the arbitrariness of our existence.

23. We might say that what becomes *too* glaring in excessively "perverse" postmodernism is the fact that, as John McGowan puts it, "the description of our condition as one of insertion within networks (or systems) of differential play is hard put to avoid transcendental claims in the process of arguing that such is our condition" (42). From this perspective, postmodernism "fails" because, in its most perverse manifestations, it fails to satisfactorily negotiate, or announce, the paradox that it can't actually do what it claims to be doing.

24. Bauman, of course, is interested in exposing the way in which the postmodern quest for purity must ultimately view its own inevitable conclusion as another form of impurity. According to Bauman, postmodernism can only maintain its epistemological dominance if it rejects its own logical extreme—that is, a state in which we are no longer willing to embrace a single governing ideology, postmodernism included: "Postmodernity . . . lives in a state of permanent pressure towards the dismantling of all collective interference into individual fate, towards deregulation and privatization. It tends to fortify itself therefore against those who—following its inherent tendency to disengagement, indifference and free-for-all—threaten to expose the suicidal potential of the strategy by pushing its implementation to the logical extreme. The most obnoxious 'impurity' of the postmodern version of purity is not revolutionaries, but those who either disregard the law or take the law into their own hands—muggers, robbers, car-thieves and shoplifters, as well as their alter egos—the vigilantes and the terrorists" (16). In other words, and quite paradoxically, postmodernism must avoid exorcising the spectrality of the specter—that is, postmodernism must avoid fulfilling the very spectral promise

it is motivated to fulfill—if it wishes to continue exorcising the spectrality of the specter. And it is at the moment when this spectral paradox becomes unavoidably apparent (as it is, I would argue, in the work of Acker) that the postmodern ethic of perversity becomes a hegemonic imperative.

25. Significantly, the narrator/protagonist is subtly different from the author. As Catharine Calloway points out, "Unlike the real Tim O'Brien, the protagonist has a nine year old daughter named Kathleen and makes a journey to Vietnam years after the war is over" (250).

26. While many would counter this claim, arguing that Beckett was a high modernist, not a postmodernist, Beckett's work does often seem (as Federman suggests) to herald the end of modernism and thus the birth of postmodernism. Consequently, I think Federman's claim is a fair one: we can, quite easily, identify Beckett's work and death with the alpha and the omega of postmodernism.

27. In the introduction to the issue—an issue that included such writers as Jayne Anne Philips, Raymond Carver, Frederick Barthelme, and Tobias Wolff—Bill Buford positions this new "dirty realism" in direct contradistinction to both traditional forms of realism and the metafictional devices of postmodernism: "It is not heroic or grand: the epic ambitions of Norman Mailer or Saul Bellow seem, in contrast, inflated, strange, even false. It is not self-consciously experimental like so much of the writing—variously described as 'postmodern,' 'postcontemporary' or 'deconstructionist'—that was published in the sixties and seventies. The work of John Barth, William Gaddis or Thomas Pynchon seems pretentious in comparison" (4). The sense we get from Buford is that this new form of realism is a type of realism that remains inflected by the lessons of postmodernism: "This is a curious, dirty realism about the belly-side of contemporary life, but it is realism so stylized and particularized—so insistently informed by discomforting and sometimes elusive irony—that it makes the more traditional realistic novels of, say, Updike and Styron seem ornate, even baroque in comparison" (4). In other words, and as I suggest below, Buford's "dirty realism" can be read as an early symptom of the current shift away from postmodernism. Indeed, works of "dirty realism" seem to clearly anticipate what critics have come to refer to as "neo-realism" or "critical realism."

28. See Tom Wolfe's "Stalking the Billion-Footed Beast: A Literary Manifesto of the New Social Novel." Rejecting the claims of postmodernism as decadent and elitist, Wolfe argues that only the realistic novel—realistic, that is, in the journalistic tradition of a writer like Zola—has the ability to be socially pertinent and captivating: "It is not merely that reporting is useful in gathering the *petits faits vrais* that create verisimilitude and make a novel gripping or absorbing, although that side of the enterprise is worth paying attention to. My contention is that, especially in an age like this, they are essential for the greatest effects literature can achieve" (55). Not surprisingly, Wolfe holds up his own book, *The Bonfire of the Vanities*, as an example of his specific brand of neo-realism, a form of narrative that rejects postmodern strategies as overly and unjustly privileged by academia.

29. In his introduction to *Beyond Postmodernism: Reassessments in Literature, Theory, and Culture*, Klaus Stierstorfer describes the situation like this: "in a

much-quoted survey Lance Olsen reported an astounding increase in occurrences of the term 'postmodern' in American newspapers from 1980 through 1984 to 1987 at a ratio of 2: 116: 247. In his turn, Hans Bertens charted a 'history of the debate on postmodernism from its tentative beginnings in the 1950s to its overwhelming self-confidence in the early 1990s.' From the later 1990s onwards, however, this narrative of the progress of postmodernism appears to lose direction. Although no statistical data are available, the quantity of references to postmodernism in scholarly publications as well as in the daily press seems to decreases, as does the heatedness of the debate" (1).

30. Federman, following Lyotard, rephrases this paradox by stating that "Postmodernism attempted to speak the impossibility of speaking the unspeakable" ("Part 2" 158).

31. In a recent article, Malcolm Bradbury, while quoting himself, puts it like this: "most of the major movements that have been regarded as essentially anti-realist have argued that they are in effect a form of realism" (15). Bradbury's point is, it would seem, that the emergent forms of realism—he identifies writers like Toni Morrison, Philip Roth, and Saul Bellow—speak to a "realist" impulse that was never completely foreign to postmodernism. Rather than simply renewing a realist impulse, then, recent works of neo-realism attempt to stress the fact that there are still a number of "realities" that have escaped literary representation. Coming, for Bradbury, mainly from the margins, neo-realism is thus an attack on the idea of literature as an exhausted form—the idea, that is, that only pastiche and self-reflexivity can represent the reality of the present. Of course, this new realism is not a simple "narrowing back to a conventional naturalistic or reportorial realism" (22); rather, it is "a late-twentieth century realism, characteristically anxious, ironic and speculative" (23). Put in spectrological terms, recent works of neo-realism reconfigure, or renew, the aesthetic relationship with the teleological, or "realist," specter that defined postmodernism from the beginning.

32. Federman, in fact, refers to artists like Lynch, Leyner, and Acker as "the new young thugs of innovation" ("Part 2" 167). As I suggest in the above chapters, though, the work of Acker is probably more accurately classed as residual, if not high, postmodernism than as what I have been calling emergent renewalism. Indeed, as Max Shechner has argued, writers like "Paul Auster and Kathy Acker . . . are responsible for what remains of the [postmodern] metafictional remnant" (33).

33. Federman, of course, is referring to the "dirty realism" identified by Buford. For Federman, dirty realism is not stylistically innovative enough to be a continuation of a distinctly postmodern project. However, I would argue that dirty realism and the new works of innovation privileged by Federman are not as distinct as Federman would like to believe; both share a very similar relationship with the specter I have been discussing. As I demonstrate below, narrative strategies after postmodernism are best defined by their willingness to ironically embrace a certain spectrological promise. The identification of aesthetic production that moves beyond postmodernism has far less to do with the identification of a specific stylistic (metafictional, realist, or otherwise) than

it does with identification of a very specific relationship with the specter of a still incomplete project of modernity.

34. See my extended discussion of Lyotard in chapter 1.

35. As Ihab Hassan argues in "Pragmatism, Postmodernism, and Beyond," the absurdity of the "politically-correct" campus is a direct result of this oddly inverted dogmatism: "For some time now theory and ideology in American universities have produced an oppressive orthodoxy, the orthodoxy of P.C. or political correctness. Conceived first in the name of pluralism, multi-cultural-ism, social justice, theory and ideology have created a climate which threatens now pluralism itself, threatens free speech and intellectual liberty" ("Fresh Air" 136). This stifling climate is, as Hassan seems to be arguing, the result of the postmodern "pretence of exuberance in fragments, the avoidance of nostalgia—or, rather, the feigned avoidance of it" (136).

36. We should, perhaps, note that Leypoldt ultimately suggests that this shift from postmodern metafiction to forms of "realism" does not signal "an ideological or epistemological paradigm shift" (26). Instead, Leypoldt argues, this shift is symptomatic of a "change" in "audiences' aesthetic preferences" (26), a change that is due to a general sense of boredom with postmodern aesthetic production. I would argue, though, that it is difficult (if not impos-sible) to identify a major shift in aesthetic taste without (at least suggesting) a larger ideological, or epistemological, upheaval.

37. As an example, McLaughlin points out the way in which a writer like Barth—while seemingly immersing himself "in the luxury of language" (59)—repeatedly articulates a deep concern for the social world. Citing Barth's most recent work, *The Book of Ten Nights and a Night*, McLaughlin argues that "Barth seems to be doing more obviously here what he's always been doing: writing fiction about fiction, but fiction that's placed in the social world" (59). However, I would argue that this subtle shift in emphasis is more important than McLaughlin is willing to admit. While Barth's late work might be sim-ply *more overt* in terms of its social claims, the fact that his early work was far more focused on the repudiation of logocentric attitudes than his more recent work—which, as Thomas Carmichael has suggested, in a manner that anticipates McLaughlin's own claims, emphasizes an inevitable "return to the discourse of the realistic enterprise" (329–30)—speaks to the very spectrologi-cal shift I have been attempting to expose.

38. It is worth noting that Hayles and Gannon see the apparent death of postmodernism as effecting a type of aesthetic "mood swing," a shift from post-modernism to an "aesthetics of ambient emergence." While far more interested in developing technologies than my own, Hayles and Gannon's discussion of a new form of aesthetic production highlights a distinctly "renewalist" desire to open up possibilities in the "wake of postmodernism." While a full exegesis of Hayles and Gannon's complex understanding of "ambient emergence" is beyond the scope of my discussion, suffice it to say that ambient emergence is defined by the work of artists, like Mark Z. Danielewski, who "are generally more interested in building than in critique, more oriented to discovery and innovation than to paranoia and suspicion" (Hayles and Gannon 136).

39. Take, for instance, the episode in which Lisa becomes a vegetarian: "Lisa the Vegetarian." On the surface, the episode appears to privilege the more marginal position of vegetarianism, while mocking the ideological assumptions that meat eaters typically employ in defense of their lifestyle. The scene in which Bart, Homer, Marge, and Maggie dance around the house singing "you don't win friends with salad" seems to be an outward condemnation of the absurd societal imperative *to eat meat*. This condemnation is even more overtly articulated when, at school, Lisa's class is subjected to an educational film on the importance of eating meat; along with a sequence in which the narrator tells the child protagonist of the film that "the killing floor" at his local abattoir is nothing more than a poorly named area where "steel grating" allows "material to sluice through so it can be collected and exported," the "educational film" includes a picture of a "food chain" in which humans are at the natural center of all worldly consumption (arrows, in fact, absurdly point from a human to all manner of animals and goods, including a single boot). However, the satire of the episode, like most *Simpsons* episodes, quickly becomes dual-edged. Indeed, Lisa's quest for an accepting "vegetarian community" grows increasingly bizarre; at one point, she is led by Apu, the token Hindu and convenience store owner, through a secret passage in the "Quickie Mart" to an edenic place where Paul McCartney resides as the guru of all vegetarians. Culminating in an impromptu "jam session" between Apu and McCartney, this scene allows us to reapproach the episode in a manner that gives the anti-vegetarian song and dance performed by Lisa's family a subtly different tone. In other words, and as we see with most of Lisa's leftist and radical ideals, the impulse behind vegetarianism is presented as symptomatic of an often "flighty" and unpractical form of idealism. The episode thus seems to condemn the ideology driving the production and consumption of meat products as outmoded while simultaneously reaffirming the suggestion that there are perfectly acceptable reasons why "you don't win friends with salad."

40. For a detailed discussion of Jonathan Franzen's often vocal rejection of postmodernism, see Robert Rebein's excellent article, "Turncoat: Why Jonathan Franzen Finally Said 'No' to Po-Mo."

41. The obvious example is, of course, John Cage. However, Cage's incredibly esoteric music hardly indicates a postmodern imperative animating popular culture. Still, a popular musician like Beck or even a "rapper" like Eminem can be identified as distinctly postmodern. Eminem's incessant irony as well his use of alter egos (i.e., "Eminem" and "Slim Shady") suggests a certain impulse to be "responsibly" postmodern. Likewise, Beck's (perhaps more academic) use of pastiche speaks to popular culture's need to be self-reflexive and overtly parodic. Take, for instance, the list of "samples," or "quotes," that make up the song "Devils Haircut" on Beck's 1996 album, *Odelay*: " 'Devils Haircut' contains a sample from 'Out of Sight' (James Brown) published by Fort Knox Music BMI, performed by Them, courtesy of Decco Record Co.: a sample from 'Soul Drums' (Bernard Purdie) published by Tenryk Music BMI, performed by Pretty Purdie, courtesy of Sony Music; and elements from

'I Can Only Give You Everything' (Philip Coulter/Thomas Scott) published by Carbert Music ASCAP.'"

42. At the same time, the dialogue that the "fictional" actors deliver is actually dialogue from past *Seinfeld* episodes.

43. Tew is, at this point, referencing Bhaskar's *Plato Etc.: The Problems of Philosophy and Their Resolution.*

44. Anticipating the claims of a critic like Leypoldt, Winfried Fluck notes that "experimental postmodernism had radicalized its linguistic playfulness and especially its experiments in dereferentialization to such a degree that it became monotonous, and, what is worse and eventually the kiss of death for any avant-garde movement, predictable" (65). What I am suggesting, though, is that this sense of monotony speaks to a period of postmodern hegemony, a period in which any narrative style that refuses to be self-referential or anti-foundationalist is ostracized as sentimentally dangerous or ideologically complicit. This becomes, as Sanford Pinsker puts it, in a manner that coincides with the anti-theory/anti-postmodern assertions of Shechner, a form of "New Puritanism" (61). Still, like Shechner, Pinsker is too obsessed with berating academia for its acceptance of theoretical "double-speak" and postmodern pluralism to be particularly useful. Indeed, Pinsker's position is outwardly conservative and reactionary. He goes so far as to label recent works of neo-realism "redskin" literature, as if (what he calls) "palefaces" are too sterile and theory-obsessed to be associated with good literature. This rather backdated and bizarrely essentialist use of racial categories is symptomatic of the way in which Pinsker's and, for that matter, Shechner's understanding of neo-realism is tainted by an outright distaste for, and misunderstanding of, postmodern theory and literature.

45. Such a list is, of course, tentative, and a careful examination of each author would be necessary before we could identify their individual works as definitively "renewalist." However, apart from Tarantino and Erdrich and the authors that I have already discussed above, the writers that make up the remainder of this list have been identified elsewhere as (in one manner or another) complicit with a certain shift away from postmodernism: in "Writing Fiction in the 90s," Malcolm Bradbury identifies Toni Morrison, along with Alice Walker, as moving beyond postmodern aesthetic imperatives; Alfred Hornung makes similar claims in "POSTMODERN-POSTMORTEM: Death and the Death of the Novel"; in "Mood Swings" (discussed above) Hayles and Gannon claim that Danielewski's work participates in a "mood swing" from postmodernism to, what they identify as, an "aesthetic of ambient emergence"; Don DeLillo is mentioned by Winfried Fluck (in an article discussed below) as a writer that, while stylistically postmodern, is engaged in a type of writing that can be categorized along with the work of Raymond Carver; and Christopher Den Tandt makes analogous claims about DeLillo, while extending his analysis to the work of Kingston, in his "Pragmatic Commitments: Postmodern Realism in Don DeLillo, Maxine Hong Kingston and James Ellroy."

46. Of course, postmodernism never resulted in a state of paralysis. This is, I am arguing, the very failure to which renewalist forms of narrative respond.

Because it strove to finally reject the ideal of mythic indecision (or, put differently, the material possibility of the specter) postmodernism necessarily and paradoxically strove toward such a state of indecision. What the persistence of postmodernism demonstrates, though, is that the rejection of either pole of indecision is impossible. Had postmodernism been successful in its aesthetic endeavor, it would have ceased to move; it would have become absolutely silent. The failure of postmodernism to carry through on its various threats to commit suicide is thus symptomatic of the impossibility of *a discourse* that is uncontaminated by the irony of indecision—which is to say, the spectrality of the specter.

47. To a degree, then, the initial portion of Kaufman's film seems to echo and, perhaps, mock the extreme solipsism of high postmodernism. Indeed, Kaufman's continual inability to get his plot "moving" directly mirrors a text like Barth's ostentatiously metafictional "Title." Like Kaufman, the writer of/in "Title" (i.e., the tenth story in *Lost in the Funhouse*) is paralyzed by his awareness of the futility of writing: "I think she comes. The story of our life. This is the final test. Try to fill in the blank. Only hope is to fill the blank. Efface what can't be faced or else fill the blank. With words or more words, otherwise I'll fill in the blank with this noun here in my prepositional object. Yes, she already said that. And I think. What now. Everything's been said already, over and over; I'm as sick of this as you are; there's nothing to say. Say nothing" (102).

48. The suggestion seems to be that a text evades artistic failure by continually emphasizing its inevitable failure as a meaningful text. Speaking of Borges' short allegory, "Pierre Menard, Author of the Quixote," Barth points out that Menard "writes a remarkable and original work of literature, the implicit theme of which is the difficulty, perhaps the unnecessity, of writing original works of literature. His artistic victory, if you like, is that he confronts an intellectual dead end and employs it to accomplish new human work" (69–70). According to Barth, then, "the literature of exhaustion" is, quite simply, an original articulation of exhaustion or narrative futility. Ultimately, though, this becomes another aesthetic dead end. Like, we might say, de Manian deconstruction, the literature of exhaustion incessantly works to expose the same ironically *finite* truth *again and again*: the infinite inexhaustibility of apparently exhausted works of art and modes of aesthetic production. As Barth suggests, "it is a matter of every moment throwing out the bath water without for a moment losing the baby" (70).

49. Of course, Hutcheon succinctly addresses this problem in her *Poetics*. Hutcheon, though, argues that, because it was, for the most part, willing to admit "that no narrative can be a natural 'master' narrative," postmodernism was able to successfully "challenge narratives that do presume 'master' status, without necessarily assuming that status for itself" (13). While I agree with Hutcheon that postmodern metafiction, at least initially, seemed to negotiate this paradox, I would argue that its eventual dominance as an aesthetic imperative exposed such a negotiation as impossible (which it is). As I suggested in chapter 1, even Hutcheon's claim that postmodernism can evade assuming the status of a master narrative necessarily positions it *as* a master

narrative—that is, as a form of narrative that can *finally* evade becoming a metanarrative.

50. Given Barth's status as one of the quintessential postmodern writers, the fact that he seems to question what I have identified as a distinctly postmodern move toward aesthetic silence is somewhat problematic. Shouldn't a postmodernist celebrate an ambition like Beckett's? There are, I think, two ways to look at this dilemma. On the one hand, Barth's early work, including "The Literature of Exhaustion," articulates the very "failure" I have been attempting to describe throughout. What we see in Barth's work, and as I demonstrate in more detail below, is a type of ethical imperative to articulate the illusory nature of such an imperative. Even for a postmodernist (and this is, perhaps, the most obvious symptom of a postmodern "failure"), the state of paralysis to which the work of Beckett points seems irresponsible. The postmodernist is compelled to continually voice the utopian ideal of such silence. As we saw with Vonnegut, this is a compulsion to articulate a type of "ethics of perversity." Not unlike Vonnegut, Barth identifies the "felt ultimacies of our time" as a cause for celebration, a reason *to write*: "By 'exhaustion' I don't mean anything so tired as the subject of physical, moral, or intellectual decadence, only the used-upness of certain forms or the felt exhaustion of certain possibilities—by no means a cause for despair" ("Exhaustion" 64). On the other hand, though, Barth's awareness of the problematic paradox animating postmodernism—its strange ability to continue *speaking toward silence*—anticipates the subtle shift we see in his later work. As I pointed out in an earlier note, critics like Thomas Carmichael have identified a certain "return of the Real" in Barth's later work. Suggesting a connection between Barth and the Žižekean "art of the ridiculous sublime," such criticism highlights the way in which a late-Barth comes to embrace a form of literature, which he continues to call postmodernism, that is uncannily similar to the forms of renewalist narrative I have been attempting to categorize. By the time Barth publishes "The Literature of Replenishment" he has begun to outwardly anticipate a type of literature that will "somehow rise above the quarrel between realism and irrealism, formalism and 'contentism' " (203). Calling for a type of ideal aesthetic unity—a type of unity that seems to echo the linking of the disciplines that Habermas' views as the aim of a "project of modernity"—Barth seems to rewrite his earlier claims regarding what constitutes postmodernism. In fact, he seems to find in his earlier criticism and fiction suggestions that this was what he was intending all along. And, I would argue, he is quite right to do so. As Carmichael argues, "What Barth's 1967 prescription finally urges is a synthesis of narrative self-consciousness and the conventions of realistic representation, and if we substitute modernism for the former and premodernism for the latter, we have a clear anticipation of the program that Barth advances for postmodernism in his 1980 essay, "The Literature of Replenishment," with the significant difference that in the later essay this synthesis is no longer couched in the rhetoric of a heroic avant-garde" (330). Put differently, the later Barth, like the later Derrida, is very much engaged in a certain shift *away from* the postmodern episteme he helped to define. Like Derrida, the later Barth, like the literature of renewalism gener-

ally, can be understood as simply shifting his emphasis, pointing to something that was necessarily present (albeit ignored, or denied) all along. With Derrida, the shift is most obvious in his outward acceptance of the necessity of the quasi-transcendental; in Barth, we see it in his much more overt insistence that postmodernism necessarily had to have "it both ways" ("Revisited" 42).

51. We might think of this paradox, as a critic like Chris Conti does, as an effect of a type of "double-directed" discourse. Following Bahktin, Conti seems to suggest that the confessional mode assumed by a narrator like Andrews is symptomatic of "the structure of a double-directed discourse [that] betrays the need for an audience precisely—and paradoxically—at the moment the narrator's independence from others is declared" (542). The sense we get from Conti is that Andrews' affirmation of nihilism and/or suicide is always and necessarily caught up in the very thing it aims to refute: the need for, or possibility of, validation: "Todd seeks to justify more than parlor nihilism, though this might be all that remains of his ideology in the end; he seeks, rather, to justify suicide as an authentic choice and a positive act. In short, he wants to display suicidal nihilism as an affirmation of life" (541). As with the "ethics of perversity" we see advocated so blatantly in the work of Vonnegut and Acker, Andrews' need to assure himself, and his readers, that an authentic or positive act is an ideological illusion that becomes the very reason for his endlessly deferred suicide. In other words, Andrews' narrative (which can be read as an effect of his hesitation, or doubt) speaks to the impossibility of being certainly right about the impossibility of being certainly right. Andrews' narrative, like Andrews himself, persists because it/he is necessarily caught up in the paradox of "indecision."

52. I should note that I am, here, referring to the original 1956 version of *The Floating Opera*, the version Barth altered so as to satisfy his publishers. Barth eventually published a "restored" version of the text in 1967, but in that particular version Andrews does not experience the moment of paralysis discussed above. While the 1967 version is apparently the novel Barth *wanted* published, I find the idea of Andrews' paralysis too significant to ignore (especially as the theme of paralysis is central in Barth's second novel—i.e., *The End of the Road*). For this reason, I am basing my discussion on the 1956 version, not the 1967 one.

53. This structure is, to a certain degree, repeated in *The End of the Road* and *Giles Goat-Boy*. In *The End of the Road*—the counterpart to *The Floating Opera*—the main character, Jacob Horner, is also subject to moments of absolute paralysis: "I left the ticket window and took a seat on one of the benches in the middle of the concourse to make up my mind. And it was there that I simply ran out of motives, as a car runs out of gas. . . . There was no reason to do anything" (74). After sitting immobile for an entire night, Horner is approached by a doctor who runs an "immobilation farm"; and, after undergoing "mythotherapy"—a process in which he is encouraged to believe in, and restructure, the fictional stories that define his existence—Horner begins a strange relationship with a seemingly "liberated" couple. Another "confessional," Horner's story, like Andrews', ultimately becomes an attempt to validate

the claim that no claim or decision can be deemed "valid." The text itself thus becomes a contingent act of mythotherapy, a narrative that is animated by a spectral desire to invalidate all reasons for being, or acting, or deciding, or whatever. The existence of Horner's narrative, though, ultimately speaks to a latent faith in the teleological claim that intentional "myth making" is the *only* "ethical" thing we can *decide* to do. This same inverted code of "ethics" seems to be the basic conceit of a text like *Giles Goat-Boy*. Playing with the idea of a prophesized messiah—that is, the GILES—*Giles Goat-Boy* continually teases the reader with the possibility that George, the "Goat-Boy," will fulfill his destiny and become the Grand Tutor. Of course, in typical postmodern fashion, the messianic promise is denied as a dangerous illusion; George's efforts, after all, to "tutor" inevitably end up causing more harm than good. By the end, when George seems to have finally become Grand Tutor (although a certain ambiguity continues to frustrate our ability to make claims about his messianic status), we realize that the entire narrative has been told years after the events described by a disillusioned and skeptical George. Still claiming to be Grand Tutor, George suggests that he has ultimately failed, that his "lessons" only resulted in two dogmatic and opposed ideologies and that he believes the narrative he has just recorded is a futile attempt to explain something that cannot be explained: "And thus it is—empowered as it were by impotence, driven by want of motives—I record this posttape" (756). The sense we get is that George *is* the *Grand Tutor*, but only insofar as he understands and preaches the impossibility of articulating the Truth, only insofar as he continually identifies his messianic role as being *without meaning or purpose*: "I had been sought out, in my obscurity, by journalism-majors with long memories, who asked whether I still maintained that I was the Grand Tutor. . . . I had replied yes, I was the Grand Tutor, for better or worse, there was no help for it; yes I knew what studentdom was pleased to call 'the answer,' though that term—indeed the whole proposition—was as misleading as another (and thus as satisfactory), since what I 'knew' neither 'I' nor anyone could 'teach,' not even my own 'tutees' " (759). Like Andrews and Horner, then, George is identified as a type of postmodern saint, an individual who has finally realized and accepted the impossibility of a final answer, a mimetic text, a telos. At the same time, though, each of their narratives is spectrally animated by the promise that an absolute and final rejection of the promise *is possible*.

54. For this reason, it is not surprising that, as Arthur Saltzman notes, the *Washington Post* "deemed" *The Mezzanine* "the most daring and thrilling novel since John Barth's 1955 [*sic*] *The Floating Opera*" (Barbara Fisher Williamson as qtd. in Saltzman 15).

55. As Søren Pold puts it, "In *The Mezzanine*, . . . one can also find a thorough awareness of the medium of print, and the novel can also be categorized as belonging to Realism" (141). In other words, Baker demonstrates "a media consciousness that is simultaneously postmodern and realistic" (152).

56. I should note that Nancy's various, and fairly recent, theories of community, and "being with," echo and run parallel to Derrida's later more overtly "renewalist" work. We might, then, easily identify Nancy as a theorist of renewalism.

Works Cited

Acker, Kathy. *Empire of the Senseless.* New York: Grove, 1988.

———. *In Memoriam to Identity.* New York: Grove, 1990.

Allen, Donald and George F. Butterick, eds. *The Postmoderns: The New American Poetry Revised.* New York: Grove, 1982.

Allen, Woody. *Without Feathers.* 1972. New York: Warner, 1976.

Anderson, Perry. *The Origins of Postmodernity.* London: Verso, 1998.

Baker, Nicholson. *The Mezzanine.* New York: Vintage, 1986.

———. *Vox.* New York: Random House, 1992.

Banks, Russell. *Continental Drift.* New York: Harper & Row, 1985.

Barth, John. *The End of the Road.* 1958. New York: Bantam, 1969.

———. *The Floating Opera.* 1956. New York: Avon, 1967.

———. *Giles Goat-Boy: Or, The Revised New Syllabus.* 1966. New York: Fawcett, 1967.

———. "The Literature of Exhaustion." 1969. *The Friday Book: Essays and Other Nonfiction.* New York: Putnam, 1984. 62–76.

———. "The Literature of Replenishment: Postmodernist Fiction." 1980. *The Friday Book: Essays and Other Nonfiction.* New York: Putnam, 1984. 193–206.

———. *Lost in the Funhouse.* New York: Bantam, 1969.

———. "Postmodernism Revisited." 1988. *The End of Postmodernism: New Directions.* Proc. of the First Stuggart Seminar in Cultural Studies 04. 08.–18. 08. 1991. Dir. Heide Ziegler. Stuttgart: M & P Verlag für Wissenschaft und Forschung, 1993. 31–45.

Barthes, Roland. *Image-Music-Text.* Trans. Stephen Heath. New York: Hill & Wang, 1977.

———. *Mythologies.* 1972. Trans. Annette Lavers. London: Granada, 1973.

———. *S/Z.* Trans. Richard Miller. New York: Noonday, 1974.

Basker, Roy. *Plato Etc.: The Problems of Philosophy and their Resolution.* London: Verso, 1994.

Baudrillard, Jean. *The Illusion of the End.* Trans. Chris Turner. Stanford: Stanford UP, 1992.

———. *Paroxysm.* Trans. Chris Turner. London: Verso, 1998.

———. *Simulacra and Simulation.* Trans. Sheila Faria Glaser. Ann Arbor: U of Michigan P, 1994.

Baugh, Bruce. *French Hegel: From Surrealism to Postmodernism.* New York: Routledge, 2003.

———. " 'Hello, Goodbye' " Derrida and Sartre's Legacy. *Sartre Studies International* 5. 2 (1999): 61–74.

Bauman, Zygmunt. *Postmodernity and Its Discontents.* Cambridge: Polity, 1997.

Beck. *Odelay.* Willowdale, ON: Geffen Records, 1996.

Bertens, Hans. *The Idea of the Postmodern: A History.* London: Routledge, 1995.

———. "The Postmodern *Weltanschauung* and its Relation with Modernism: An Introductory Survey." *Approaching Postmodernism.* Eds. Douwe Fokkema and Hans Bertens. Philadelphia: John Benjamins, 1986. 9–48.

Bradbury, Malcolm. "Writing Fiction in the 90s." *Neo-Realism in Contemporary Fiction.* Ed. Kristiaan Versluys. Amsterdam: Rodopi, 1992. 13–25.

Bradley, Arthur. "Thinking the Outside: Foucault, Derrida and Negative Theology." *Textual Practice* 16. 1 (2002): 57–74.

Brooks, Neil and Josh Toth, eds. *The Mourning After: Attending the Wake of Postmodernism.* Amsterdam: Rodopi, 2007.

Buford, Bill. "Editorial." *Granta 8: Dirty Realism* (1983): 4–5.

Burke, Kenneth. *A Rhetoric of Motives.* Berkeley: U of California P, 1969.

———. *Language as Symbolic Action: Essays on Life, Literature, Method.* Berkeley: U of California P, 1966.

Calloway, Catherine. " 'How to Tell a True War Story': Metafiction in *The Things They Carried.*" *Critique* 36. 4 (1995): 249–57.

Caputo, John D. "Apostles of the Impossible: On God and the Gift in Derrida and Marion." *God, the Gift, and Postmodernism.* Ed. John D. Caputo and Michael J. Scanlon. Bloomington: Indiana UP, 1999. 185–222.

———. and Michael J. Scanlon. "Introduction." *God, the Gift, and Postmodernism.* Ed. John D. Caputo and Michael J. Scanlon. Bloomington: Indiana UP, 1999. 1–19.

———. "On Not Circumventing the Quasi-Transcendental: The Case of Rorty and Derrida." *Working Through Derrida.* Ed. Gary B. Madison. Evanston: Northwestern UP, 1993. 147–69.

———. *The Prayers and Tears of Jacques Derrida: Religion without Religion.* Bloomington: Indiana UP, 1997.

Carmichael, Thomas. "Postmodernism Reconsidered: The Return of the Real in John Barth's *Sabbatical* and *The Tidewater Tales.*" *Revue Française d'Etudes Américaines* 17. 62 (1994): 329–38.

Carver, Raymond. "Why Don't You Dance?" *What We Talk About When We Talk About Love.* 1974. New York: Vintage, 1989. 3–10.

Chen, Tina. " 'Unraveling the Deeper Meaning': Exile and the Embodied Poetics of Displacement in Tim O'Brien's *The Things They Carried.*" *Contemporary Literature* 39. 1 (1998): 77–98.

Coen, Joel, dir. *The Big Lebowski.* Perfs. Jeff Bridges, John Goodman, and Julianne Moore. Polygram, 1998.

————. *The Man Who Wasn't There*. Perfs. Billy Bob Thorton, Frances McDormand, and James Gandolfini. Good Machine, 2001.

Conte, Joseph Mark. *Design and Debris: A Chaotics of Postmodern American Fiction*. London: U of Alabama P, 2002.

Conti, Chris. "The Confessions of Todd Andrews: Double-Directed Discourse in *The Floating Opera*." *Studies in the Novel* 36. 4 (2004): 533–51.

Couturier, Maurice. "From Displacement to Compactness: John Barth's *The Floating Opera*." *Critique* 33. 1 (1991): 3–21.

Critchley, Simon. *Ethics-Politics-Subjectivity: Essays on Derrida, Levinas and Contemporary French Thought*. London: Verso, 1999.

Crockett, Clayton. "Post-Modernism and its Secrets: Religion without Religion." *Cross Currents* 52. 4 (2003): 499–515.

Culler, Jonathan. *On Deconstruction: Theory and Criticism after Structuralism*. Ithaca: Cornell UP, 1982.

Curb Your Enthusiasm. Created by Larry David. HBO, 2000–2006

DeKoven, Marianne. *Utopia Limited: The Sixties and the Emergence of the Postmodern*. Durham: Duke UP, 2004.

Den Tandt, Christopher. "Pragmatic Commitments: Postmodern Realism in Don DeLillo, Maxine Hong Kingston and James Ellroy." *Beyond Postmodernism: Reassessments in Literature, Theory, and Culture*. Ed. Klaus Stierstorfer. Berlin: Walter de Gruyter, 2003. 121–42.

Derrida, Jacques. "Differance." *Speech and Phenomena and Other Essays on Husserl's Theory of Signs*. Trans. David B. Allison. Evanston: Northwestern UP, 1973. 129–60.

————. "The Ends of Man." *The Margins of Philosophy*. Trans. Alan Bass. Chicago: U of Chicago P, 1982. 109–36.

————. *Envois*. *The Postcard: From Socrates to Freud*. Trans. Alan Bass. Chicago: U of Chicago P, 1987. 1–256.

————. *Force of Law: The "Mystical Foundation of Authority." Acts of Religion*. Trans. Mary Quaintance. Ed. Gil Anidjar. New York: Routledge, 2002. 228–98.

————. *Of Grammatology*. 1974. Trans. Gayatri Chakrovorty Spivak. Baltimore: John Hopkins UP, 1997.

————. *Politics of Friendship*. Trans. George Collins. London: Verso, 1997.

————. *Positions*. Trans. Alan Bass. Chicago: U of Chicago P, 1981.

————. *Specters of Marx: The State of the Debt, the Work of Mourning, and the New International*. Trans. Peggy Kamuf. New York: Routledge, 1994.

————. *Writing and Difference*. Trans. Alan Bass. Chicago: U of Chicago P, 1978.

Federman, Raymond. "Before Postmodernism and After (Part One)." *The End of Postmodernism: New Directions*. Proc. of the First Stuggart Seminar in Cultural Studies 04. 08.–18. 08. 1991. Dir. Heide Ziegler. Stuttgart: M & P Verlag für Wissenschaft und Forschung, 1993. 47–64.

————. "Before Postmodernism and After (Part Two)." *The End of Postmodernism: New Directions*. Proc. of the First Stuggart Seminar in Cultural Studies 04. 08.–18. 08. 1991. Dir. Heide Ziegler. Stuttgart: M & P Verlag für Wissenschaft und Forschung, 1993. 153–70.

————. "Critifictional Reflections on the Pathetic Condition of the Novel in our Time." *Symploke* 12. 1–2 (2004): 155–70.

Fenves, Peter. "Marx, Mourning and Messianicity." *Violence, Identity, and Self-Determination.* Ed. Hent de Vries. Stanford: Stanford UP, 1997. 253–70.

Fiedler, Leslie. "Cross the Border—Close the Gap: Postmodernism." *American Literature Since 1900.* Ed. Marcus Cunliffe. London: Sphere Books, 1975. 344–66.

Fluck, Winfried. "Surface and Depth: Postmodernism and Neo-Realist Fiction." *Neo-Realism in Contemporary Fiction.* Ed. Kristiaan Versluys. Amsterdam: Rodopi, 1992. 65–85.

Foucault, Michel. *Discipline and Punish: The Birth of the Prison.* 1977. Trans. Alan Sheridan. New York: Vintage, 1995.

————. *The Order of Things: An Archaeology of the Human Sciences.* 1970. New York: Vintage Books, 1994.

————. What is an Author? *The Foucault Reader.* Ed. Paul Rabinow. New York: Pantheon Books, 1984. 101–20.

Fox, Nik Farrell. *The New Sartre: Explorations in Postmodernism.* New York: Continuum, 2003.

Frow, John. "What was Postmodernism?" *Time and Commodity Culture: Essays in Cultural Theory and Postmodernity.* New York: Oxford UP, 1997. 1–13.

Gasché, Rodolphe. *Inventions of Difference: On Jacques Derrida.* Cambridge: Harvard UP, 1994.

Geddes, Jennifer, ed. *Evil after Postmodernism: Histories, Narratives, and Ethics.* New York: Routledge, 2001.

Graff, Gerald. *Literature Against Itself: Literary Ideas in Modern Society.* Chicago: U of Chicago P, 1979.

Habermas, Jürgen. *Legitimation Crisis.* Trans. Thomas McCarthy. Boston: Beacon P, 1975.

————. "Modern and Postmodern Architecture." *Critical Theory and Public Life.* Ed. John Forester. Cambridge: MIT P, 1985. 317–29.

————. "Modernity—An Incomplete Project." *The Anti-Aesthetic: Essays on Postmodern Culture.* Ed. Hal Foster. Port Townsend: Bay, 1983. 1–16.

————. *The Philosophical Discourse of Modernity: Twelve Lectures.* Trans. Frederick Lawrence. Cambridge: Polity, 1987.

Hamacher, Werner. "Lingua Amissa: The Messianism of Commodity-Language and Derrida's *Specters of Marx.*" *Futures: Of Jacques Derrida.* Trans. Kelly Barry. Ed. Richard Rand. Stanford: Stanford UP, 2001. 130–78.

Harvey, David. *The Condition of Postmodernity: An Enquiry into the Origins of Cultural Change.* New York: Blackwell, 1989.

Harvey, Irene. *Derrida and the Economy of Différance.* Bloomington: Indiana UP, 1986.

Hassan, Ihab. "Beyond Postmodernism: Toward an Aesthetic of Trust." *Beyond Postmodernism: Reassessments in Literature, Theory, and Culture.* Ed. Klaus Stierstorfer. Berlin: Walter de Gruyter, 2003. 199–212.

————. "Let the Fresh Air In: Critical Perspectives of the Humanities." *The End of Postmodernism: New Directions.* Proc. of the First Stuggart Seminar in

Cultural Studies 04. 08.–18. 08. 1991. Dir. Heide Ziegler. Stuttgart: M & P Verlag für Wissenschaft und Forschung, 1993. 135–52.

———. *The Postmodern Turn: Essays in Postmodern Theory and Culture.* Columbus: Ohio State UP, 1987.

Hayles, Katherine N., and Todd Gannon. "Mood Swings: The Aesthetics of Ambient Emergence." *The Mourning After: Attending the Wake of Postmodernism.* Eds. Neil Brooks and Josh Toth. Amsterdam: Rodopi, 2007. 99–142.

Hornung, Alfred. "POSTMODERN-POSTMORTEM: Death and the Death of the Novel." *Neo-Realism in Contemporary Fiction.* Ed. Kristiaan Versluys. Amsterdam: Rodopi, 1992. 87–110.

Howe, Irving. "Mass Society and Post-Modern Fiction." *Partisan Review* 26 (1959): 420–36.

Howells, Christina. *Derrida: Deconstruction from Phenomenology to Ethics.* Cambridge: Polity, 1998.

———. "Derrida and Sartre: Hegel's Death Knell." *Derrida and Deconstruction.* Ed. Hugh J. Silverman. New York: Routledge, 1989. 169–81.

———. "Sartre and Derrida: *Qui Perd Gagne.*" *Sartre: And Investigation of Some Major Themes.* Aldershot: Avebury, 1987. 147–58.

———. "Sartre and Negative Theology." *The Modern Language Review* 76. 3 (1981): 549–55.

Hutcheon, Linda. *The Poetics of Postmodernism: History, Theory, Fiction.* New York: Routledge, 1988.

———. *The Politics of Postmodernism.* 2nd ed. New York: Routledge, 2002.

———. "Postmodern Afterthoughts." *Wascana Review of Contemporary Poetry and Short Fiction* 37. 1 (2002): 5–12.

Huyssen, Andreas. *After the Great Divide.* Bloomington: Indiana UP, 1987.

Jameson, Fredric. *The Political Unconscious: Narrative as a Socially Symbolic Act.* Ithaca: Cornell UP, 1981.

———. "Postmodernism and Consumer Society." *The Anti-Aesthetic: Essays on Postmodern Culture.* Ed. Hal Foster. Port Townsend: Bay, 1983. 111–25.

———. *Postmodernism, Or, The Cultural Logic of Late capitalism.* Durham: Duke UP, 1991.

———. "Preface." *The Postmodern Condition: A Report on Knowledge.* By Jean-François Lyotard. Trans. Geoff Bennington and Brian Massumi. Minneapolis: U of Minnesota P, 1979. vii–xxi.

Jencks, Charles. *The Language of Post-Modern Architecture.* London: Academy, 1977.

Johnston, John. "Toward the Schizo-Text: Paranoia as Semiotic Regime" in *The Crying of Lot 49. New Essays on The Crying of Lot 49.* Ed. Patrick O'Donnell. Cambridge: Cambridge UP, 1991. 47–8.

Jonze, Spike, dir. *Adaptation.* Perfs. Nicolas Cage, Meryl Streep, and Chris Cooper. Columbia Pictures, 2002.

Kamuf, Peggy. "Violence, Identity, Self-Determination, and the Question of Justice: On *Specters of Marx.*" *Violence, Identity, and Self-Determination.* Ed. Hent de Vries. Stanford: Stanford UP, 1997. 271–83.

Kaplan, Steve. "The Undying Uncertainty of the Narrator in Tim O'Brien's *The Things They Carried*." *Critique* 35. 1 (1993): 43–52.

Kearney, Richard. "Desire of God." *God, the Gift, and Postmodernism*. Ed. John D. Caputo and Michael J. Scanlon. Bloomington: Indiana UP, 1999. 112–45.

Keenan, Thomas. "Deconstruction and the Impossibility of Justice." *Critical Encounters: Reference and Responsibility in Deconstructive Writing*. Ed. Cathy Caruth and Deborah Esch. New Brunswick, NJ: Rutgers UP, 1995. 262–74.

Keskinen, Mikko. "Voces Intimae: Electro-Erotic Speech in Nicholson Baker's *Vox*." *Critique* 45. 2 (2004): 99–114.

Kristeva, Julia. *Revolution in Poetic Language*. Trans. Margaret Waller. New York: Columbia UP, 1984.

Lacan, Jacques. "The Mirror Stage as Formative of the Function of the I Function in Psychoanalytic Experience." *Écrits*. Trans. Bruce Fink. New York: Norton, 1977. 75–81.

Laclau, Ernesto. " 'The Time Is Out of Joint.' " *Diacritics* 25. 2 (1995): 86–94.

Levin, Harry. "What Was Modernism?" *Varieties of Literary Experience*. Ed. Stanley Burnshaw. New York: New York UP, 1962. 307–52.

Leyner, Mark. *My Cousin, My Gastroenterologist*. New York: Vintage, 1990.

———. *The Tetherballs of Bougainville*. New York: Vintage, 1998.

Leypoldt, Günter. "Recent Realist Fiction and the Idea of Writing 'After Postmodernism.' " *Amerikastudien/American Studies* 49. 1 (2004): 19–34.

Little, William G. "Figuring Out Mark Leyner: A Waste of Time." *Arizona Quarterly* 52. 4 (1996): 135–61.

López, José, and Garry Potter, eds. *After Postmodernism: An Introduction to Critical Realism*. London: Sage, 1994.

Luckhurst, Roger. " 'Impossible Mourning' in Toni Morrison's *Beloved* and Michèle Roberts' *Daughters of the House*." *Critique* 37. 4 (1996): 243–60.

Lynch, David, dir. *Lost Highway*. Perfs. Bill Pullman, Patricia Arquette, and Balthazar Getty. Asymmetrical Productions, 1997.

———. *Mulholland Dr.* Perfs. Naomi Watts, Laura Harring, and Ann Miller. Asymmetrical Productions, 2001.

Lyotard, Jean-François. "Answering the Question: What Is Postmodernism?" Trans. Regis Durand. *The Postmodern Condition: A Report on Knowledge*. Trans. Geoff Bennington and Brian Massumi. Minneapolis: U of Minnesota P, 1984. 71–82.

———. "Note on the Meaning of 'Post-' " *The Postmodern Explained: Correspondence 1982–1985*. Trans. Don Berry. Ed. Julian Pefanis and Morgan Thomas. Minneapolis: U of Minnesota P, 1992. 75–80.

———. *The Postmodern Condition: A Report on Knowledge*. Trans. Geoff Bennington and Brian Massumi. Minneapolis: U of Minnesota P, 1984. 3–67.

———. *Postmodern Fables*. Trans. Georges Van Den Abbeele. Minneapolis: U of Minnesota P, 1997.

———. "Rewriting Modernity." *The Inhuman: Reflections on Time*. Trans. Geoff Bennington and Rachel Bowlby. Stanford: Stanford UP, 1991. 24–36.

Martinot, Steve. *Forms in the Abyss: A Philosophical Bridge Between Sartre and Derrida.* Philadelphia: Temple UP, 2006.

Marx, Karl. "Manifesto of the Communist Party." 1848. *The Marx-Engels Reader.* 2nd ed. Ed. Robert Tucker. New York: Norton, 1978. 469–500.

Mazzaro, Jerome. *Postmodern American Poetry.* Urbana: U of Illinois P, 1980.

McDermott, Ryan P. "Silence, Visuality, and the Staying Image: The 'Unspeakable Scene' of Toni Morrison's *Beloved.*" *Angelaki* 8. 1 (2003): 75–89.

McGowan, John. *Postmodernism and Its Critics.* Ithaca: Cornell UP, 1991.

McLaughlin, Robert L. "Postmodernism in the Age of Distracting Discourses." *The Mourning After: Attending the Wake of Postmodernism.* Eds. Neil Brooks and Josh Toth. Amsterdam: Rodopi, 2007. 53–64.

———. "Post-Postmodern Discontent: Contemporary Fiction and the Social World." *Symploke* 12. 1–2 (2004): 53–68.

Milletti, Christina. "Violent Acts, Volatile Words: Kathy Acker's Terrorist Aesthetic." *Studies in the Novel* 36. 3 (2004): 352–73.

Morrison, Toni. *Beloved.* 1987. New York: Knopf, 1988.

Nancy, Jean-Luc. *Being Singular Plural.* Trans. Robert D. Richardson and Anne E. O'Byrne. Stanford: Stanford UP, 2000.

Norris, Christopher. *Deconstruction and the 'Unfinished Project of Modernity.'* London: Alhlone, 2000.

———. *Derrida.* Cambridge: Harvard UP, 1987.

———. *What's Wrong with Postmodernism?* Baltimore: John Hopkins UP, 1990.

O'Brien, Tim. *In the Lake of the Woods.* Boston: Houghton Mifflin, 1994.

———. *The Things They Carried.* 1990. Boston: Houghton Mifflin, 1998.

Olson, Charles. *Charles Olson and Robert Creeley: The Complete Correspondence.* Vol. 7. Ed. George F. Butterick. Santa Rosa: Black Sparrow, 1987.

———. "The Present Is Prologue." 1952. *Collected Prose.* Ed. Donald Allen and Benjamin Friedlander. Berkeley: U of California P, 1997. 205–7.

Pinsker, Sanford. "Theoretical Palefaces/Neo-Realistic Redskins, or Why the Ghost of Philip Rahv Would Cry 'Uncle!' " *Neo-Realism in Contemporary Fiction.* Ed. Kristiaan Versluys. Amsterdam: Rodopi, 1992. 51–64.

Pold, Søren. "Novel Media: On Typographical Consciousness and Marginal Realism in Nicholson Baker." *Reinventions of the Novel: Histories and Aesthetics of a Protean Genre.* Ed. Karen-Margrethe Simonsen, Marianne Ping Huang, and Mads Rosendahl Thomsen. Amsterdam: Rodopi, 2004.

Pynchon, Thomas. *The Crying of Lot 49.* 1965. New York: Harper & Row, 1986.

———. *Gravity's Rainbow.* New York: Viking, 1973.

———. *Mason & Dixon.* New York: Henry Holt, 1997.

Rabaté, Jean-Michel. "The 'Mujic of the Footure': Future, Ancient, Fugitive." *Futures: Of Jacques Derrida.* Ed. Richard Rand. Stanford: Stanford UP, 2001. 130–78.

Rackstraw, Loree. "The Paradox of 'Awareness' and Language in Vonnegut's Fiction." *Kurt Vonnegut: Images and Representations.* Ed. Marc Leeds and Peter J. Reed. Westport: Greenwood, 2000. 51–66.

Rajan, Tilottama. *Deconstruction and the Remainders of Phenomenology.* Stanford: Stanford UP, 2002.

Rebein, Robert. *Hicks, Tribes and Dirty Realists: American Fiction after Postmodernism.* Lexington: UP of Kentucky, 2001.

———. "Turncoat: Why Jonathan Franzen Finally Said "No" to Po-Mo." *The Mourning After: Attending the Wake of Postmodernism.* Eds. Neil Brooks and Josh Toth. Amsterdam: Rodopi, 2007. 201–22.

Reed, Peter J. "Kurt Vonnegut's Bitter Fool: Kilgore Trout." *Kurt Vonnegut: Images and Representations.* Eds. Marc Leeds and Peter J. Reed. Westport: Greenwood, 2000. 67–80.

Reitman, Ivan, dir. *Ghostbusters.* Perfs. Bill Murray, Dan Ackroyd, and Sigourney Weaver. Columbia Pictures, 1984.

Rorty, Richard. *Contingency, Irony, and Solidarity.* New York: Cambridge UP, 1989.

———. "Is Derrida a Transcendental Philosopher?" *Working Through Derrida.* Ed. Gary B. Madison. Evanston: Northwestern UP, 1993. 137–46.

———. *Philosophical Papers, Volume 2: Essays on Heidegger and Others.* New York: Cambridge UP, 1991.

———. "Remarks on Deconstruction and Pragmatism." *Deconstruction and Pragmatism.* Ed. Chantal Mouffe. London: Routledge, 1996. 13–18.

———. "Response to Simon Critchley." *Deconstruction and Pragmatism.* Ed. Chantal Mouffe. London: Routledge, 1996. 41–46.

Saltzman, Arthur. *Understanding Nicholson Baker.* Columbia: U of South Carolina P, 1999.

Sartre, Jean-Paul. *Being and Nothingness.* Trans. Hazel E. Barnes. New York: Washington Square, 1956.

Schaub, Thomas. *American Fiction in the Cold War.* Madison: U of Wisconsin P, 1991.

Seinfeld. Created by Jerry Seinfeld and Larry David. Castle Rock Entertainment, 1990–1998.

Shechner, Mark. "American Realism, American Realities." *Neo-Realism in Contemporary Fiction.* Ed. Kristiaan Versluys. Amsterdam: Rodopi, 1992. 27–50.

Simmons, Philip E. "Toward the Postmodern Historical Imagination: Mass Culture in Walker Percy's *The Moviegoer* and Nicholson Baker's *The Mezzanine.*" *Contemporary Literature* 33. 4 (1992): 601–24.

Simpson, Josh. " 'This Promising of Great Secrets': Literature, Ideas, and the (Re)Invention of Reality in Kurt Vonnegut's *God Bless You, Mr. Rosewater, Slaughterhouse-Five,* and *Breakfast of Champions,* Or 'Fantasies of an Impossibly Hospitable World': Science Fiction and Madness in Vonnegut's Troutean Trilogy." *Critique* 45. 3 (2004): 261–71.

The Simpsons. Created by Matt Groening. Twentieth Century Fox, 1989–2006.

Sontag, Susan. *Against Interpretation and Other Essays.* New York: Dell, 1967.

Spheeris, Penelope, dir. *Wayne's World.* Perfs. Mike Myers and Dana Carvey. Paramount Pictures, 1992.

Spivak, Gayatri Chakrovorty. "Ghostwriting." *Diacritics* 25. 2 (1995): 65–84.

Stierstorfer, Klaus. "Introduction: Beyond Postmodernism—Contingent Referentiality?" *Beyond Postmodernism: Reassessments in Literature, Theory, and Culture.* Ed. Klaus Stierstorfer. Berlin: Walter de Gruyter, 2003. 1–10.

Taylor, Mark. "Tim O'Brien's War." *Centennial Review* 39. 2 (1995): 213–30.

Taylor, Mark C. *Disfiguring: Art, Architecture, Religion.* Chicago: U of Chicago P, 1992.

Tew, Philip. "A New Sense of Reality? A New Sense of Text?" *Beyond Postmodernism: Reassessments in Literature, Theory, and Culture.* Ed. Klaus Stierstorfer. Berlin: Walter de Gruyter, 2003. 29–50.

Toth, Josh. "A *Différance* of Nothing: Sartre, Derrida and the Problem of Negative Theology." *Sartre Studies International* 13. 1 (2007): 16–34.

———. "A Certain Perhaps: Touching on the Decisiveness of Derrida's Indecision." *Mosaic* 40. 2 (2007): 245–60.

Toynbee, Arnold. *A Study of History: Volume IX.* London: Oxford UP, 1954.

Varsava, Jerry A. "Thomas Pynchon and Postmodern Liberalism." *Canadian Review of American Studies / Revue canadienne d'études américianes* 25. 3 (1995): 63–100.

Venturi, Robert, Denise Scott Brown, and Steven Izenour. *Learning from Las Vegas: The Forgotten Symbolism of Architectural Form.* Cambridge: MIT P, 1977.

Versluys, Kristiaan. "Introduction." *Neo-Realism in Contemporary Fiction.* Ed. Kristiaan Versluys. Amsterdam: Rodopi, 1992. 7–12.

Vonnegut, Kurt. *Breakfast of Champions.* 1973. New York: Random House, 1999.

———. *Jailbird.* 1979. New York: Delacorte, 1980.

Wallace, David Foster. *Infinite Jest.* Boston: Little, Brown, 1996.

Wieczorak, Marek. Introduction. *The Art of the Ridiculous Sublime: On David Lynch's* Lost Highway. By Slavoj Žižek. Seattle: U of Washington P, 2000. viii–xiii.

Wolfe, Tom. "Stalking the Billion-Footed Beast: A Literary Manifesto for the New Social Novel." *Harper's Magazine* 279. 1674 (Nov. 1989): 45–56.

Žižek, Slavoj. *The Art of the Ridiculous Sublime: On David Lynch's* Lost Highway. Seattle: U of Washington P, 2000.

———. *The Sublime Object of Ideology.* London: Verso, 1989.

Index